MW00699845

The Christ Myth

The

Christ
Myth

Arthur Drews

Translated from the Third Edition
(Revised and Enlarged)
By C. Delisle Burns

WESTMINSTER COLLEGE–OXFORD: CLASSICS IN THE STUDY OF RELIGION

Amherst, New York • Oxford, England

Published 1998 by Prometheus Books
59 John Glenn Drive, Amherst, New York 14228–2197,
716–691–0133. FAX: 716–691–0137.

Library of Congress Cataloging-in-Publication Data

Drews, Arthur, 1865–1935.
    [Christusmythe. English]
    The Christ myth / Arthur Drews ; translated by C. Delisle Burns.
        p.   cm. — (Westminster College-Oxford classics in the study
of religion)
    Originally published: Chicago : Open Court, 1910.
    Includes bibliographical references and index.
    ISBN 1–57392–190–4 (alk. paper)
    1. Jesus Christ—Historicity. 2. Bible. N.T.,Criticism, interpretation,
etc. I. Title. II. Series.
BT303.2.D753   1998
232.9'08—dc21   97–46443
                                                                      CIP

Printed in the United States of America on acid-free paper

TO

MY FRIEND

WILHELM VON SCHNEHEN

PREFACE TO THE FIRST AND
SECOND EDITIONS

SINCE David Frederick Strauss, in his "Life of Jesus," attempted for the first time to trace the Gospel stories and accounts of miracles back to myths and pious fictions, doubts regarding the existence of an historical Jesus have never been lulled to rest. Bruno Bauer also in his "Kritik der evangelischen Geschichte und der Synoptiker" (1841–42, 2nd ed. 1846),* disputed the historical existence of Jesus; later, in his "Christ und die Cäsaren, der Ursprung des Christentums aus dem römischen Griechentum" (1877), he attempted to show that the life of Jesus was a pure invention of the first evangelist, Mark, and to account for the whole Christian religion from the Stoic and Alexandrine culture of the second century, ascribing to Seneca especially a material influence upon the development of the Christian point of view. But it was reserved for the present day, encouraged by the essentially negative results of the so-called critical theology, to take up the subject energetically, and thereby to attain to results even bolder and more startling.

In England John M. Robertson, in "Christianity and Mythology" (1900), in "A Short History of Christianity" (1902), as well as in his work "Pagan Christs: Studies in Comparative Hierology" (1903), has traced the picture

* Cf. also his "Kritik der Evangelien," 2 vols. (1850–51).

7

of Christ in the Gospels to a mixture of mythological elements in heathenism and Judaism.

In France, as early as the end of the eighteenth century, Dupuis ("L'origine de tous les cultes" (1795) and Voltaire ("Les Ruines," 1791) traced back the essential points of the history of the Christian redemption to astral myths, while Émile Burnouf ("La science des religions," 4th ed., 1885) and Hochart ("Études d'histoire religieuse," 1890) collected important material for the clearing up of the origin of Christianity, and by their results cast considerable doubt upon the existence of an historical Christ.

In Italy Milesbo (Emilio Bossi) has attempted to prove the non-historicity of Jesus in his book "Gesù Christo non è mai esistito" (1904).

In Holland the Leyden Professor of Philosophy, Bolland, handled the same matter in a series of works ("Het hijden en Sterven van Jezus Christus," 1907; "De Achtergrond der Evangèlien. Eene Bijdrage tot de kennis van de Wording des Christendoms," 1907; "De evangelische Jozua. Eene poging tot aanwijzing van den oorsprong des Christendoms," 1907).

In Poland the mythical character of the story of Jesus has been shown by Andrzej Niemojewski in his book "Bóg Jezus" (1909), which rests on the astral-mythological theories of Dupuis and the school of Winckler.

In Germany the Bremen Pastor Kalthoff, in his work, "Das Christusproblem, Grundlinien zu einer Sozialtheologie" (1903), thought that the appearance of the Christian religion could be accounted for without the help of an historical Jesus, simply from a social movement of the lower classes under the Empire, subsequently attempting to remove the one-sidedness of this view by his work "Die Entstehung des Christentums. Neue Beiträge zum Christusproblem" (1904). (Cf. also his work " Was wissen wir von Jesus ? Eine Abrechnung mit Professor D. Bousset," 1904.) A supplement to the works of Kalthoff in question is furnished by Fr. Steudel in " Das Christusproblem und die Zukunft des Protestantismus " (Deutsche Wiedergeburt, 1909).

Finally, the American, William Benjamin Smith, in his work, " The Pre-Christian Jesus " (1906), has thrown so clear a light upon a number of important points in the rise of Christianity, and elucidated so many topics which give us a deeper insight into the actual correlation of events, that we gradually commence to see clearly in this connection.

" The time is passed," says Jülicher, " when among the learned the question could be put whether an ' historical ' Jesus existed at all." * The literature cited does not appear to justify this assertion. On the contrary, that time seems only commencing. Indeed, an unprejudiced judge might find that even Jülicher's own essay, in which he treated of the so-called founder of the Christian religion in the " Kultur der Gegenwart," and in which he declared it " tasteless " to look upon the contents of the Gospels as a myth, speaks rather against than for the historical reality of Jesus. For the rest, official learning in Germany, and especially theology, has, up to the present, remained, we may almost say, wholly unmoved by all the above-mentioned publications. To my mind it has not yet taken up a serious position regarding Robertson. Its sparing citations of his " Pagan Christs " do not give the impression that there can be any talk of its having a real knowledge of his expositions.†

* " Kultur d. Gegenwart : Gesch. d. christl. Religion," 2nd ed., 1909, 47.

† The same is true of Clemen, who, judging by his " Religionsgeschichtl. Erklärung d. N.T." (1909), appears to be acquainted with Robertson's masterpiece, " Christianity and Mythology," only from a would-be witty notice of Réville, and furthermore only cites the author when he thinks he can demolish him with ease.

It has, moreover, passed Kalthoff over with the mien of a better informed superiority or preferably with silent scorn, and up to the present it has avoided with care any thoroughgoing examination of Smith.*   And yet such a distinguished theologian as Professor Paul Schmiedel, of Zürich, who furnished a foreword to Smith's work, laid such an examination upon his colleagues as a "duty of all theologians making any claim to a scientific temper," and strongly warned them against any under-estimation of Smith's highly scientific work ! "How can one then confidently stand by his former views," Schmiedel cries to his theological colleagues, "unless he investigates whether they have not in whole or in part been undermined by these new opinions? Or is it a question of some secondary matter merely, and not rather of exactly what for the majority forms the fundamental part of their Christian conviction? But if these new opinions are so completely futile, then it must be an easy matter, indeed a mere nothing, to show this."

In the meantime there are many voices which speak out against the existence of an historical Jesus. In wide circles the doubt grows as to the historical character of the picture of Christ given in the Gospels. Popular works written with a purpose, such as the investigations of the Frenchman Jacolliot, worked up by Plange into "Jesus ein Inder " (1898), have to serve to alleviate this

---

* A. Hausrath, in his work "Jesus u. die neutestamentlichen Schriftsteller," vol. i. (1908), offers a striking example of how light a matter our theologians make it to overthrow the attacks of the opponents of an historical Jesus. In scarcely three pages at the commencement of his compendious work he rejects the myth theory of Bruno Bauer with the favourite appeal to a few individual and historical features of the Gospel tradition which are intrinsically of no significance, finishing up this "refutation" with a reckless citation from Weinel which proves nothing for the historical character of Jesus.

thirst for knowledge and confuse views more than they clear them. In a short work, "Die Entstehung des Christentums" (1905), Promus has afforded a brief *résumé* of the most important matter bearing on the point, without any working up of it on its own account, and attacked the existence of an historical Jesus. Lately Karl Voller, the prematurely deceased Jena Orientalist, in his valuable work, "Die Weltreligionen in ihrem geschichtlichen Zusammenhange" (1907), voiced the opinion "that weighty reasons favour this radical myth interpretation, and that no absolutely decisive arguments for the historicity of the person of Jesus can be brought forward" (*op. cit.* i. 163).

Another Orientalist, P. Jensen, in his work "Das Gilgamesch-Epos in der Weltliteratur" (1906), even thinks that he can show that both the main lines of the Old Testament story and the whole narrative of the life of Jesus given in the Gospels are simply variations of the Babylonian Gilgamesch Epic (about 2000 B.C.), and consequently a pure myth.*

While criticism of the Gospel documents is advancing more boldly and always leaving in existence less of an historical Jesus, the number of works in popular religious literature intended to glorify Jesus the man grows enormously. These endeavour to make up for the deficiency in certain historical material by sentimental phrases and the deep tone of conviction; indeed, the rhetoric which is disseminated with this design † seems to find more sympathy in proportion as it works with less historical restraint. And yet learning as such has long come to the point when the historical Jesus threatens to disappear from under its hands. The latest results in the

* Cf. also his work "Moses, Jesus, Paulus. Drei sagen varianten des babylonischen Gottmenschen Gilgamesch," 2nd ed., 1909.
† Cf., for example, "Jesus Vier Vorträge, geh. in Frankf." 1910.

province of Oriental mythology and religion, the advances in the comparative history of religion, that are associated in England with the names of Frazer and Robertson especially, and in Germany with those of Winckler, Jeremias, Gunkel, Jensen, &c., have so much increased our knowledge of the religious position of Nearer Asia in the last century before Christ, that we are no longer obliged to rely exclusively upon the Gospels and the other books of the New Testament for the rise of Christianity.* The critical and historical theology of Protestantism has itself thrown so deep a light upon the origins of the Christian religion that the question as to the historical

---

* In other respects the "progress" in the province of religious history is not so great as I formerly believed I could assume. That is to say, in essentials modern learning in this connection has only brought facts to light and given a new focus to points of view which were already possessed (cf. Dupuis and Volney) by the eighteenth century. In the twenties and forties of the nineteenth century investigations, unprejudiced and independent of theology, had already reached in the case of some of their representatives, such as Gfrörer, Lützelberger, Ghillany, Nork, and others, the point which is to-day again represented by the most advanced learning. The revolution of 1848 and the reaction consequent on it in ecclesiastical matters then again shook, on account of their radical tendency, those views which had been already arrived at. The liberal Protestantism, too, that rose as a recoil against orthodoxy in its effort to work out the "historical" Jesus as the kernel of Christianity on its part had no interest in again bringing up the old results. Indeed, it actually makes it a reproach to a person of the present day if he quotes the works of those earlier investigators, and reminds him that religious learning did not begin only with the modern Coryphaei, with Holtzman, Harnack, &c. Whoever looks upon things from this point of view can most probably agree in the melancholy reflection of a reviewer of the first edition of "The Christ Myth," when he says with reference to the "latest investigations": "Apparently the whole learning of the nineteenth century so far as relates to investigations into the moving forces of civilisation and national upheavals will be considered by future research as an arsenal of errors" (O. Hauser in the *Neue Freie Presse*, August 8, 1909).

existence of Jesus loses all paradox which hitherto may have attached to it in the eyes of many. So, too, Protestant theology no longer has any grounds for becoming excited if the question is answered in a sense opposed to its own answer.

The author of the present work had hoped until lately that one of the historians of Christianity would himself arise and extract the present results of the criticisms of the Gospel, which to-day are clear. These hopes have not been fulfilled. On the contrary, in theological circles religious views continue to be quietly drawn from the "fact" of an historical Jesus, and he is considered as the impassable height in the religious development of the individual, as though nothing has occurred and the existence of such a Jesus was only the more clearly established by the investigations of critical theology in this connection. The author has accordingly thought that he should no longer keep back his own views, which he long since arrived at out of the works of specialists, and has taken upon himself the thankless task of bringing together the grounds which tell against the theory of an historical Jesus.

Whoever, though not a specialist, invades the province of any science, and ventures to express an opinion opposed to its official representatives, must be prepared to be rejected by them with anger, to be accused of a lack of scholarship, "dilettantism," or "want of method," and to be treated as a complete ignoramus. This has been the experience of all up to now who, while not theologians, have expressed themselves on the subject of an historical Jesus. The like experience was not spared the author of the present work after the appearance of its first edition. He has been accused of "lack of historical training," "bias," "incapacity for any real historical way of thinking," &c., and it has been held up against him that in his investigations their result was settled beforehand—as if this was not precisely the case with theologians, who write on the subject of a historical Jesus, since it is just the task of theology to defend and establish the truth of the New Testament writings. Whoever has looked about him in the turmoil of science knows that generally each fellow-worker is accustomed to regard as "method" that only which he himself uses as such, and that the famous conception of "scientific method" is very often ruled by points of view purely casual and personal. *

* It has also been reckoned as a want of "method" in this work that I have often made use of a cautious and restrained mode of expression, that I have spoken of mere "suppositions" and employed locutions such as "it appears," &c., when it has been for the time being impossible for science or myself to give complete certainty to an assertion. This reproach sounds strange in the mouths of such as plume themselves upon "scientific method." For I should think that it was indeed more scientific in the given cases to express oneself in the manner chosen by me, than by an unmeasured certainty in assertions to puff out pure suppositions into undoubted facts. I must leave such a mode of proceeding to the historical theologians. They work purely with hypotheses. All their endeavours to obtain an historical kernel from the Gospels rest upon conjectures simply. Above everything, their explanation of the origin of Christianity simply from an historical Jesus is, in spite of the certainty and self-confidence with which it comes out, a pure hypothesis, and that of very doubtful value. For that in reality the new religion should have been called into life by the "all-subduing influence of the personality of Jesus" and its accompaniments, the visions and hallucinations of the disciples worked up into ecstasies, is so improbable, and the whole view is psychologically so assailable, and, moreover, so futile, that even a liberal theologian like Gunkel declares it entirely insufficient ("Zum religionsgesichtl. Verständnis d. N.T.," 89 *sq.*). With this explanation, however, stands or falls the whole modern Jesus-religion. For if they cannot show how the Pauline and Johannine Christology could develop from the mere existence of an historical Jesus, if this now forms "the problem of problems of New testament research" (Gunkel, *op. cit.*), then their

Thus, for example, we see the theologian Clemen, in his investigation into the method of explaining the New Testament on religious-historical lines, seriously put the question to himself whether one " could not dispense himself from refuting such books as finally arrive at the unauthenticity of all the Pauline epistles and the non-historicity of the whole, or at least of almost the whole, tradition concerning Jesus ; for example, not only that of Bauer, but also those of Jensen and Smith." This same Clemen advances the famous methodological axiom: " An explanation on religious-historical lines is impossible if it of necessity leads to untenable consequences or sets out from such hypotheses," * obviously thinking here of the denial of an historical Christ. For the rest, the " method " of " critical theology " consists, as is well known, in applying an already settled picture of Jesus to the Gospels and undertaking the critical sifting of their contents according to this measure. This picture makes the founder of the Christian religion merely a pious preacher of morality in the sense of present-day liberalism, the " representative of the noblest individuality," the incarnation of the modern ideal of personality, or of some other fashionable theological view. Theologians commence with the conviction that the historical Jesus was a kind of " anticipation of modern religious consciousness." They think that they discern the real historical import of the Gospels in their " moral-religious kernel " so far as this is good for all time, and they arrive in this manner at its " strictly scientific conception " of Jesus by casting out all such features as

whole conception of the rise of Christianity disappears into air, and they have no right to hold up against others who seek a better explanation the partially hypothetical character of the views advanced by them.

* *Op. cit.*, 10 *sq.*

do not fit this picture, thus recognising only the "ever-lasting human" and the "modern" as historical.*

* Cf. K. Dunkmann, "Der historische Jesus, der mythologische Christus, und Jesus der Christ" (1910). Cf. also Pfleiderer, "Das Christusbild des urchristlichen Glaubens in religionsgeschichtlicher Beleuchtung" (1903), 6 *sq.* Here, too, it is pointed out that modern scientific theology in its description of the figure of Christ proceeds in anything but an unprejudiced manner. Out of the belief in Christ as contained in the New Testament it "only draws forth what is acceptable to present modes of thinking—passing over everything else and reading in much that is its own—in order to construct an ideal Christ according to modern taste." Pfleiderer declares it a "great illusion" to believe that the pictures of Christ in works such as Harnack's "Wesen des Christentums," each differently drawn according to the peculiarities of their composers, but all more or less in the modern style, are the result of scientific historical research, and are related to the old conceptions of Christ like truth to error. "One should," he says, "be reasonable and honourable enough to confess that both the modern and the antique conceptions of Christ are alike creations of the common religious spirit of their times and sprung from the natural need of faith to fix its special prin-ciple in a typical figure and to illustrate it. The differences between the two correspond to the differences of the times, the former a simple mythical Epic, the latter a sentimental and conscious Romance." In the same sense Alb. Schweitzer also characterises the famous "method" of historical theology as "a continual experi-mentation according to settled hypotheses in which the leading thought rests in the last resort upon an intuition" ("Von Reimarus bis Wrede," 1906). Indeed, Weinel himself, who cannot hold up against the author with sufficient scorn his lack of method and his dilettantism has to confess that the same blemishes which in his opinion characterise dilettantism are to be found even in the most prominent representatives of historical theology, in a Wrede or a Wellhausen. He reproaches both of these with the fact that in their researches "serious faults of a general nature and in method" are present (21). He advises the greatest prudence in respect to Wellhausen's Gospel Commentaries "on account of their serious general blemishes" (26). He objects to Wrede that to be consistent he must himself go over to radical dilettantism (22). He charges Schweitzer actually with dilettantism and blind bias which cause every literary consideration to be lacking (25 *sq.*). Indeed, he finds himself, in face of the "dilettante endeavours" to deny the

If one keeps this before his eyes he will not be particularly moved by the talk about "method" and "lack of scientific system." One could then at most wonder that it should be forbidden to philosophers particularly to have a say in theological matters. As though the peace at present reigning between philosophy and theology and their mutual efforts at a *rapprochement* did not clearly indicate that upon one of the two sides, or upon both, something cannot be in order, and that consequently it was high time, if no one else undertakes it, for a philosopher to notice theology in order to terminate the make-believe peace which is for both so fateful. For what does Lessing say? "With orthodoxy God be thanked one had arrived at a tolerable understanding. Between it and philosophy a partition had been raised behind which each could continue its way without hindering the other. But what is now being done? The partition is again being demolished, and under the pretext of making us reasonable Christians we are being made unreasonable philosophers."

historical Jesus, compelled even to admit that liberal theology for the future "must learn to express itself with more caution and to exhibit more surely the method of religious historical comparison" (14). He blames Gunkel for imprudence in declaring Christianity to be a syncretic religion, and demands that the historical works of liberal theology "should be clearer in their results and more convincing in their methods" (16). He says that the method which they employ is at present not sure and clear enough since "it has been spoken of generally in very loose if not misleading terms," and he confesses : "We have apparently not made the measure, according to which we decide upon what is authentic and what not so in the tradition, so plain that it can always be recognised with security" (29). Now, if matters are in such a position, we non-theologians need not take too tragically the reproach of dilettantism and lack of scientific method, since it appears very much as though historical theology, with the exception at most of Herr Weinel, has no sure method.

The author of this book has been reproached with following in it tendencies merely destructive. Indeed, one guardian of Zion, particularly inflamed with rage, has even expressed himself to this effect, that the author's researches do not originate in a serious desire for knowledge, but only in a wish to deny. One who, as I have done, has in all his previous work emphasised the positive nature of the ethical and religious life against the denying and destroying spirit of the age, who has in his work "Die Religion als Sebst-Bewusstein Gottes" (1906) sought to build up anew from within the shattered religious outlook upon the world, who in the last chapter of the present work has left no doubt remaining that he regards the present falling away of religious consciousness as one of the most important phenomena of our spiritual life and as a misfortune for our whole civilisation, should be protected against such reproaches. In reality, "The Christ Myth" has been written pre-eminently in the interests of religion, from the conviction that its previous forms no longer suffice for men of to-day, that above all the "Jesuanism" of historical theology is in its deepest nature irreligious, and that this itself forms the greatest hindrance to all real religious progress. I agree with E. v. Hartmann and W. v. Schnehen in the opinion that this so-called Christianity of the liberal pastors is in every direction full of internal contradiction, that it is false through and through (in to saying naturally no individual representative of this movement is accused of subjective untruthfulness). I agree that by its moving rhetoric and its bold appearance of being scientific it is systematically undermining the simple intellectual truthfulness of our people; and that on this account this romantic cult of Jesus must be combated at all costs, but that this cannot be done more effectually than by

taking its basis in the theory of the historical Jesus *
from beneath its feet.

This work seeks to prove that more or less all the
features of the picture of the historical Jesus, at any rate
all those of any important religious significance, bear a
purely mythical character, and no opening exists for
seeking an historical figure behind the Christ myth. It
is not the imagined historical Jesus but, if any one, Paul
who is that " great personality " that called Christianity
into life as a new religion, and by the speculative range
of his intellect and the depth of his moral experience
gave it the strength for its journey, the strength which
bestowed upon it victory over the other competing
religions. Without Jesus the rise of Christianity can be
quite well understood, without Paul not so. If in spite of
this any one thinks that besides the latter a Jesus also
cannot be dispensed with, this can naturally not be
opposed ; but we know nothing of this Jesus. Even in
the representations of historical theology he is scarcely
more than the shadow of a shadow. Consequently it is
self-deceit to make the figure of this " unique " and
"mighty " personality, to which a man may believe he
must on historical grounds hold fast, the central point of
religious consciousness. Jesus Christ may be great and
worthy of reverence as a religious idea, as the symbolical
personification of the unity of nature in God and man, on
the belief in which the possibility of the " redemption "
depends. As a purely historical individual, as liberal
theology views him, he sinks back to the level of other
great historical personalities, and from the religious point
of view is exactly as unessential as they, indeed, more

---

* Cf. W. v. Schnehen, " Der moderne Jesuskultus," 2nd ed.,
1907, p. 41, a work with which even a Pfleiderer has agreed in the
main points ; also the same author's " Fr. Naumann vor dem Bankrott
des Christentums," 1907.

capable of being dispensed with than they, for in spite of all rhetoric he is in the light of historical theology of to-day, even at best only " a figure swimming obscurely in the mists of tradition." *

PROFESSOR DR. ARTHUR DREWS.

KARLSRUHE, *January*, 1910.

* The excursus on " The Legend of Peter " which was contained in the first edition of this work, and there appears to have been rather misunderstood, has recently (1910) appeared more closely worked out and reasoned in an independent form in the *Neuer Frankfurter Verlag* under the title " Die Petrus Legende. Ein Beitrag zur Mythologie des Christentums."

PREFACE TO THE THIRD EDITION

THE time since the appearance of the second edition was too short for any material alterations to be undertaken in the third edition now appearing. However, the phraseology here and there has been improved and many things put more strongly. Above all, the famous passage in Tacitus and the passage 1 Cor. ii. 23 *et seq.* has been so handled that its lack of significance as regards the existence of an historical Jesus should now appear more clearly than hitherto. That Paul in reality is not a witness for an historical Jesus and is wrongly considered as the "foundation" of the faith in such a figure, should be already established for every unprejudiced person as the result of the discussion so far on the "Christ Myth." The *Protestantenblatt* finds itself now compelled to the admission that the historical image of the person of Jesus as a matter of fact "can no longer be clearly recognised" (No. 6, 1910). How then does it fare with the new "bases" of Schmiedel? To no refutation of the assertions which I represent has greater significance been hitherto ascribed on the theological side than to those supposed supports of a "really scientific life of Jesus" (in the discussions of "the Christ Myth" this has again received the strongest expression). And yet these bases were advanced by their originator obviously with a view to a conception quite different from mine, and, as I have now shown, do not

affect, generally speaking, the view represented by me
regarding the rise of the supposed historical picture of
Jesus. When, above all, the "historical references to
Jesus" are supposed to be contained in them, and these,
according to the *Protestantenblatt*, lie "like blocks of
granite" in my path—then this is a pure illusion of the
theologians.

As can be conceived, my assertion that a pre-Christian
cult of Jesus existed has found the most decisive rejec-
tion. This, however, is for the most part only due to
the fact that the researches in this connection of the
American, Smith, and the Englishman, Robertson, were
not known, and, moreover, the opinion was held that one
need not trouble about these "foreigners," who further
were not "specialists." And yet Gunkel, in his work
"Zum religionsgeschichtlichen Verständnis des Neuen
Testaments," had already sufficiently prepared that view,
as one might have thought, when, among other things,
he declares "that even before Jesus there existed in
Jewish syncretistic circles a belief in the death and
resurrection of Christ."* Again, it can only be rejected
without more ado by such as seek the traces of the
pre-Christian cult of Jesus in well-worn places and will
only allow that to be "proved" which they have
established by direct original documentary evidence
before their eyes. In this connection it is forgotten that
we are dealing with a secret cult, the existence of which
we can decide upon only by indirect means. It is forgotten also that the hypothesis of a pre-Christian cult of
Jesus, if urged upon us from another quarter, cannot be
forthwith rejected because it does not suit the current
views, and because it may be that it is impossible for the
time being to place it beyond all doubt. Where everything is so hypothetical, uncertain, and covered with dark-

* *Op cit.*, 82.

ness, as is the case with the origins of Christianity, every hypothesis should be welcomed and tested which appears to be in some way or the other suitable for opening up a new point of view and clearing away the darkness. For as Dunkmann says in his sympathetic and genuine discussion of " The Christ Myth " : " Irregularities and even violences of combination must be borne in science for the simple reason that our sources are too scanty and full of contradictions. Our hypotheses will in all such cases have something rash, bold, and surprising in them ; if even they are in the main correct, *i.e.*, if they are irrefutable according to the method of investigation " (" Der historische Jesus, der mythologische Jesus, und Jesus der Christ," 1910, 55). But if that very hypothesis is not established, yet this makes no difference in the fact that there existed a pre-Christian Jesus Christ, at least as a complex myth, and this quite suffices for the explanation of the Pauline Christology and the so-called " original community " of Jerusalem. I can, accordingly, only regard it as a misleading of the public when the other side, after rejecting the hypothesis of a pre-Christian cult of Jesus, bear themselves as though they had thereby taken away the foundations for the whole body of my views regarding an historical Jesus.

Meanwhile the storm which has been raised against my book in theological circles and in the Press, and has even led to mass meetings of protest in the Busch Circus and in the Dom at Berlin, shows me that I have " hit the bull's-eye " with my performance and have in truth touched the sore point of Christianity. The way in which the battle is being waged, the means by which my opponents attempt to disparage the author of " The Christ Myth," or to make me ridiculous in the eyes of the public by personal slanders, their habit of trying to injure me by throwing doubt on my intellectual capabilities, and to undermine my scientific honour and official position (Bornemann, Beth)—all this can only make me more determined to continue the work of illumination that I have begun, and only proves to me that my "Christ Myth" cannot be so absolutely "unscientific" and so completely a *quantité négligeable* as its opponents are disposed to represent it.

The means by which the "Christ Myth" is opposed to-day are exactly the same as those which were employed against Strauss's "Leben Jesu," without, however, the least result being attained. I accordingly await the further attacks of the enemy with complete coolness of mind, confident in the fact that what is true in my book will make its way of itself, and that a work which, like mine, has arisen from serious motives, and has been carried through with a disregard of personal advantages, cannot be lost but will be serviceable to the spiritual progress of mankind. The attacks which have so far come to my notice in pamphlets (Bornemann, v. Soden, Delbrück, Beth) and in the Press have not had the effect of making any weaker my fundamental convictions. On the contrary, they have only served to reveal to me still further the weakness of the opposing position, which is much greater than I myself had hitherto imagined. I am, however, at all times ready and pleased—and I have shown this too by the corrections undertaken since the first edition of this work—to give attention to real objections and to put right possible errors. All that matters to me is simply the fact as such. The question before us in "The Christ Myth," as it is not unnecessary to point out here once again, is a purely scientific one. For possible suggestions and advice in this direction I will accordingly at all times be grateful. On the contrary, I am left perfectly cold by personal slanders, anonymous threats, and pious corrections, meetings of protest in which the Minister of Public Worship takes part with obbligato trombone choirs and professions of faith, as well as by the uproar of the multitude roused to fanaticism in this manner by the " guardian of their souls." They are everything except refutations.

PROFESSOR DR. ARTHUR DREWS.

KARLSRUHE, *March,* 1910.

CONTENTS

THE PRE-CHRISTIAN JESUS

THE CHRIST MYTH

THE PRE-CHRISTIAN JESUS

"IF you see a man undaunted by dangers, undisturbed by passions, happy when fortune frowns, calm in the midst of storms, will you not be filled with reverence for him? Will you not say that here is something too great and grand to be regarded as of the same nature as the trivial body in which it dwells? A divine force has descended here—a heavenly power moves a soul so wonderful, so calm, one which passes through all life as though it were of small account, and smiles at all our hopes and fears. Nothing so great can exist without the help of God, and therefore in the main it belongs to that from which it came down. Just as the rays of the sun touch the earth, but belong to that from which they are sent, so a great and holy spirit, sent here that we may have a more intimate knowledge of deity, lives indeed in our midst, but remains in contact with its source. On that it depends, thither its eyes are turned, thither its life tends: among men it dwells as a noble guest. What then is this soul? One which relies upon no goodness but its own. What is proper to man is his soul and the perfect reason in the soul: for man is a rational animal: therefore his highest good is reached when he is filled with that of which he is born."

With these words the Roman philosopher Seneca

(4 B.C.–65 A.D.) portrays the ideally great and good
man that we may be moved to imitate him.* "We must
choose some good man," he says, "and always have him
before our eyes ; and we must live and act as if he were
watching us. A great number of sins would remain
uncommitted were there a witness present to those
about to sin. Our heart must have some one whom it
honours, and by whose example its inner life can be
inspired. Happy is he whose reverence for another
enables him to fashion his life after the picture living in
his memory. We need some one upon whose life we may
model our own : without the rule you cannot correct
what is amiss" (Ep. 11). "Rely on the mind of a
great man and detach yourself from the opinions
of the mob. Hold fast to the image of the most
beautiful and exalted virtue, which must be worshipped not with crowns but with sweat and blood"
(Ep. 67). "Could we but gaze upon the soul of a
good man, what a beautiful picture should we see,
how worthy of our reverence in its loftiness and peace.
There would justice shine forth and courage and prudence and wisdom : and humanity, that rare virtue,
would pour its light over all. Every one would declare
him worthy of honour and of love. If any one saw that
face, more lofty and splendid than any usually found
among men, would he not stand in dumb wonder as
before a God, and silently pray that it might be for his
good to have seen it ? Then, overcome by the inviting
grace of the vision, he would kneel in prayer, and after
long meditation, filled with wondering awe, he would
break forth into Virgil's words : ' Hail to thee, whoe'er
thou art ! O lighten thou our cares ! ' There is no one,
I repeat, who would not be inflamed with love were it
given him to gaze upon such an ideal. Now indeed

* Ep. ad Luc. 41.

much obscures our vision : but if we would only make our eyes pure and remove the veil that covers them, we should be able to behold virtue even though covered by the body, and clouded by poverty, lowliness and shame. We should see its loveliness even through the most sordid veils " (Ep. 115).

The attitude expressed in these words was widespread in the whole of the civilised world at the beginning of the Christian era. A feeling of the uncertainty of all things human weighed like a ghastly dream upon most minds. The general distress of the time, the collapse of the nation states under the rough hand of the Roman conquerors, the loss of independence, the uncertainty of political and social conditions, the incessant warfare and the heavy death-roll it involved—all this forced men back upon their own inner life, and compelled them to seek there for some support against the loss of outer happiness in a philosophy which raised and invigorated the soul. But the ancient philosophy had spent itself. The naïve interplay of nature and spirit, that ingenuous trust in external reality which had been the expression of a youthful vigour in the Mediterranean peoples, from which indeed the ancient civilisation was derived, now was shattered. To the eyes of men at that time Nature and Spirit stood opposed as hostile and irreconcilable facts. All efforts to restore the shattered unity were frustrated by the impossibility of regaining the primitive attitude. A fruitless scepticism which satisfied no one, but out of which no way was known, paralysed all joy in outward or inner activities, and prevented men from having any pleasure in life. Therefore all eyes were turned towards a supernatural support, a direct divine enlightenment, a revelation; and the desire arose of finding once again the lost certainty in the ordering of life by dependence upon an ideal and superhuman being.

Many saw in the exalted person of the Emperor the incarnation of such a divine being. It was not then always pure flattery, but often enough the expression of real gratitude towards individual Imperial benefactors, combined with a longing for direct proximity with and visible presence of a god, which gave to the worship of the Emperor its great significance throughout the whole Roman Empire.

An Augustus who had put an end to the horrors of the civil war must, in spite of everything, have appeared as a prince of peace and a saviour in the uttermost extremity, who had come to renew the world and to bring back the fair days of the Golden Age. He had again given to mankind an aim in life and to existence some meaning. As the head of the Roman State religion, a person through whose hands the threads of the policy of the whole world passed, as the ruler of an empire such as the world had never before seen, he might well appear to men as a God, as Jupiter himself come down to earth, to dwell among men. " Now at length the time is passed," runs an inscription, apparently of the ninth year before Christ, found at Priene not long ago, " when man had to lament that he had been born. That providence, which directs all life, has sent this man as a saviour to us and the generations to come. He will put an end to all feuds, and dispose all things nobly. In his appearance are the hopes of the past fulfilled. All earlier benefactors of mankind he has surpassed. It is impossible that a greater should come. The birthday of the God has brought for the world the messages of salvation (Gospels) which attend him. From his birth a new epoch must begin." *

* E. v. Mommsen and Wilamowitz in the *Transactions* of the German Archæological Institute, xxiii. Part iii. ; " Christl. Welt," 1899, No. 57. Compare as a specially characteristic expression of that

It was not only the longing of mankind for a new structure of society, for peace, justice, and happiness upon earth, which lay at the root of the cult of the Emperors. Deeper minds sought not only an improvement in political and social circumstances, but felt disturbed by thoughts of death and the fate of the soul after its parting from its bodily shell. They trembled at the expectation of the early occurrence of a world-wide catastrophe, which would put a terrible end to all existence. The apocalyptic frame of mind was so widespread at the commencement of the Christian era that even a Seneca could not keep his thoughts from the early arrival of the end of the world. Finally, there also grew up a superstitious fear of evil spirits and Dæmons, which we can scarcely exaggerate. And here no philosophic musings could offer a support to anxious minds, but religion alone. Seldom in the history of mankind has the need for religion been so strongly felt as in the last century before and the first century after Christ. But it was not from the old hereditary national religions that deliverance was expected. It was from the unrestrained commingling and unification of all existing religions, a religious syncretism, which was specially furthered by acquaintance with the strange, but on that account all the more attractive, religions of the East. Already Rome had become a Pantheon of almost all religions which one could believe, while in the Far East, in Nearer Asia, that breeding-place of ancient Gods and cults, there were continually appearing new, more daring and secret forms of religious activity. These, too, in a short while obtained their place in the consciousness of Western humanity. Where the public worship of the

period's longing for redemption the famous Fourth Eclogue of Virgil. Also Jeremias, " Babylonisches im Neuen Testament," 1905, pp. 57 *sqq.* Lietzmann, " Der Weltheiland," 1909.

recognised Gods did not suffice, men sought a deeper satisfaction in the numberless mystic associations of that time, or formed themselves with others of like mind into private religious bodies or pious brotherhoods, in order to nourish in the quiet of private ritualistic observance an individual religious life apart from the official State religion.

I

THE INFLUENCE OF PARSEEISM ON THE BELIEF IN A MESSIAH

AMONG no people was the longing for redemption so lively and the expectation of a speedy end of the world so strong as among the Jews. Since the Babylonian captivity (586–536 B.C.) the former Jewish outlook upon the world had undergone a great change. Fifty years had been spent by the Israelites in the land of the stranger. For two hundred years after their return to their own land they were under Persian overlordship. As a consequence of this they were in close connection politically and economically with the Achæmenidean Empire, and this did not cease when Alexander overthrew the Persian power and brought the whole Eastern world under Greek influence. During this lengthy period Persian modes of thinking and Persian religious views had influenced in many ways the old Jewish opinions, and had introduced a large number of new ideas. First of all the extreme dualism of the Persians had impressed a distinctly dual character upon Jewish Monotheism. God and the world, which in the old ideas had often mingled with one another, were separated and made to stand in opposition to each other. Following the same train of thought, the old national God Jahwe, in imitation of the Persian Ahuramazda (Ormuzd), had developed from a God of fire, light, and

37

sky into a God of supernatural purity and holiness. Surrounded by light and enthroned in the Beyond, like Ahuramazda, the source of all life, the living God held intercourse with his creatures upon the earth only through the instrumentality of a court of angels. These messengers of God or intermediate beings in countless numbers moved between heaven and earth upon his service. And just as Angromainyu (Ahriman), the evil, was opposed to Ahuramazda, the good, and the struggle between darkness and light, truth and falsehood, life and death, was, according to Persian ideas, reproduced in the course of earthly events, so the Jews too ascribed to Satan the rôle of an adversary of God, a corrupter of the divine creation, and made him, as Prince of this world and leader of the forces of hell, measure his strength with the King of Heaven.*

In the struggle of the two opposing worlds, according to Persian ideas, Mithras stood in the foreground, the spirit of light, truth, and justice, the divine " friend " of men, the " mediator," " deliverer," and " saviour " of the world. He shared his office with Honover, Ahuramazda's Word of creation and revelation; and indeed in most

* It is certain that the old Israelite Jahwe only attained that spiritualised character for which he is nowadays extolled under the influence of the Persians' imageless worship of God. All efforts to construct, in spite of this admission, a " qualitative " difference between Jahwe and Ahuramazda, as, for example, Stave does in his work (" Der Einfluss des Parsismus auf das Judentum," 1898, 122 sq.) are unavailing. According to Stave, the conception of good and evil is not grasped in Mazdeism in all its purity and truth, but " has been confused with the natural." But is that distinction "grasped in all its purity " in Judaism with its ritualistic le ality? Indeed, has it come to a really pure realisation even in Christianity, in which piety and attachment to the Church so often pass as identical ideas? Let us give to each religion its due, and cease to be subtle in drawing such artificial distinctions in favour of our own—distinctions which fall into nothingness before every unprejudiced consideration.

things their attributes were mingled. An incarnation of fire or the sun, above all of the struggling, suffering, triumphant light, which presses victoriously through night and darkness, Mithras was also connected with death and immortality, and passed as guide of souls and judge in the under-world. He was the "divine son," of whom it was said that Ahuramazda had fashioned him as great and worthy of reverence as his own self. Indeed, he was in essence Ahuramazda himself, proceeding from his supernatural light, and given a concrete individuality. As companion in creation and "protector" of the world he kept the universe standing in its struggle against its enemies. At the head of the heavenly host he fought for God, and with his sword of flame he drove the Dæmons of Darkness in terror back into the shadows. To take part in this combat on the side of God, to build up the future kingdom of God by the work of a life-giving civilisation, by the rendering fruitful of sterile wastes, the extinction of noxious animals, and by moral self-education, seemed the proper end of human existence. But when the time should have been fulfilled and the present epoch come to an end, according to Persian belief, Ahuramazda was then to raise up from the seed of Zarathustra, the founder of this religion, the "virgin's son," Saoshyant (Sraosha, Sosiosch, which signifies the Saviour), or, as it ran according to another rendering, Mithras himself should descend upon the earth and in a last fierce struggle overwhelm Angromainyu and his hosts, and cast them down into the Nether World. He would then raise the dead in bodily shape, and after a General Judgment of the whole world, in which the wicked should be condemned to the punishments of hell and the good raised to heavenly glory, establish the "millennial Kingdom of Peace." Hell itself was not to last for ever, for a great reconciliation was to be finally held out even to the damned. Then Angromainyu also would make peace with Ahuramazda, and upon a new earth beneath a new heaven all were to be united to one another in everlasting blessedness.

These ideas entered the circle of Jewish thought and there brought about a complete transformation of the former belief in a Messiah.

Messiah—that is, the Anointed (in Greek, Christos)— originally signified the king as representative of Jahwe before the people and of the people before Jahwe. According to 2 Sam. vii. 13 *sq.*, he was placed in the same relation of an obedient " son " to his " father," in which the whole people was conscious of standing.* Then the opposition between the holy dignity of the " Anointed " of God and the humanly imperfect personality of the Jewish kings led to the ideal of the Messiah being transferred to the future and the complete realisation of the rule of Jahwe over his people being expected only then. In this sense the ancient prophets had already celebrated the Messiah as an ideal King of the future, who would experience in the fullest sense the high assurances of Jahwe's favour, of which David had been deemed worthy, since he would be completely worthy of them. They had described him as the Hero, who would be more than Moses and Joshua, who would establish the promised glory of Israel, dispose the people anew, and bring Jahwe's religion even to the heathen.† They had glorified him in that he would span the heavens afresh, establish a new earth, and make Israel Lord over all nations.‡ In this they had at first understood the Messiah only as a human being, as a new David or of his seed—theocratic king, divinely favoured prince of peace and just ruler over his people, just as the

---

* Exod. iv. 22; Deut. xxxii. 6; Hosea xi. 1.
† Isa. xlix. 6, 8. ‡ *Id.* li. 16.

Persian Saoshyant was to be a man of the seed of Zarathustra. In this sense a Cyrus, the deliverer of the people from the Babylonian captivity, the rescuer and overlord of Israel, had been acclaimed Messiah.* But just as Saoshyant had been undesignedly transfigured in the imagination of the people into a divine being and made one with the figure of Mithras,† so also among the prophets the Messiah was more and more assigned the part of a divine king. He was called " divine hero," " Father of Eternity," and the prophet Isaiah indulged in a description of his kingdom of peace, in which the wolf would lie down by the lamb,men would no longer die before their time, and would enjoy the fruit of their fields without tithe, while right and justice would reign upon earth under this king of a golden age as it had never done before.‡ Secret and supernatural, as was his nature, so should the birth of the Messiah be. Though a divine child, he was to be born in lowly state.§ The personality of the Messiah mingled with that of Jahwe himself, as though it were God himself of whose ascending the throne and journey heavenwards the Psalmists sing.‖

These alternations of the Messiah between a human and a divine nature appear still more clearly in the Jewish apocalyptics of the last century before and the first century after Christ. Thus the Apocalypse of Daniel (about 165 B.C.) speaks of one who as Son of Man will descend upon the clouds of heaven and will be brought before the " Ancient of Days." The whole tone of the passage leaves no doubt that the Son of Man (barnasa) is a superhuman being representing the Deity. To him the

* Isa. xliv. 28, xlv. 1 *sq.*
† Cumont, " Textes et monuments figurés relatifs aux mystères de Mithra," 1899, vol. i. 188.   ‡ Isa. xi. 65, 17 *sqq.*
§ Isa. ix. 6; Micah v. 1.   ‖ Psa. xlvii. 6, 9, lvii. 12.

majesty and kingdom of God have been entrusted in order that, at the end of the existing epoch, he should descend upon the clouds of heaven, surrounded by a troop of angels, and establish an everlasting power, a Kingdom of Heaven. In the picture-language of Enoch (in the last decade before Christ) the Messiah, the "Chosen One," the " Son of Man," appears as a supernatural pre-existing being, who was hidden in God before the world was created, whose glory continues from eternity to eternity and his might from generation to generation, in whom the spirit of wisdom and power dwells, who judges hidden things, punishes the wicked, but will save the holy and just.* Indeed, the Apocalypse of Esdras (the so-called fourth Book of Esdras) expressly combats the opinion that the judgment of the world will come through another than God, and likewise describes the Messiah as a kind of "second God," as the " Son of God," as the human incarnation of the Godhead.†

In all of this the influence of Persian beliefs is unmistakable, whether these arose in Iran itself directly, or whether the idea of a God-appointed king and deliverer of the world was borrowed by the Persians from the circle of Babylonian ideas. Here this conception had taken deep root and was applied at different times now to this king, now to that.‡ Just as in the Persian religion the image of Saoshyant, so also in the Jewish view the picture of the Messiah wavered between a human king of the race of David and a supernatural being of divine nature descended from heaven. And just as in the Persian representation of the coming of Saoshyant and the final victory of the Kingdom of Light

* Ch. xlv.–li.
† Ch. vi. 1 *sqq.*
‡ Cf. Gunkel, " Zum religionsgesch. Verständnis des Neuen Testaments," 1903, p. 23, note 4.

there would be a preceding period during which threatening signs would appear in the heavens, the whole of nature would find itself in upheaval and mankind would be scourged with fearful plagues, so also the Jewish Apocalypse speaks of the "woes" of the Messiah and describes a period of terror which would precede the coming of the Messiah. The coming of the power of God was looked upon as a miraculous catastrophe suddenly breaking in from on high, as a conflagration of the world followed by a new creation. The Jewish agreed with the Persian view in this also, that it made a heavenly kingdom of undisturbed bliss " in the light of the everlasting life and in likeness of the angels " follow the earthly world-wide empire of the Messiah. This they imagined on exactly the same lines as the Persian Paradise. There would the holy drink of the "Water of Life" and nourish themselves on the fruit which hang upon the "Tree of Life." The wicked, on the other hand, would be cast into hell and suffer in fearful torments the just punishment of their sins.*

The conception of a resurrection of the dead and a last judgment had hitherto been strange to the Jews. In pre-exilic days they allowed the body to die and the soul after death to go down as a shadow without feeling into Hades (Sheol), without disturbing themselves further about its fate. Now, however, with the doctrine of the destruction of the world by fire and the general judgment, the idea of personal immortality entered the world of Jewish thought. Thus it is said by Daniel that on the day of judgment the dead will rise again, some waking to everlasting life, others to everlasting perdition. "But the teachers will shine as the brightness of heaven, and those who led the multitude to

---

* Revelation xxii.; cf. Pfleiderer, "Das Urchristentum. Seine Schriften und seine Lehren," 2nd edit., 1902, vol. ii. 54 *sqq.*

justice as the stars for ever and ever." * With the acceptance of personal immortality the whole tone of religious thought was deepened and enriched in the direction of thought for the individual. Former Jewish morality had been essentially of a collective kind. It was not so much the individual as the people viewed collectively that was looked upon as the object of divine solicitude. At this point the position, the road to which had been already prepared by the prophets, was definitely established, that the individual hoped for a personal religious salvation and as a consequence felt in direct personal relationship with Jahwe. God indeed remained, as the Persians had taught them to understand him, the superhuman lord of heaven enthroned in pure light, the source of all life, the living God. His metaphysical qualities, however, his dazzling glory and unconquerable might were ever more and more overshadowed by his moral attributes: goodness, grace, and mercy appeared as the most prominent features in the character of Jahwe. God seemed a loving father who leads his children through life with kindly care, and without whose consent not a hair of one of his creatures could be touched. The strong tendency within Judaism, represented by the upper currents of pharisaic rabbinism, continually drew the national boundaries closer, and was ever more anxiously occupied with a painfully strict observance of the letter of the law and a conscientious observance of ritualistic ordinances. Ethics threatened to be extinguished under a system of conventional rules of an essentially juristic nature. Yet all the while a more human and natural morality was arising, an inward piety, warm-hearted, popular, and sound, which broke through the narrow limits of Jewish nationalism, and sent a fresh current into the heavy atmosphere of

* Dan. xii. 3.

official legality. It was then that the groundwork of later Christian ethics was laid in the purified morality of the psalms, aphorisms, and other edificatory writings of a Job, Baruch, Jesus son of Sirach, &c. It was then that the Jewish Monotheism set itself to extend its sway beyond the boundaries of its own land and to enter into competition with the other religions of antiquity, from which it was to draw back vanquished only before a matured Christianity.

II

THE HELLENISTIC IDEA OF A MEDIATOR (PHILO)

WITH Alexander's conquest of the Persian Empire Palestine also was drawn within the circle of Hellenistic culture. It was at first a vassal state of the Egyptian Ptolemies, and consequently at the commencement of the second century before Christ came under the overlordship of the Syrian Seleucids. The customs and intellectual life of Greece forced their way into the quiet isolation of the priest-ruled Jewish state and could not be expelled again, despite the national reaction under the Maccabees against foreign influences. Above all, however, the dispersal of the Jews contributed to bring about a settlement of opposing views. Since the Exile the Jews had spread over all the countries of the East Mediterranean. Some had remained in Babylon, others were permanently settled especially in the ports as tradesmen, bankers, and merchants. They controlled the entire money market and trade of the East through their assiduous industry, mercantile sharpness, their lack of scruples, and the tenacity with which they held together, supported therein by their worship in common in the Synagogue. In the atmosphere of Greek philosophy and morality a still further transformation and purification of Jahwe took place. All common human and material lineaments were dropped, and he developed into a spiritual being of perfect goodness, such as Plato had described the Godhead. Here the Jews found themselves face to face with the same problem that had long occupied the Greek philosophers. This was the reconciliation of the supernatural loftiness and aloofness from the world of their God with the demands of the religious consciousness that required the immediate presence of Godhead.

Among the ideas which were borrowed by Judaism from the Persian religion belonged those connected with the mediatory " Word." As the creative power of the Godhead, the bearer of revelation and representative of God upon earth, the expression " the word " had already appeared in aphoristic literature. Under Græco-Egyptian influence the term " wisdom " (*sophia*) had become the naturalised expression for it. " Wisdom " served to describe the activities in regard to man of the God who held aloof from the world. In this connection it may be noted that according to Persian ideas " Wisdom " under the name of Spenta Armaiti was considered as one of the six or seven Amesha Spentas (Amshaspands), those spirits that stood as a bodyguard closest to the throne of God and corresponded to the Jewish archangels. She was considered by the Persians as the daughter or spouse of Ahuramazda. Already, in the so-called " Wisdom of Solomon," written by an Alexandrian Jew in the last century before Christ, she was declared to be a separately existing spirit in close relation to God. Under the guise of a half-personal, half-material being—a power controlling the whole of nature—she was described as the principle of the revelation of God in the creation, maintenance, and ruling of the world, as the common principle of life from on high and as the intermediary organ of religious salvation. Just as Plato had sought to overcome the dualism of the ideal and the material world by the conception of a " world-soul," so " Wisdom " was intended to serve as an intermediary between the opposites, the God of the Jews and his creation. These efforts were continued by the Alexandrian Jew Philo (30 B.C. to 50 A.D.), who tried to bring the Perso-Jewish conception of the "Word" or "Wisdom" into closer accord with the ideas of Greek philosophy than the author of the "Book of Wisdom" had already done. Philo, too, commenced with the opposition between an unknowable, unnameable God, absolutely raised above the world, and material created existence. He imagined this opposition bridged over by means of "powers" which, as relatively self-existing individuals, messengers, servants, and representatives of God, at one time more closely resembled Persian angels or Greek Dæmons, at another time the Platonic "Ideas," the originals and patterns of God in creating. Essentially, however, they bore the character of the so-called "Fructifying powers," those creative forces which infused a soul and design into formless matter and by means of which the Stoic philosophers sought to explain existence. As the first of these intermediate forces, or, indeed, as the essence of them all, Philo considered the "Logos," efficacious reason or the creative word of God. He called him the "firstborn son of God" or the "second God," the representative, interpreter, ambassador, Archangel of God, or Prince of Angels. He considered him as the High Priest, who made intercession with God for the world, the affairs of which he represented before him as the paraclete, the advocate and consoler of the world, who was the channel to it of the divine promises; as the tool with which God had fashioned the world, the original and ideal of it to which God had given effect in its creation—that which operated in all things; in a word, as the soul or spirit of the world, which the Stoics had identified with their God, but which Philo distinguished from the other-world Divinity and looked upon as his revelation and manifestation.

In essence only an expression for the sum total of all divine forces and activities, the Logos of Philo also was sometimes an impersonal metaphysical principle, simply the efficacy of the Godhead, and sometimes an independent personality distinct from God. Just as the Stoics had personified their world-reason in Hermes, the messenger of the Gods, so the Egyptians had raised Amun Ra's magic word of creation to a self-existing personal mediatory being in Thoth the guide of souls; the Babylonians, the word of fate of the great God Marduk in the shape of Nabu; the Persians, the word of Ahuramazda in Vohu mano as well as in the Spenta Armaiti, the good thought of the creative God. And just as according to Persian ideas it was at one time the divine " son " and mediator " Mithras," the collectivity of all divine forces, at another the ideal man Saoshyant who appeared as Saviour and Deliverer of the world, and just as both mingled in one form, so Philo also at one time described the Word as the collectivity of all creative ideas, at another only as the unembodied idea of man, the ideal man, the direct divine image and immaterial pattern of the material exemplars of humanity, that is effective therein as the subject of all religious redemption. Indeed, he occasionally identified him with the tree of life in Paradise, since both were everlasting and " stood in the middle."

According to Philo, man is unable of his own strength to free himself from the bonds of earthly existence. All deliverance depends upon the emancipation of the soul from the body and its sensuous desires. In conformity with his true spiritual and godlike nature, to become as perfect as God, is the highest virtue and at the same time true happiness. This is attained by an insight into the divine reality of things, by whole-hearted trust in God, by grateful recognition of the goodness and love bestowed by him, showing itself in piety towards God as well as in charity and justice towards other men. But in addition the Logos itself must be in us and cause for us the insight into our divine nature. The Logos must guide us, come to the aid of our human weakness with his supernatural strength in the struggles against the world and sin and raise us up to God. Thus the apotheosis of man is the goal aimed at in all religious activity. The Logos, however, is the only means to this end, in so far as we are raised through union with him in faith and love to our true origin and life's source, "the vision of God," and thereby have participation in his life.

III

JESUS AS CULT-GOD IN THE CREED OF JEWISH SECTS

ALL religious spirits of the time longed to secure this happy vision and communion with God, and to obtain even here on earth a foretaste of the heavenly life. The Jews sought to attain this end by a painfully exact observance of the ordinances of their law, but in so doing they became entangled in a mesh of such minute and tiresome regulations that the more they applied themselves to the service of the law the more difficult it appeared. It seemed to be no longer possible to reconcile the demands of everyday life with one's religious duties. Some therefore withdrew from the life of the world and in retirement and quiet endeavoured to devote themselves exclusively to the "inner life." In Egypt the Therapeutes or Physicians, a religious association composed of Jews and their proselytes, with their headquarters in the neighbourhood of Alexandria, sought in this manner, as Philo informs us in his work "On the Contemplative Life," to give effect to the claims of religion as expressed by Philo himself.* Their religious

---

* The assertion advanced by Grätz and Lucius that the work mentioned is a forgery of a fourth-century Christian foisted upon Philo with the object of recommending the Christian "Ascesis," and that a sect of Therapeutes never existed, can now be considered disposed of, since its refutation by Massebiau and Conybeare. Cf. Pfleiderer, " Urchristentum," ii. 5 *sq*.

observances resembled those of the Orphic-Pythagorean sects, as in abstinence from flesh and wine, admiration for virginity, voluntary poverty, religious feasts and community singing, and the use of white garments.

They made a deep study of the mystical writings of revelation that had been handed down, and these they used as a guide in the allegorical explanation of the Mosaic law. They united a contemplative piety with a common religious observance, and thus sought to strengthen themselves mutually in the certainty of religious salvation. Beyond the Jordan the Jewish sect of the Essenes (from the Syrian word *chase*, plural *chasen* or *chasaja*) had their chief settlement. These called themselves, as is expressed by their name, the " Pious " or " Godfearing." In their esteem of temperance, celibacy, and poverty, their reprobation of slavery, private property, the taking of oaths, and blood-sacrifice, in the honour they paid the sun as a visible manifestation of the divine light, they agreed with the Therapeutes. They differed from them, however, in their monastic organisation and the regular manner in which the life of the community was divided among different classes, their strict subordination to superiors, their maintenance of a novitiate of several years, the secrecy of the traditions of the sect, and their cultivation of the healing art and magic. The Therapeutes passed their lives in leisurely contemplation and spiritual exercises ; the Essenes, on the other hand, engaged in the rearing of stock, farming, and bee-culture, or they pursued a handicraft, and in the country places or towns of Judæa, where they often dwelt together in houses of the order, they lived as dwellers in a desert the life of purity and sanctity. Both sects, again, were alike in expecting an early end of the world and in seeking to prepare themselves for the reception of the promises of God by the cultivation of brotherly dispositions amongst themselves, by justice, good works, and benevolence towards their fellow-men, finding therein the special occupation of their lives.*

Of what nature were the secret traditions upon which these sects rested? We know from the Jewish historian Josephus that the Essenes clung to an extreme dualism of soul and body, in which, indeed, they agreed with the other religious associations of antiquity. Like all mystical sects, they regarded the body as the grave and prison-house of the immortal soul, to which it had been banished from an earlier life in light and blessedness. They also grounded their longing for deliverance from the world of sense and their strivings towards the glory of a better life of the soul beyond the grave upon pessimism in regard to human existence. They even regarded the performance of secret rites as a necessary condition of redemption. But in the opinion of the Essenes it was essential above all to know the names of the angels and dæmons who opened the passage to the different heavens, disposed one above another. This knowledge was to be revealed to men by one of the higher gods, a god-redeemer. A conception allied to that lay at the root of the Book of Wisdom, as well as of Philo's work—the belief in the magic power of the redemptive word of God, mingled by the Essenes with many strange Egyptian, Persian, and Babylonian ingredients and removed from the sphere of philosophic thought to the region of a rankly luxuriant superstition. Thus the closely related Jewish Apocalypse had expressly supported the revelation of a secret divine wisdom.†

* Cf. as regards the Essenes, Schürer, " Geschichte des jüdischen Volkes im Zeitalter Jesu Christi," 1898, TT. 573–584.

† Regarding the connection between the Essenes and the Apocalypse, cf. Hilgenfeld, " Die jüdische Apokalyptik," 1857, p. 253 *sqq.*

Indeed, we now know that this whole world of thought belonged to an exceedingly manifold syncretic religious system, composed of Babylonian, Persian, Jewish, and Greek ingredients, which ruled the whole of Western Asia in the last centuries before Christ. Its followers called themselves Adonæi, after the name of its supposed founder, Ado (? Adonis). It is, however, generally described as the Mandaic religion, according to another name for its followers, the so-called Mandæi (Gnostics).*

Of the numberless sects into which this religion split only a few names have come down to us, of which some played a part in the history of the heresies of early Christianity; for example, the Ophites or Nassenes, the Ebionites, Perates, Sethianes, Heliognostics, Sampsæes, &c.† We are thus much better acquainted with their fundamental ideas, which were very fantastic and complicated. They all subscribed to the belief in the redemption of the soul of man from its grave of darkness by a mediatory being, originally hidden in God and then expressly awakened or appointed by him for this purpose. In original Mandaism he bore the name of Mandâ de hajjê—that is, Gnosis, or " word " of life. In the form of Hibil-ziwâ, the Babylonian Marduk or Nabu, he was to descend from heaven with the keys thereof, and by means of his magic obtain the dominion of the world. He was to conquer those dæmons that had fallen away from God, introduce the end of the world, and lead back the souls of light to the highest Godhead.

As the Apocalyptics show, this view had numerous adherents among the Jews of Palestine also. All those who found no satisfaction in the literalness of the

---

* On this point, cf. Brandt, " Die mandäische Religion," 1899 ; " Realenzyklop, f.d. protest. Theologie u. Kirche," xii. 160 *sqq.* ; Gunkel, *op. cit.*, 18 *sqq.*

† Cf. Hilgenfeld, " Ketzergeschichte des Urchristentums," 1884.

Pharasaic beliefs and the business-like superficiality of the official Jewish religion, found edification in ideas of this sort, which excited the imagination. They dealt with them as "mysteries," and sought, as may well be from fear of conflicts with traditional religion, to keep them secret from the public.* Hence it is that we have such an incomplete knowledge of this side of the religious life of the Jews. At any rate they clothed their expected Messiah with the attributes of the Mandaic God of Mediation, and they appear, as is clear from the Apocalypse of Daniel and that of John, to have taken particular pleasure in the description of the scene where God calls (" awakes ") the Redeemer to his mediatory office and installs him as Deliverer, Ruler of the World, and Judge of the living and the dead.

We are accustomed to look upon the Jewish religion as strictly monotheistic. In truth, it never was, even in the Mosaic times, until after the return from Exile. And this is clear, in spite of the trouble which the composers of the so-called historic books of the Old Testament have taken to work up the traditions in a monotheistic sense and to obliterate the traces of the early Jewish polytheism, by transforming the ancient gods into patriarchs, heroes, angels, and servants of Jahwe. It was not entirely Babylonian, Persian, and Greek opinions which influenced Judaism in a polytheistic direction; from the beginning, besides the theory of one God, emphasised by the priesthood and official world, there existed a belief in other Gods. This constantly received fresh nourishment from foreign influences, and it appears to have been chiefly cultivated in the secret societies. On the descent of the Israelites into Canaan each tribe brought with it its special God, under whose specific guidance it believed its deeds were accomplished. By the reforms of the

* Gunkel, *op. cit.*, 29.

Prophets these Gods were suppressed; but the higher grew the regard for Jahwe (apparently the God of the tribe of Judah), and the further he was in consequence withdrawn from the world to an unapproachable distance, the more strongly the remembrance of the ancient Gods again arose and assumed the form of the recognition of divine intermediate beings, the so-called "Sons of God." In these the longing for the direct presence and visible representation of God sought expression. Such appears to have been the "Presence," or "Angel of God," with whom Jacob wrestled in the desert,[*] who led the Israelites out of Egypt and went before them as a pillar of flame,[†] who fought against their enemies, drove the Canaanites from their homes,[‡] held intercourse with the prophets Elijah and Ezekiel,[§] and stood by the people of Jahwe in every difficulty.[||] He is also called the "King" (Melech), or "Son" of Jahwe,[¶] and thus exactly resembles the Babylonian Marduk, the Persian Mithras, the Phœnician Hercules or Moloch, "the first-born son" of God (Protogonos), who also appeared among the Orphics under the name of Phanes (*i.e.,* Countenance), who wrestles with Zeus at Olympia as Jacob with Jahwe, and, like him, dislocates his hip in the struggle with Hippokoon. In the rabbinic theology he is compared with the mystic Metatron, a being related to the Logos, "The Prince of the Presence," "Leader of Angels," "Lord of Lords," "King of Kings," "Commencement of the Way of God." He was also called the "Protector," "Sentinel," and "Advocate" of Israel, who lays petitions before God, and "in whom is the name of the Lord."[**] Thus he is identical with that Angel

---

[*] Gen. xxxii. 24.

[†] Numb. xx. 16 ; Exod. xiii. 21.

[‡] Exod. xxxiii. 14 ; 2 Sam. v. 23.

[§] 1 Kings i. 3 ; Ezek. xliii. 5.

[||] Isa. lxiii. 9 *sqq.*

[¶] Psa. ii.

[**] Cf. Ghillany, "Die Menschenopfer der alten Hebräer," 1842,

promised in the second Book of Moses, in whom also is
the name of Jahwe, who was to lead Israel to victory over
the Amorites, Hittites, Perizzites, Canaanites, Hivites,
and Jebusites.* But he, again, is no other than Joshua,
who was said to have overthrown these nations with
Jahwe's aid.† But Joshua himself is apparently an
ancient Ephraimitic God of the Sun and Fruitfulness,
who stood in close relation to the Feast of the Pasch
and to the custom of circumcision.‡

Now, many signs speak in favour of the fact that
Joshua or Jesus was the name under which the expected
Messiah was honoured in certain Jewish sects. In Zech.
iii. Joshua, who, according to Ezra iii. 2, led back the
Jews into their old homes after the Babylonian captivity,
just as the older Joshua brought back the Israelites into
Canaan, the promised land of their fathers, was invested
as High Priest by the "Angel of the Lord," and promised
the continuance of his priesthood so long as he walked in
the ways of the Lord. In Zech. vi. 9–15 the High Priest
Joshua is crowned as Messiah and brought into connection with the " branch " under which the glory of God's
kingdom will come to pass. It is true that in this passage
under the title of Messiah Zerubbabel, the leader of the
Jews of the race of David, was originally understood.

326–334 ; Eisenmenger, " Entdecktes Judentum," 1711, i. 311, 395
sqq. Also Movers, " Die Phönizier," 1841 ; i. 398 *sq.*

* Exod. xxiii. 20 *sqq.*

† Jos. xxiv. 11.

‡ Jos. v. 2–10. The unhistorical nature of Joshua is admitted also
by Stade. Stade counts him an Ephraimitic myth, recalling to mind
in so doing that the Samaritans possessed an apocryphal book of
the same name in place of our Book of Joshua (" Gesch. d. Volkes
Israel," 1887, i. 64 *sqq.*, 135). The Samaritan Book of Joshua
(Chronicum Samaritanum, published 1848) was written in Arabic
during the thirteenth century in Egypt, and is based upon an old
work composed in the third century B.C. containing stories which
in part do not appear in our Book of Joshua.

In him the prophet thought he could discern that "branch" by which, in accordance with Isaiah xi. 1, the House of David was again to obtain the rule. Since, however, the great hopes set upon Zerubbabel as Messiah were not fulfilled, a correction was made (and this before the Bible was translated into Greek) in the text of the prophet, as follows : The name of Zerubbabel was struck out, the plural changed into the singular, so that Joshua alone was represented as having been crowned, the promises regarding the Messiah accordingly also passing over to him (Stade, "Gesch. des Volkes Israel," 1888, ii. 126, note. Hühn, "Die messianischen Weissagungen des israel. Volkes," 1889, 62 et sq.).

Jesus was a name given, as will be still more clearly shown, not only to the High Priest of Zechariah and to the successor of Moses, both of whom were said to have led Israel back into its ancient home, both having a decidedly Messianic character. The name in ancient times also belonged to the Healthbringer and Patron of the Physician—namely, Jasios or Jason, the pupil of Chiron skilled in healing *—who in general shows a remarkable resemblance to the Christian Redeemer. Consider also the significant fact that three times at decisive turning-points in the history of the Israelites a Joshua appears who leads his people into their promised home, into Canaan and Jerusalem, into the Kingdom of God—the "New Jerusalem." Now, as Epiphanius remarks in his "History of the Heretics," Jesus bears in the Hebrew language the same meaning as curator, therapeutes—that is, physician and curer. But the Therapeutes and Essenes regarded themselves as

---

* That the hypothesis of Smith here mentioned is quite admissible from the linguistic point of view has lately been maintained by Schmiedel in opposition to Weinel (*Protestantenbl.*, 1910, No. 17, 438).

physicians, and, above all, physicians of the soul. It
is accordingly by no means improbable that they too
honoured the God of their sect under this name.* We,
moreover, read in a Parisian magic-papyrus recently
found and published by Wessely (line 3119 *et sq.*) :
" I exort thee by Jesus the God of the Hebrews." The
words are found in an ostensibly "Hebrew Logos" of
that papyrus, the tone of which is quite ancient, moreover shows no trace of Christian influence, and is ascribed
by the transcriber to "the Pure," under which name,
according to Dieterich, the Essenes or Therapeutes are
to be understood.† The Jessaes or Jessenes (Jessaioi)
named themselves after Jesus, or after " the branch from
the root of Jesse." ‡ They were closely connected on one
side with the Essenes and on the other side with the Jewish
sect of the Nazarenes or Nazoraes (Nazoraiori), if they
were not absolutely identical. These were, as Epiphanius
shows, in existence long before Christ, and had no knowledge of him.§ They were, however, called Nazoraes (Nazarenes (Nazarenos) is only a linguistic variation of it, cf.
Essaes and Essenes) because they honoured the Mediator
God, the divine "son," as a protector and guardian
(Syrian, Nasaryá; Hebrew, Ha-nôsrî) (cf. "the Protector of Israel," also the fact that Mithras was honoured
as "Protector of the World"). According to Acts
xxiv. 5 the first followers of Jesus were also called
Nazoraes or Nazarenes. The expressions "Jesus" and
"Nazorean" were therefore originally of almost like meaning, and by the addition of " the Nazorean" or " Nazarene " Jesus is not characterised as the man of Nazareth,
as the Evangelists represent it, but as the Healer and
Deliverer.

Whether there was a place called Nazareth in pre-

* Epiph., " Hæresiol." xxix. Smith, *op. cit.*, 37 *sq.*, 54.
‡ Isa. ii. 1. Cf. Epiphanius, *op. cit.* § *Id.* xxix. 6.

Christian days must be considered as at least very
doubtful. Such a place is not mentioned either in the
Old Testament or in the Talmud, which, however, mentions more than sixty Galilean towns ; nor, again, by
the Jewish historian Josephus, nor in the Apocrypha.
Cheyne believes himself justified by this in the conclusion that Nazareth in the New Testament is a pure
geographical fiction.*

It is only in the later phases of the tradition that the
name appears in the New Testament as a place-name. In
the earlier ones the Nazorean (Nazarene) only signifies
the follower of a particular sect, or is a surname of Jesus
which characterises the significance attached to him in
the thoughts of his followers. " The Nazorean" appears
here only as an integral part of the whole name of Jesus,
as Zeus Xenios, Hermes Psychopompos, Apollo Pythios,
&c., &c. It is applied to Jesus only as Guardian of the
world, Protector and Deliverer of Men from the power of
sin and Dæmons, but without any reference to a quite
obscure and entirely unknown village named Nazareth,
which is mentioned in documents beyond any dispute,
only from the fourth century on (see Eusebius, Jerome, and
Epiphanius). Or where else is a sect named after the
birthplace of its founder? † Moreover, even in the Gospels
it is not Nazareth but Capernaum which is described as

---

* " Enc. Bibl.," art. "Nazareth."

† " Since ha-nosrîm was a very usual term for guardians or protectors, it follows that when the term or its Greek equivalent hoi
Nazoraioi was used the adoption of its well-known meaning was unavoidable. Even if the name was really derived from the village of
Nazareth, no one would have thought of it. Every one would have
unavoidably struck at once upon the current meaning. If a class of
persons was called protectors, every one would understand that as
meaning that they protected something. No one would hit upon it to
derive their name from an otherwise unknown village named
Protection " (Smith, op. cit., 47).

his city; while Nazareth does not play any part at all in the life of Jesus. For the passages Matt. xiii. 53–58 and Mark vi. 1–6, according to which he had no success with his miracles in his "patris" on account of the unbelief of the people, leave the question open whether under the name of "patris" one is to understand his father-city Nazareth or somewhere else. The corresponding passage, Luke iv. 16–31, mentions Nazareth, it is true, in connection with this incident; but it is in discrepancy with the older versions of Matthew and Mark, and it appears otherwise recognisable as a later redaction of the passages in the other Gospels.*

Now the expression nazar or netzer in the sense of twig (sprout) is found not only in the well-known passage Isaiah xi. 1, where the Messiah is described as the "rod from the tree of Jesse" or "the twig from its root." In fine, was not the twig looked upon as a symbol of the Redeemer in his character of a God of vegetation and life, as was the case in the worship of Mithras, of Men, a god of Asia Minor, of Attis, Apollo,† &c., and did not this idea also make itself felt in the name of the Nazareans? "He shall be called a Nazarene,"‡ accordingly, does not signify that he was to be born in the small village of Nazareth, which probably did not exist in the time of Jesus, but that he is the promised netzer or Zemah, who makes all new, and restores the time when "one loads the other beneath vine and fig-tree,"§ and wonderful increase will appear.‖ Again, the possibility is not excluded of the name of the Nazareans having been confused with that of the Nasiraes (Nazirites), those "holy" or "dedicated" ones, who were a survival in Judea from the times when the Israelite tribes were nomads. These

---

* Cf. in this connection Smith, *op. cit.*, 36 *sq.*, 42 *sqq.*
† Cf. Cumont, *op. cit.*, 195 *sq.* ‡ Matt. ii. 25.
§ Zech. iii. 10. ‖ Jeremias, *op. cit.*, 56; cf. also 33 and 46, notes.

sought to express their opposition to the higher civilisation of the conquered land by patriarchal simplicity and purity of life, abstinence from the use of oil, wine, and the shears, &c.*

According to this, Jesus (Joshua) was originally a divinity, a mediator, and God of healing of those pre-Christian Jewish sectaries, with reference to whom we are obliged to describe the Judaism of the time—as regards certain of its tendencies, that is—as a syncretic religion.† " The Revelation of John " also appears to be a Christian redaction of an original Jewish work which in all likelihood belonged to a pre-Christian cult of Jesus. The God Jesus which appears in it has nothing to do with the Christian Jesus. Moreover, its whole range of ideas is so foreign even to ancient Judaism that it can be explained only by the influence of heathen religions upon the Jewish.‡ It is exactly the same with the so-called "Doctrine of the Twelve Apostles." This too displays a Jewish foundation, and speaks of a Jesus in the context of the words of the supper, who is in no wise the same as the Christian Redeemer.§ It is comprehensible that the later Christians did all they could in order to draw the veil of forgetfulness over these things. Nevertheless Smith has succeeded in his book, " The Pre-Christian Jesus," in showing clear evidences even in the New Testament of a cult of an old God Jesus. Among other things the phrase " τὰ περὶ τοῦ Ἰησοῦ " (" the things concerning Jesus ")|| which according to all appearance has no reference to the history of Jesus, but only means the

---

* Robertson, " A Short History of Christianity," 1902, 9 *sqq.*

† Gunkel, *op. cit.*, 34.

‡ *Id., op. cit.*, 39–63 ; cf. also Robertson, " Pagan Christs," 1903, 155 *seq.*

§ Cf. Robertson, *op. cit.*, 156.

|| Mark v. 27 ; Luke xxiv. 19 ; Acts xviii. 25, xxviii. 31.

doctrines concerning him, and in any case could originally only have had this meaning, involves a pre-Christian form of belief in a Jesus. But this point is above all supported by the circumstance that even at the earliest commencement of the Christian propaganda we meet with the name of Jesus used in such a manner as to point to a long history of that name. For it is employed from the beginning in the driving out of evil spirits, a fact that would be quite incomprehensible if its bearer had been merely a man. Now we know from the Gospels and Acts of the Apostles that it was not only the disciples of the Jesus of the Gospels, but also others even in his lifetime (*i.e.*, even in the first commencement of the Christian propaganda), healed diseases, and drove out evil spirits in the name of Jesus. From this it is to be concluded that the magic of names was associated from of old with the conception of a divine healer and protector, and that Jesus, like Marduk, was a name for this God of Healing.* Judging by this the Persian, but above all the Babylonian, religion must have influenced the views of the above-named sects. For the superstition regarding names, the belief in the magic power attributed to the name of a divine being, as well as the belief in Star Gods and Astral mythology, which is a characteristic of Mandaism, all have Babylon as their home. The Essenes also appear to have exercised the magical and healing art of which they boasted in the form of wonder-working and the driving out of evil spirits by a solemn invocation of the name of their God of Healing.†

---

* Luke ix. 49, x. 17; Acts iii. 16; James v. 14 *sq.* For more details regarding Name magic, see W. Heitmüller, "Im Namen Jesu," 1903.

† Cf. on whole subject Robertson, *op. cit.*, 153–160.

IV

THE SUFFERINGS OF THE MESSIAH

IN the most different religions the belief in a divine Saviour and Redeemer is found bound up with the conception of a suffering and dying God, and this idea of a suffering and dying Messiah was by no means unknown to the Jews. It may be of no importance that in the Apocalypse of Esdras* the death of Christ is spoken of, since in the opinion of many this work only appeared in the first century after Christ ; but Deutero-Isaiah too, during the Exile, describes the chosen one and messenger of God as the "suffering servant of God," as one who had already appeared, although he had remained unknown and despised, had died shamefully and been buried, but as one also who would rise up again in order to fulfil the splendour of the divine promise.† This brings to mind the suffering, death, and resurrection of the Gods of Babylon and of the whole of Nearer Asia ; for example, Tammuz, Mithras, Attis, Melkart, and Adonis, Dionysus, the Cretan Zeus, and the Egyptian Osiris. The prophet Zechariah, moreover, speaks of the secret murder of a God over which the inhabitants of Jerusalem would raise their lament, "as in the case of Hadad-rimmon (Rammân) in the valley of Megiddon," that is, as at the death of Adonis, one of the chief figures among the Gods

* Ch. vii. 29.   † Isa. iii.

believed in by the Syrians.* Ezekiel also describes the women of Jerusalem, sitting before the north gate of the city and weeping over Tammuz.† The ancient Israelites, too, were already well acquainted with the suffering and dying Gods of the neighbouring peoples. Now, indeed, it is customary for Isaiah's " servant of God " to be held to refer to the present sufferings and future glory of the Jewish people, and there is no doubt that the prophet understood the image in that sense. At the same time Gunkel rightly maintains that in the passage of Isaiah referred to, the figure of a God who dies and rises again stands in the background, and the reference to Israel signifies nothing more than a new symbolical explanation of the actual fate of a God.‡

Every year the forces of nature die away to reawaken to a new life only after a long period. The minds of all peoples used to be deeply moved by this occurrence —the death whether of nature as a whole beneath the influence of the cold of winter, or of vegetable growth under the parching rays of the summer sun. Men looked upon it as the fate of a fair young God whose death they deeply lamented and whose rebirth or resurrection they greeted with unrestrained rejoicing. On this account from earliest antiquity there was bound up with the celebration of this God an imitative mystery under the form of a ritualistic representation of his death and resurrection. In the primitive stages of worship, when the boundaries between spirit and nature remained almost entirely indistinct, and man still felt himself inwardly in a sympathetic correspondence with surrounding nature, it was believed that one could even exercise an influence upon nature or help it in its interchange between life and death, and turn the course of events

---

* Ch. xii. 10 *sqq.* ; cf. Movers, *op. cit.*, i. 196.
† Ch. viii. 14.   ‡ *Op. cit.*, 78.

to one's own interest. For this purpose man was obliged
to imitate it. "Nowhere," says Frazer, to whom we
are indebted for a searching inquiry into all ideas and
ritualistic customs in this connection, "were these efforts
more strictly and systematically carried out than in
Western Asia. As far as names go they differed in
different places, in essence they were everywhere alike.
A man, whom the unrestrained phantasy of his adorers
clothed with the garments and attributes of a God, used
to give his life for the life of the world. After he had
poured from his own body into the stagnating veins of
nature a fresh stream of vital energy, he was himself
delivered over to death before his own sinking strength
should have brought about a general ruin of the forces of
nature, and his place was then taken by another, who,
like all his forerunners, played the ever-recurring drama
of the divine resurrection and death." * Even in historic
times this was frequently carried out with living persons.
These had formerly been the kings of the country or
the priests of the God in question, but their place was
now taken by criminals. In other cases the sacrifice
of the deified man took place only symbolically, as with
the Egpytian Osiris, the Persian Mithras, the Phrygian
Attis, the Syrian Adonis, and the Tarsic (Cilician) Sandan
(Sandes). In these cases a picture of the God, an effigy,
or a sacred tree-trunk took the place of the " God man."
Sufficient signs, however, still show that in such cases
it was only a question of a substitute under milder forms
of ritual for the former human victim. Thus, for example, the name of the High Priest of Attis, being also
Attis, that is, "father," the sacrificial self-inflicted wound
on the occasion of the great feast of the God (March 22nd
to 27th), and the sprinkling with his blood of the picture
of the God that then took place, makes us recognise

* Frazer, " The Golden Bough," 1900, ii. 196 *sq.*

still more plainly a later softening of an earlier custom of self-immolation.* With the idea of revivifying dying nature by the sacrifice of a man was associated that of the " scapegoat." The victim did not only represent to the people their God, but at the same time stood for the people before God and had to expiate by his death the misdeeds committed by them during the year.† As regards the manner of death, however, this varied in different places between death by his own sword or that of the priest, by the pyre or the gibbet (gallows).

In this way we understand the 53rd chapter of Isaiah : " Surely he hath borne our griefs, and carried our sorrows : yet we did esteem him stricken, smitten of God, and afflicted. But he was wounded for our transgressions, he was bruised for our iniquities : the chastisement of our peace was upon him ; and with his stripes we are healed. All we like sheep have gone astray ; we have turned every one to his own way ; and the Lord hath laid on him the iniquity of us all. He was oppressed, yet he humbled himself, and opened not his mouth ; as a lamb that is led to the slaughter, and as a sheep that before her shearers is dumb ; yea, he opened not his mouth. He was cut off out of the land of the living; for the transgression of my people was he stricken. And they made his grave with the wicked and with the rich in his death ; although he had done no violence, neither was any deceit in his mouth. When thou shalt make his soul an offering for sin, he shall see his seed, he shall prolong his days, and the pleasure of the Lord shall prosper in his hand. He shall see of the travail of his soul [? sufferings], and shall be satisfied : by his knowledge shall my righteous servant justify many, and he shall bear their iniquities. There-

---

* Frazer, " Adonis, Attis, Osiris," 1908, 128 *sqq.*

† " The Golden Bough," i., iii. 20 *sq.*

fore will I divide him a portion with the great, and he shall divide the spoil with the strong ; because he poured out his soul unto death, and was numbered with the transgressors ; yet he bare the sin of many, and made intercession for the transgressors." Here we obviously have to do with a man who dies as an expiatory sacrifice for the sins of his people, and by his death benefiting the lives of the others is on that account raised to be a God. Indeed, the picture of the just man suffering, all innocent as he is, itself varies between a human and a divine being.

And now let us enter into the condition of the soul of such an unhappy one, who as " God man " suffers death upon the gibbet, and we understand the words of the 22nd Psalm : " My God, my God, why hast thou forsaken me ? Why art thou so far from helping me, and from the words of my roaring ? O my God, I cry in the day time, but thou answereth not ; and in the night season, and am not silent. But thou art holy, O thou that inhabitest the praises of Israel. Our fathers trusted in thee ; they trusted, and thou didst deliver them. They cried unto thee, and were delivered ; they trusted in Thee, and were not ashamed. But I am a worm, and no man ; a reproach of men, and despised of the people. All they that see me laugh me to scorn : they shoot out the lip, they shake the lip, saying, Commit thyself unto the Lord, let him deliver him : let him deliver him, seeing he delighteth in him. . . . Many bulls have compassed me : strong bulls of Bashan have beset me round. They gape upon me with their mouth, as a ravening and a roaring lion. I am poured out like water. And all my bones are out of joint : my heart is like wax : it is melted in the midst of my bowels. . . . They pierced my hands and my feet. I may tell all my bones. They look and stare upon me : they part my garments among them, and upon my vesture do they cast lots. But be not thou far off, O Lord : O Thou, my succour, haste Thee to help me. . . . Save me from the lion's mouth, yea, from the horns of the wild oxen. . . . ."

When the poet of the psalms wished to describe helplessness in its direst extremity, before his eyes there came the picture of a man, who, hanging upon the gibbet, calls upon God's aid, while round about him the people gloat over his sufferings, which are to save them ; and the attendants who had taken part in the sacrifice divide among themselves the costly garments with which the God-king had been adorned.

The employment of such a picture presupposes that the occurrence depicted was not unknown to the poet and his public, whether it came before their eyes from acquaintance with the religious ideas of their neighbours or because they were accustomed to see it in their own native usages. As a matter of fact in ancient Israel human sacrifices were by no means unusual. This appears from numberless passages of the Old Testament, and has been already exhaustively set forth by Ghillany in his book "Die Menschenopfer der alten Hebräer" (1842), and by Daumer in his "Der Feuer- und Molochdienst der alten Hebräer." Thus we read in 2 Sam. xxi. 6–9 of the seven sons of the House of Saul, who were delivered over by David to the Gibeonites, who hung them on the mountain before the Lord. Thus was God appeased towards the land.* In Numb. xxv. 4 Jahwe bade Moses hang the chiefs of the people " to the Lord before the sun, in order that the bitter wrath of the Lord might be turned from Israel." And according to the Book of Joshua this latter dedicated the inhabitants of the city of Ain to the Lord, and after the capture of the

* Verse 14.

city hung their king upon a tree,* while in the tenth chapter (15–26) he even hangs five kings at one time. Indeed, it appears that human sacrifice formed a regular part of the Jewish religion in the period before the Exile ; which indeed was but to be expected, considering the relationship between Jahwe and the Phœnician Baal. Jahwe himself was, moreover, originally only another form of the old Semitic Fire- and Sun-God ; the God-king (Moloch or Melech), who was honoured under the image of a Bull, was represented at this time as a " smoking furnace " † and was gratified and propitiated by human sacrifices.‡ Even during the Babylonian captivity, despite the voices raised against it by some prophets in the last years of the Jewish state, sacrifices of this kind were offered by the Jews ; until they were suppressed under the rule of the Persians, and in the new Jewish state were expressly forbidden. But even then they continued in secret and could easily be revived at any time, so soon as the excitement of the popular mind in some time of great need seemed to demand an extraordinary victim.§

Now the putting to death of a man in the rôle of a divine ruler was in ancient times very often connected

---

* *Op. cit.*, viii. 24–29. † 1 Gen. xv. 17.

‡ Ghillany, *op. cit.*, 148, 195, 279, 299, 318 *sqq.* Cf. especially the chapter " Der alte hebräische Nationalgott Jahve," 264 *sqq.*

§ J. M. Robertson, " Pagan Christs," 140–148. It cannot be sufficiently insisted upon that it was only under Persian influence that Jahwe was separated from the Gods of the other Semitic races, from Baal, Melkart, Moloch, Chemosh, &c., with whom hitherto he had been almost completely identified ; also that it was only through being worked upon by Hellenistic civilisation that he became that "unique" God, of whom we usually think on hearing the name. The idea of a special religious position of the Jewish people, the expression of which was Jahwe, above all belongs to those myths of religious history which one repeats to another without thought, but which science should finally put out of the way.

with the celebration of the new year. This is brought to our mind even at the present day by the German and Slav custom of the " bearing out" of death at the beginning of spring, when a man or an image of straw symbolising the old year or winter, is taken round amidst lively jesting and is finally thrown into the water or ceremonially burnt, while the "Lord of May," crowned with flowers, makes his entrance. Again, the Roman Saturnalia, celebrated in December, during which a mock king wielded his sceptre over a world of joy and licence and unbounded folly, and all relationships were topsy-turvy, the masters playing the part of slaves and *vice-versâ*, in the most ancient times used to be held in March as a festival of spring. And in this case, too, the king of the festival had to pay for his short reign with his life. In fact, the Acts of St. Dasius, published by Cumont, show that the bloody custom was still observed by the Roman soldiers on the frontiers of the Empire in the year 303 A.D.*

In Babylon the Feast of the Sakæes corresponded to the Roman Saturnalia. It was ostensibly a memorial of the inroad of the Scythian Sakes into Nearer Asia, and according to Frazer was identical with the very ancient new year's festival of the Babylonians, the Zakmuk. This too was associated with a reversal of all usual relationships. A mock king, a criminal condemned to death, was here also the central figure—an unhappy being, to whom for a few days was accorded absolute freedom and every kind of pleasure, even to the using of the royal harem, until on the last day he was divested of his borrowed dignity, stripped naked, scourged, and then burnt.† The Jews gained a knowledge of this feast during the Babylonian captivity, borrowed it from their

---

* "Golden Bough," iii. 138–146.
† Movers, *op. cit.*, 480 *sqq.*

oppressors, and celebrated it shortly before their Pasch under the name of the Feast of Purim, ostensibly, as the Book of Esther is at pains to point out, as a memorial of a great danger from which in Persia during the reign of Ahasuerus (Xerxes) they were saved by the craft of Esther and her uncle Mordecai. Jensen, however, has pointed out in the Vienna *Zeitschrift für die Kunde des Morgenlandes* * that the basis of the narrative of Esther is an opposition between the chief Gods of Babylon and those of hostile Elam. According to his view under the names of Esther and Mordecai are hidden the names of Istar, the Babylonian Goddess of fertility, and Marduk, her " son " and " beloved." At Babylon during the Feast of the Sakæes, under the names of the Elamite Gods Vashti and Haman (Humman), they were put out of the way as representatives of the old or wintry part of the year in order that they might rise up again under their real names and bring into the new year or the summer half of the year.† Thus the Babylonian king of the Sakæes also played the part of a God and suffered death as such upon the pyre. Now we have grounds for assuming that the later Jewish custom at the Feast of Purim of hanging upon a gibbet and burning a picture or effigy representing the evil Haman, originally consisted, as at Babylon, in the putting to death of a real man, some criminal condemned to death. Here, too, then was seen not only a representative of Haman, but one also of Mordecai, a representative of the old as well as of the new year, who in essence was one and the same being. While the former was put to death at the Purim feast, the latter, a criminal chosen by lot, was given his freedom

* VI. 47 *sqq.*, 209 *sqq.*
† Cf. Gunkel, "Schöpfung und Chaos in Urzeit und Endzeit," 1895. 309 *sq.* E. Schrader, " Die Keilinschriften und das Alte Testament," 1902, 514–520.

on this occasion, clothed with the royal insignia of the dead man and honoured as the representative of Mordecai rewarded by Ahasuerus for his services. " Mordecai," it is said in the Book of Esther, " went out from the king in royal attire, gold and white, with a great crown of gold, and covered with a robe of linen and purple. And the town of Susa rejoiced and was merry." * Frazer has discovered that in this description we have before us the picture of an old Babylonian king of the Sakæes, who represented Marduk, as he entered the chief town of the country side, and thus introduced the new year. At the same time it appears that in reality the procession of the mock king was less serious and impressive than the author of the Book of Esther would out of national vanity make us believe. Thus Lagarde has drawn attention to an old Persian custom which used to be observed every year at the beginning of spring in the early days of March, which is known as " the Ride of the Beardless One." † On this occasion a beardless and, when possible, one-eyed yokel, naked, and accompanied by a royal body-guard and a troop of outriders, was conducted in solemn pomp through the city seated upon an ass, amidst the acclamations of the crowd, who bore branches of palm and cheered the mock king. He had the right to collect contributions from the rich people and shopkeepers along the route which he followed. Part of these went into the coffers of the king, part were assigned to the collector, and he could without more ado appropriate the property of another in case the latter refused his demands. He had, however, to finish his progress and disappear within a strictly limited time, for in default of this he exposed himself to the danger of

* Ch. viii. 15. Cf. also vi. 0, 0.
† " Abhandlungen d. Kgl. Ges. d. Wissenschaften zu Göttingen," xxxiv.

being seized by the crowd and mercilessly cudgelled to death. People hoped that from this procession of "the Beardless One" an early end of winter and a good year would result. From this it appears that here too we have to do with one of those innumerable and multiform spring customs, which at all times and among the most diverse nations served to hasten the approach of the better season. The Persian "Beardless One" corresponded with the Babylonian king of the Sakæes, and appears to have represented the departing winter. Frazer concludes from this that the criminal also who played the [part of the Jewish "Mordecai" with similar pomp rode through the city like "the Beardless One," and had to purchase his freedom with the amusement which he afforded the people. In this connection he recalls a statement of Philo according to which, on the occasion of the entry of the Jewish King Agrippa into Alexandria, a half-crazy street sweeper was solemnly chosen by the rabble to be king. After the manner of "the Beardless One," covered with a robe and bearing a crown of paper upon his head and a stick in his hand for a sceptre, he was treated by a troop of merry-makers as a real king.* Philo calls the poor wretch Karabas. This is probably only a corruption of the Hebrew name Barabbas, which means "Son of the Father." It was accordingly not the name of an individual, but the regular appellation of whoever had at the Purim feast to play the part of Mordecai, the Babylonian Marduk, that is, the new year. This is in accordance with the original divine character of the Jewish mock king. For as "sons" of the divine father all the Gods of vegetation and fertility of Nearer Asia suffered death, and the human representatives of these gods had to give their lives for the welfare

---

* Cf. also P. Wendland, "Ztschr. Hermes," xxxiii., 1898, 175 *sqq.*, and Robertson, *op. cit.*, 138, note 1.

of their people and the renewed growth of nature.* It thus appears that a kind of commingling of the Babylonian Feast of the Sakæes and the Persian feast of " the Beardless One " took place among the Jews, owing to their sojourn in Babylon under Persian overlordship. The released criminal made his procession as Marduk (Mordecai) the representative of the new life rising from the dead, but it was made in the ridiculous rôle of the Persian " Beardless One "—that is, the representative of the old year—while this latter was likewise represented by another criminal, who, as Haman, had to suffer death upon the gallows. In their account of the last events of the life of the Messiah, Jesus, the custom at the Jewish Purim feast, already referred to, passed through the minds of the Evangelists. They described Jesus as the Haman, Barabbas as the Mordecai of the year, and in so doing, on account of the symbol of the lamb of sacrifice, they merged the Purim feast in the feast of Easter, celebrated a little later. They, however, transferred the festive entry into Jerusalem of " the Beardless One," his hostile measures against the shopkeepers and money-changers, and his being crowned in mockery as " King of the Jews," from Mordecai-Barabbas to Haman-Jesus, thus anticipating symbolically the occurrences which should only have been completed on the resurrection of the Marduk of the new year.†
According to an old reading of Math. xxvii. 18 et seq., which, however, has disappeared from our texts since

---

* In the same way the Phrygian Attis, whose name characterises him as himself the " father," was also honoured as the " son," beloved and spouse of Cybele, the mother Goddess. He thus varied between a Father God, the high King of Heaven, and the divine Son of that God.

† Frazer, op. cit., iii. 138–200. Cf. also Robertson, " Pagan Christs," 136–140.

Origen, Barabbas, the criminal set against the Saviour, is called " Jesus Barabbas "—that is, " Jesus, the son of the Father." * May an indication of the true state of the facts not lie herein, and may the figure of Jesus Barabbas, the God of the Year, corresponding to both halves of the year, that of the sun's course upwards and downwards, not have separated into two distinct personalities on the occasion of the new year's feast ?

The Jewish Pasch was a feast of spring and the new year, on the occasion of which the firstfruits of the harvest and the first-born of men and beasts were offered to the God of sun and sky. Originally this was also associated with human sacrifices. Here too such a sacrifice passed, as was universal in antiquity, for a means of expiation, atoning for the sins of the past year and ensuring the favour of Jahwe for the new year.† " As representing all the souls of the first-born are given to God ; they are the means of union between Jahwe and his people; the latter can only remain for ever Jahwe's own provided a new generation always offers its first-born in sacrifice to God. This was the chief dogma of ancient Judaism ; all the hopes of the people were fixed thereon ; the most far - reaching promises were grounded upon the readiness to sacrifice the first-born." ‡ The more valuable such a victim was, the higher the rank which he bore in life, so much the more pleasing was his death to God. On this account they were "kings" who, according to the Books of Joshua and Samuel, were " consecrated " to the Lord. Indeed, in the case of the seven sons of the house of Saul whom David caused to be hung, the connection between their death and the Pasch is perfectly clear,

* Keim, " Geschichte Jesu," 1873, 331 note.
† Ghillany, op. cit., 510 sqq.
‡ Id. 505.

when it is said that they died " before the Lord " at the
time of the barley harvest (*i.e.*, of the Feast of the
Pasch).* Thus there could be no more efficacious
sacrifice than when a king or ruler offered his first-born.
It was on this account that, as Justin informs us, † the
banished Carthaginian general Maleus caused his son
Cartalo, decked out as a king and priest, to be hung
in sight of Carthage while it was being besieged by him,
thereby casting down the besiegers so much that he
captured the city after a few days. It was on this
account that the Carthaginian Hamilcar at the siege
of Agrigentum (407 B.C.) sacrificed his own son, and
that the Israelites relinquished the conquest of Moab,
when the king of this country offered his first-born to
the Gods. ‡ Here, too, the human victim seems to have
been only the representative of a divine one, as when, for
example, the Phœnicians in Tyre until the time of the
siege of that city by Alexander sacrificed each year,
according to Pliny, a boy to Kronos, *i.e.*, Melkart or
Moloch (king).§ This Tyrian Melkart, however, is the
same as he to whom, as Porphyry states, a criminal
was annually sacrificed at Rhodes. According to Philo
of Byblos the God was called " Israel " among the
Phœnicians, and on the occasion of a great pestilence,
in order to check the mortality, he is said to have
sacrificed his first-born son Jehud (Judah), *i.e.*, " the Only
one," having first decked him out in regal attire.‖ Thus
Abraham also sacrificed his first-born to Jahwe.
Abraham (the " great father ") is, however, only another
name for Israel, " the mighty God." This was the
earliest designation of the God of the Hebrews, until

* 2 Sam. xxi. 9 ; cf. Lev. xxiii. 10–14.   † " Hist.," xviii. 7.
‡ 2 Kings iii. 27.   § " Hist. Nat.," xxxiv. 4, § 26.
‖ Mentioned in Eusebius, " Praeparatio Evangelica," i. 10. Cf.
Movers, *op. cit.*, 303 *sq.*

it was displaced by the name Jahwe, being only employed henceforth as the name of the people belonging to him. The name of his son Isaac (Jishâk) marks the latter out as " the smiling one." This, however, does not refer, as Goldzither * thinks, to the smiling day or the morning light, but to the facial contortions of the victim called forth by the pains he endured from the flames in the embrace of the glowing oven. These contortions were anciently called "sardonic laughter," on account of the sacrifices to Moloch in Crete and Sardinia.† When, as civilisation increased, human sacrifices were done away with in Israel, and with the development of monotheism the ancient Gods were transformed into men, the story of Genesis xxii. came into existence with the object of justifying " historically " the change from human to animal victims. The ancient custom according to which amongst many peoples of antiquity, kings, the sons of kings, and priests were not allowed to die a natural death, but, after the expiration of a certain time usually fixed by an oracle, had to suffer death as a sacrificial victim for the good of their people, must accordingly have been in force originally in Israel also. Thus did Moses and Aaron also offer themselves for their people in their capacity of leader and high priest. ‡ But since both, and especially Moses, passed as types of the Messiah, the opinion grew up quite naturally that the expected great and mighty leader and high priest of Israel, in whom Moses should live again,§ had to suffer the holy death of Moses and Aaron as sacrificial victims.‖

---

* " Der Mythus bei den Hebräern," 1876, 109–113.

† Cf. Ghillany, *op. cit.*, 451 *sqq.* ; Daumer, *op. cit.*, 34 *sqq.*, 111.

‡ Numb. xx. 22 *sqq.*, xxvii. 12 *sqq.*, xxxiii. 37 *sqq.*, Deut. xxxii. 48 *sqq.* Cf. Ghillany, *op. cit.*, 709–721.

§ Deut. xviii. 15.

‖ Cf. Heb. v.

The view that the idea of a suffering and dying Messiah was unknown to the Jews cannot accordingly be maintained. Indeed, in Daniel ix. 26 mention is made of a dying Christ. We saw above that among the Jews of the post-exilic period the thought of the Messiah was associated with the personality of Cyrus. Now of Cyrus the story goes that this mighty Persian king suffered death upon the gibbet by the order of the Scythian queen Tomyris.* But in Justin the Jew Trypho asserts that the Messiah will suffer and die a death of violence. † Indeed, what is more, the Talmud looks upon the death of the Messiah (with reference to Isaiah liii.) as an expiatory death for the sins of his people. From this it appears " that in the second century after Christ, people were, at any rate in certain circles of Judaism, familiar with the idea of a suffering Messiah, suffering too as an expiation for human sins." ‡

The Rabbinists separate more accurately two conceptions of the Messiah. According to one, in the character of a descendant of David and a great and divine hero he was to release the Jews from servitude, found the promised world-wide empire, and sit in judgment over men. This is the Jewish conception of the Messiah, of which King David was the ideal.§ According to the other he was to assemble the ten tribes in Galilee and lead them against Jerusalem, only to be overthrown, however, in the battle against Gog and Magog under the leadership of Armillus on account of Jeroboam's sin— that is, on account of the secession of the Israelites from the Jews. The Talmud describes the last-mentioned

* Diodorus Siculus, ii. 44.
† Justin, " Dial. cum Tryphone," cap. xc.
‡ Böhürer, *op. cit.*, ii. 555. Cf. also Wünsche, "Die Leiden des Messias," 1870.
§ See above, page 40 *sqq.*

Messiah, in distinction from the first, as the son of Joseph or Ephraim. This is done with reference to the fact that the kingdom of Israel included above all the tribes of Ephraim and Manasseh, and that these traced back their origin to the mythical Joseph. He is thus the Messiah of the Israelites who had separated from the Jews, and especially, as it appears, of the Samaritans. This Messiah, " the son of Joseph," it is said, " will offer himself in sacrifice and pour forth his soul in death, and his blood will atone for the people of God." He himself will go to heaven. Then, however, the other Messiah, "the son of David," the Messiah of the Jews in a narrower sense, will come and fulfil the promises made to them, in which connection Zech. xii. 10 *sq.* and xiv. 3 *sq.* seem to have influenced this whole doctrine.*
According to Dalman,† the figure of the Messiah ben Joseph first appeared in the second or third century after Christ. Bousset too appears to consider it a "later" tradition, although he cannot deny that the Jewish Apocalypses of the end of the first thousand years after Christ, which are the first to make extensive mention of the matter, may have contained "very ancient" traditions. According to Persian beliefs, too, Mithras was the suffering Redeemer and mediator between God and the world, while Saoshyant, on the other hand, was the judge of the world who would appear at the end of all time and obtain the victory over Ariman (Armillus). In the same way the Greek myth distin-

---

* Cf. Eisenmenger, *op. cit.*, ii. 720 *sqq.* ; Gfrörer, "Das Jahrhundert des Heils," 1838, ii. 260 *sqq.* ; Lützelberger, "Die kirchl. Tradition über den Apostel Johannes u. s. Schriften," 1840, 224–229 ; Dalman, "Der leidende und der sterbende Messias der Synagoge im ersten nachchristlichen Jahrtausend," 1888 ; Bousset, "Die Religion des Judentums, im neutestamentlichen Zeitalter," 1903, 218 *sq.*; Jeremias, *op. cit.*, 40 *sq.*

† *Op. cit.*, 21.

guished from the older Dionysius, Zagreus, the son of Persephone, who died a cruel death at the hands of the Titans, a younger God of the same name, son of Zeus and Semele, who was to deliver the world from the shackles of darkness. Precisely the same relationship exists between Prometheus, the suffering, and Heracles, the triumphant deliverer of the world. We thus obviously have to do here with a very old and wide-spread myth, and it is scarcely necessary to point out how closely the two figures of the Samaritan and Jewish Messiahs correspond to the Haman and Mardachai of the Jewish Purim feast, in order to prove the extreme antiquity of this whole conception. The Gospel united into one the two figures of the Messiah, which had been originally separate. From the Messiah ben Joseph it made the human Messiah, born in Galilee, and setting out from there with his followers for Jerusalem, there to succumb to his adversaries. On the other hand, from the Messiah ben David it made the Messiah of return and resurrection. At the same time it elevated and deepened the whole idea of the Messiah in the highest degree by commingling the conception of the self-sacrificing Messiah with that of the Paschal victim, and this again with that of the God who offers his own son in sacrifice. Along with the Jews it looked upon Jesus as the " son " of King David, at the same time, however, preserving a remembrance of the Israelite Messiah in that it also gave him Joseph as father; and while it said with respect to the first idea that he was born at Bethlehem, the city of David, it assigned him in connection with the latter Nazareth of Galilee as his birthplace, and invented the abstruse story of the journey of his parents to Bethlehem in order to be perfectly impartial towards both views.

And now, who is this Joseph, as son of whom the

Messiah was to be a suffering and dying creature like any ordinary man ?   Winckler has pointed out in his " Geschichte Israels " that under the figure of the Joseph of the Old Testament, just as under that of Joshua, an ancient Ephraimitic tribal God is concealed.   Joseph is, as Winckler expresses it, "the heroic offspring of Baal of Garizim, an offshoot of the Sun-God, to whom at the same time characteristics of Tammuz, the God of the Spring Sun, are transferred." *   Just as Tammuz had to descend into the under-world, so was Joseph cast into the well, in which, according to the " Testament of the twelve Patriarchs," † he spent three months and five days. This betokens the winter months and five additional days during which the sun remains in the under-world.   And again he is cast into prison; and just as Tammuz, after his return from the under-world, brings a new spring to the earth, so does Joseph, after his release from confinement, introduce a season of peace and happiness for Egypt.‡   On this account he was called in Egypt Psontomphanech, that is, Deliverer of the World, in view of his divine nature, and later passed among the Jews also as a prototype of the Messiah.   Indeed, it appears that the Evangelists themselves regarded him in such a light, for the story of the two fellow-prisoners of Joseph, the baker and cupbearer of Pharaoh, one of whom, as Joseph foretold, was hanged,§ while the other was again received into favour by the king, was transformed by them into the story of the two robbers who were executed at the same time as Jesus, one of whom mocked the Saviour while the other besought him

---

* *Op. cit.*, 71 *sq.*

† Kautzsch, " Pseudoepigraphen," 500.

‡ Winckler, *op. cit.*, 67–77.   Cf. also Jeremias, *op. cit.*, 40, and his " Das Alte Testament im Lichte des alten Orients," 1904, 239 *sq.*

§ Gen. xl.

to remember him when he entered into his heavenly kingdom.*

But the Ephraimitic Joshua too must have been a kind of Tammuz or Adonis. His name (Joshua, Syrian, Jeshu) characterises him as saviour and deliverer. As such he also appears in the Old Testament, finally leading the people of Israel into the promised land after long privations and sufferings. According to the Jewish Calendar the commencement of his activity was upon the tenth of Nisan, on which the Paschal lamb was chosen, and it ended with the Feast of the Pasch. Moses introduced the custom of circumcision and the redemption of the first-born male, and Joshua was supposed to have revived it.† At the same time he is said to have replaced the child victims, which it had been customary to offer to Jahwe in early days, by the offering of the foreskin of the male and thereby to have established a more humane form of sacrificial worship. This brings to our mind the substitution of an animal victim for a human one in the story of Isaac (Jishâks). It also brings to mind Jesus who offered his own body in sacrifice at the Pasch as a substitute for the numberless bloody sacrifices of expiation of prior generations. Again, according to an ancient Arabian tradition, the mother of Joshua was called Mirzam (Mariám, Maria), as the mother of Jesus was, while the mother of Adonis bore the similar sounding name of Myrrha, which also expressed the mourning of the women at the lament for Adonis ‡ and characterised the mother of the Redeemer God as " the mother of sorrow." §

But what is above all decisive is that the son of the

* Luke xxiii. 39–43 ; cf. also Isa. lxxx. 12.
† Jos. v. 2 *sqq.*
‡ Amos viii. 10 ; cf. Movers, *op cit.*, 243.
§ Cf. Robertson, " Pagan Christs," 157.

" Ploughman " Jephunneh, Caleb (*i.e.*, the Dog), stands by Joshua's side as a hero of equal rank. His name points in the same way to the time of the summer solstice, when in the mouth of the "lion" the dog-star (Sirius) rises, while his descent from Nun, the Fish or Aquarius, indicates Joshua as representing the winter solstice.* Just as Joshua belonged to the tribe of Ephraim, to which according to the Blessing of Jacob the Fishes of the Zodiac refer,† so Caleb belonged to the tribe of Judah, which Jacob's Blessing likened to a lion; ‡ and while the latter as Calub (Chelub) has Shuhah for brother, that is, the Sun descending into the kingdom of shadows (the Southern Hemisphere),§ in like manner Joshua represents the Spring Sun rising out of the night of winter. They are thus both related to one another in the same way as the annual rise and decline of the sun, and as, according to Babylonian ideas, are Tammuz and Nergal, who similarly typify the two halves of the year. When Joshua dies at Timnath-heres, the place of the eclipse of the Sun (*i.e.*, at the time of the summer solstice, at which the death of the Sun-God was celebrated ‖), he appears again as a kind of Tammuz, while the "lamentation" of the people at his death¶ alludes possibly to the lamentation at the death of the Sun-God.**

It cannot be denied after all this that the conception of a suffering and dying Messiah was of extreme antiquity amongst the Israelites and was connected with the earliest nature-worship, although later it may indeed have become restricted and peculiar to certain exclusive circles.††

* Numb. xiv.   † *Id.* xiii. 9; Gen. xlviii. 16.

‡ *Id.* xiii. 7 ; Gen. xlix. 9.   § 1 Chron. iv. 11.

‖ Judges ii. 9.   ¶ *Id.* iv.

** Cf. Nork, " Realwörterbuch," 1843–5, ii. 301 *sq.*

†† Cf. on whole subject Martin Brückner, "Der sterbende und auferstehende Gottheiland in den orientalischen Religionen und ihr Verhältnis zum Christentum. Religionsgesch. Volksbücher," 1908.

The Jewish representative of Haman suffered death at the Feast of Purim on account of a crime, as a deserved punishment which had been awarded him. The Messiah Jesus, on the other hand, according to the words of Isaiah, took the punishment upon himself, being "just." He was capable of being an expiatory victim for the sins of the whole people, precisely because he least of all deserved such a fate.

Plato had already in his "Republic" sketched the picture of a "just man" passing his life unknown and unhonoured amidst suffering and persecution. His righteousness is put to the proof and he reaches the highest degree of virtue, not allowing himself to be shaken in his conduct. "The just man is scourged, racked, thrown into prison, blinded in both eyes, and finally, when he has endured all ills, he is executed, and he recognises that one should be determined not to be just but to appear so." In Pharisaic circles he passed as a just man who by his own undeserved sufferings made recompense for the sins of the others and made matters right for them before God, as, for example, in the Fourth Book of the Maccabees the blood of the martyrs is represented as the expiatory offering on account of which God delivered Israel. The hatred of the unjust and godless towards the just, the reward of the just and the punishment of the unjust, were favourite themes for aphoristic literature, and they were fully dealt with in the Book of Wisdom, the Alexandrian author of which was presumably not unacquainted with the Platonic picture of the just man. He makes the godless appear conversing and weaving plots against the just. "Let us then," he makes them say, "lie in wait for the righteous; because he is not to our liking and he is clean contrary to our doings; he upbraideth us with our offending the law and reproacheth us with our sins against our training. He professeth to have the knowledge of God ; and he calleth himself the child of the Lord. He proved to be to us for the reproof of our designs. He is grievous unto us even to behold : for his life is not like other men's, his ways are of another fashion. We are esteemed of him as counterfeits ; he abstaineth from our ways as from filth ; he pronounceth the end of the just to be blessed and maketh his boast that God is his father. Let us see if his words be true : and let us prove what will happen in the end of him. For if the just man be the son of God, he will help him, and deliver him from the hand of his enemies. Let us examine him with despitefulness and torture that we may know his meekness and prove his patience. Let us condemn him with a shameful death : thus will he be known by his words." * "But the souls of the just," continues the author of the Book of Wisdom, "are in the hands of God, and there shall no torment touch them. In the sight of the unwise they seemed to die : and their departure is taken for misery, and their going from us for utter destruction : but they are in peace. For though they be punished in the sight of men yet is their hopes full of immortality. And having been a little chastised, they shall be greatly rewarded : for God proved them and found them worthy for himself. As gold in the furnace hath he tried them, and received them as a burnt offering. And in the time of their visitation they shall shine and run to and fro like sparks among the stubble. They shall judge the nations and have dominion over the people and their Lord will rule for ever." † It could easily be imagined that these words, which were understood by the author of the Book of Wisdom of the just man in general, referred to the just man *par excellence*, the Messiah, the "son" of God in the highest sense of the word, who gave his life for the sins

* Ch. ii. 12–20.   † Ch. iii. 1–8.

of his people. A reason was found at the same time for the shameful death of the Messiah. He died the object of the hatred of the unjust; he accepted contempt and scorn as did the Haman and Barabbas of the Feast of Purim, but only in order that by this deep debasement he might be raised up by God, as is said of the just man in the Book of Wisdom: "That is he whom we had sometimes in derision and a proverb of reproach: We fools accounted his life madness and his end to be without honour: Now is he numbered among the children of God, and his lot is among the saints." *

Now we understand how the picture of the Messiah varied among the Jews between that of a divine and that of a human being; how he was "accounted just among the evil-doers"; how the idea became associated with a human being that he was a "Son of God" and at the same time "King of the Jews"; and how the idea could arise that in his shameful and undeserved death God had offered himself for mankind. Now too we can understand that he who died had after a short while to rise again from the dead, and this in order to ascend into heaven in splendour and glory and to unite himself with God the Father above. These were ideas which long before the Jesus of the Gospels were spread among the Jewish people, and indeed throughout the whole of Western Asia. In certain sects they were cherished as secret doctrines, and were the principal cause that precisely in this portion of the ancient world Christianity spread so early and with such unusual rapidity.

* Ch. v. 3–5.

V

THE BIRTH OF THE MESSIAH. THE BAPTISM

IT is not only the idea of the just man suffering, of the Messiah dying upon the gibbet, as "King of the Jews" and a criminal, and his rising again, which belongs to the centuries before Christ. The stories which relate to the miraculous birth of Jesus and to his early fortunes also date back to this time. Thus in the Revelation of John* we meet with the obviously very ancient mythical idea of the birth of a divine child, who is scarcely brought into the world before he is threatened by the Dragon of Darkness, but is withdrawn in time into heaven from his pursuer; whereupon the Archangel Michael renders the monster harmless. Gunkel thinks that this conception must be traced back to a very ancient Babylonian myth.† Others, as Dupuis ‡ and Dieterich, have drawn attention to its resemblance to the Greek myth of Leto,§ who, before the birth of the Light god Apollo, being pursued by the Earth dragon Pytho, was carried by the Wind god Boreas to Poseidon, and was brought safely by the latter to the Island of Ortygia, where she was able to bring forth her son unmolested by the hostile monster. Others again, like Bousset, have compared the Egyptian myth of Hathor, according to which Hathor or Isis sent her young son,

* Ch. xii.   † " Zum religionsgesch. Verst. d. N.T.," 54.

‡ "L'origine de tous les cultes," 1795,v.183. §"Abraxas," 117.

the Light god Horus, fleeing out of Egypt upon an ass before the pursuit of his uncle Seth or Typhon. Pompeian frescoes represent this incident in such a manner as to recall feature for feature the Christian representations of the flight of Mary with the Child Jesus into Egypt; and coins with the picture of the fleeing Leto prove how diffused over the whole of Nearer Asia this myth must have been. The Assyrian prince Sargon also, being pursued by his uncle, is said to have been abandoned on the Euphrates in a basket made of reeds, to have been found by a water-carrier, and to have been brought up by him—a story which the Jews have interwoven into the account of the life of their fabulous Moses.* And very similar stories are related both in East and West, in ancient and in later times, of other Gods, distinguished heroes and kings, sons of the Gods, of Zeus, Attis, Dionysus, Œdipus, Perseus, Romulus and Remus, Augustus, and others. As is well known, the Indian God-man Krishna, an incarnation of Vishnu, is supposed to have been sought for immediately after his birth by his uncle, King Kansa, who had all the male children of the same age in his country put to death, the child being only saved from a like fate by taking refuge with a poor herdsman.† This recalls Herodotus's story of Cyrus,‡ according to which Astyages, the grandfather of Cyrus, being warned by a dream, ordered his grandson to be exposed, the latter being saved from death, however, through being found by a poor herdsmen and being brought up in his house. Now

---

* Cf. regarding the mythical nature of Moses, who is to be looked upon as an offshoot of Jahwe and Tammuz, Winckler, *op. cit.*, 86–95.

† Cf. also O. Pfleiderer, "Das Christusbild des urchristlichen Glaubens in religionsgesch. Beleuchtung," 1903, 37. Also Jeremias, " Das A.T. im Lichte des alten Orients," 254.

‡ I. 107.

in Persian the word for son is Cyrus (Khoro,* Greek Kyros), and Kyris or Kiris is the name of Adonis in Cyprus.† Thus it appears that the story of the birth of Cyrus came into existence through the transfer to King Cyrus of one of the myths concerning the Sun-God, the God in this way being confused with a human individual. Now since Cyrus, as has been said, was in the eyes of the Jews a kind of Messiah and was glorified by them as such, we can understand how the danger through which the Messianic child is supposed to have passed found a place in the Gospels. Again, a similar story of a king, who, having been warned by a dream or oracle, orders the death of the children born within a specified time, is found in the " Antiquities " of Josephus‡ in connection with the story of the childhood of Moses. Moses, however, passed like Cyrus for a kind of forerunner and anticipator of Christ; and Christ was regarded as a Moses reappearing.§ Again Joab, David's general, is said to have slaughtered every male in Edom ; the young prince Hadad, however, escaped the massacre by fleeing into Egypt. Here he grew up and married the sister of the king, and after the death of his enemy King David he returned to his home.‖ But Hadad is, like Cyrus, (Kyrus) a name of the Syrian Adonis.

Another name of Adonis or Tammuz is Dôd, Dodo, Daud, or David. This signifies " the Beloved " and indicates " the beloved son " of the heavenly father, who offers himself for mankind, or " the Beloved " of the Queen of heaven (Atargatis, Mylitta, Istar).¶ As is well known, King David was also called "the man after the heart of God," and there is no doubt that characteristics of the divine Redeemer and Saviour of the same

* Cf. Plutarch, " Artaxerxes," ch. i.   † Movers, *op. cit.*, 228.
‡ II. 9, 2.   § Bousset, "Das Judentum," 220.   ‖ 1 Kings xi. 14 *sq.*
¶ Schrader, " Die Keilinschriften u. d. A.T.," 225.

name have been intermingled in the story of David in the same way as in that of Cyrus.* According to Jeremiah xxx. 8 and Ezekiel xxxiv. 22 *sqq.* and xxxvii. 21, it was David himself who would appear as the Messiah and re-establish Israel in its ancient glory. Indeed, this even appears to have been the original conception of the Messiah. The Messiah David seems to have been changed into a descendant of David only with the progress of the monotheistic conception of God, under the influence of the Persian doctrine concerning Saoshyant, the man "of the seed of Zarathustra." Now David was supposed to have been born at Bethlehem. But in Bethlehem there was, as Jerome informs us,† an ancient grove and sanctuary of the Syrian Adonis, and as Jerome himself complains the very place where the Saviour first saw the light resounded with the lamentations over Tammuz.‡ At Bethlehem, the former Ephrata (*i.e.,* Place of Ashes), Rachel is said to have brought forth the youngest of the twelve month-sons of Jacob. She herself had christened him Benoni, son of the woeful lament. He was, however, usually called Benjamin, the Lord or Possessor of light. In the Blessing of Moses he is also called "a Darling of the Lord," and his father Jacob loved him especially.§ He is the God of the new year born of the ashes of the past, at whose appearance lament and rejoicings are commingled one with another; and thus he is only a form of Tammuz (Hadad) bringing to mind the Christian Redeemer in that he presided over the month of the Ram.‖

---

* Winckler, *op. cit.,* 172 *sqq.,* Jeremias, "Das A.T. im Lichte d. a. O.," 2nd. ed., 488 *sqq.*; cf. also " Baentsch, " David und sein Zoitalter. Wissenschaft u. Bildung," 1907.

† Ep. viii. 3.   ‡ *Id.* xlii. 58.   § Ch. v. 1.

‖ Gen. xxxv. 11–19; Deut. xxxiii. 12; Gen. xliv. 26.

Now we understand the prophecy of the prophet
Micah : " Thou Bethlehem Ephrathah, which art little
to be among the thousands of Judah, out of thee shall
one come forth unto me that is to be a ruler in Israel,
whose going forth is from of old, from everlasting." *
Now, too, the story of the slaughter of the children at
Bethlehem has its background in religious history. It
is said in Matt. ii. 18, with reference to Jer. xxxi. 15,
"A voice was heard in Ramah, weeping and great mourning, Rachel weeping for her children, and she would not
be comforted, because they are not." It is the lamentation of the women over the murdered Adonis which
was raised each year at Bethlehem. This was transformed by the Evangelists into the lament over the
murder of the children which took place at the birth of
Hadad who was honoured at Bethlehem.†

---

* Cf. Nork, " Realwörterbuch," i. 240 *sq.*

† The other famous " prophecy " supposed to refer to the birth of
the Messiah, viz., Isaiah vii. 14, is at present no longer regarded as
such by many. The passage obviously does not refer to the Messiah.
This is shown by a glance at the text, and it would hardly have been
considered so long as bearing that meaning, if any one had taken
the trouble to read it in its context. Consider the situation. Queen
Rezin of Syria and Pekah of Israel march against the Jewish King
Ahaz, who is therefore much troubled. At the command of Jahwe
the prophet goes to the king in order to exhort him to courage, and
urges him to pray for a sign of the happy outcome of the fight. He,
however, refuses to tempt God. Thereupon Isaiah himself gives him
a sign. " Behold," he says, " a virgin shall conceive and bear a son,
and shall call his name Immanuel, God be with us. Before the
child shall know to refuse the evil and choose the good, the land whose
two kings thou abhorrest shall be forsaken." And undisturbed by
the fact that this prophecy for the moment can give but little
encouragement to the king, Isaiah goes with the help of two witnesses(!)
to a prophetess and gets her with child in order to make his words
true (!). The text does not say in what relationship the woman stood
to Isaiah. The Hebrew word Almah may mean " young woman "
as well as " virgin." The Septuagint, however, thoughtlessly making

Hadad-Adonis is a God of Vegetation, a God of the rising sap of life and of fruitfulness: but, as was the case with all Gods of a similar nature, !the thought of the fate of the sun, dying in winter and being born anew in the spring, played its part in the conception of this season God of Nearer Asia. Something of this kind may well have passed before the mind of Isaiah, when he foretold the future glory of the people of God under the image of a new birth of the sun from out of the blackness of night, with these "prophetic" words: "Arise, shine, for thy light has come and the glory of the Lord is risen upon thee. For behold darkness shall cover the earth and gross darkness the peoples: but the Lord shall arise upon thee, and his glory shall be seen upon thee. And nations shall come to thy light, and kings to the brightness of thy rising . . . The abundance of the sea shall be turned unto thee, the wealth of the nations shall come unto thee. The multitude of camels shall cover thee, the dromedaries of Midian and Ephah. They all shall come from Sheba : they shall bring gold and frankincence, and shall proclaim the praises of the Lord." *

As is well known, later generations were continually setting out this idea in a still more exuberant form. The imagination of the enslaved and impoverished Jews feasted upon the thought that the nations and their princes would do homage to the Messiah with gifts, while uncounted treasures poured into the temple at Jerusalem : "Princes shall come out of Egypt, Ethiopia shall haste to stretch out her hands unto God. Sing

the passage refer to the Messiah, and having before its eyes very possibly the stories of the miraculous birth of the heathen Redeemer Gods, translates the word straightway by "virgin," without thinking what possible light it thereby threw upon Isaiah.

* Ch. lx. 1 *sqq.*

unto God ye kingdoms of the earth.* This is the foundation of the Gospel story of the " Magi," who lay their treasures at the feet of the new-born Christ and his "virgin mother." But that we have here in reality to do with the new birth of the sun at the time of the winter solstice appears from the connection between the Magi, or kings, and the stars. For these Magi are nothing else than the three stars in the sword-belt of Orion, which at the winter solstice are opposed in the West to the constellation of the Virgin in the East; stars which according to Persian ideas at this time seek the son of the Queen of Heaven—that is, the lately rejuvenated sun, Mithras.† Now, as it has been said, Hadad also is a name of the Sun-God, and the Hadad of the Old Testament returns to his original home out of Egypt, whither he had fled from David. Thus we can understand how Hosea xi. 1, " I called my son out of Egypt," could be referred to the Messiah and how the story that Jesus passed his early youth in Egypt was derived from it.‡

It may be fairly asked how it was that the sun came to be thus honoured by the people of Western Asia, with lament at its death and rejoicing at its new birth. For winter, the time of the sun's " death," in these southern countries offered scarcely any grounds at all for lament. It was precisely the best part of the year. The night, too, having regard to its coolness after the heat of the day, gave no occasion for desiring the new birth of the sun in the morning.

We are compelled to suppose that in the case of all the Gods of this nature the idea of the dying away of vegetation during the heat of the year and its revival had become intertwined and commingled with that of the declining and reviving strength of the sun. Thus, from this ming-

* Psa. lxviii. 32 *sq.*   † Dupuis, *op. cit.*, 268.   ‡ Matt. i. 14 *sq.*

ling of two distinct lines of thought, we have to explain the variations of the double-natured character of the Sun-Gods and Vegetation-Gods of Western Asia.* It is obvious, however, that the sun can only be regarded from such a tragic standpoint in a land where, and in the myths of a people for whom, it possesses in reality such a decisive significance that there are grounds for lamenting its absence or lack of strength during winter and for an anxious expectation of its return and revival.† But it is chiefly in the highlands of Iran and the mountainous

---

* The feasts of the Gods in question also correspond to this in character. They fell upon the solstice (the birthday or day of death of the sun), so far as their connection with the sun was emphasized. On the contrary, upon the equinoxes, so far as their connection with vegetation was concerned, sowing and harvest were brought into prominence. Usually, however, death and reappearance were joined in one single feast, and this was celebrated at the time in spring when day and night were of equal length, when vegetation was at its highest, and in the East the harvest was begun. Cf. Jeremias, " Babylonisches im N.T.," 10 *sq.*

† One should compare the description given by Hommel of the climate of Babylonia (*op. cit.*, 186) with the picture of the natural occurrences which, according to Gunkel, gave occasion for the myth of the birth of Marduk, and the threatening of the child by the " Winter Dragon," Tiâmat. " Before spring descends to the earth from heaven, winter has had its grim (!) rule upon the earth. Men pine away (in the country of the two rivers!) beneath its sway, and look up to heaven wondering if deliverance will not come. The myth consoles them with the story that the God of spring who will overthrow winter has already been born. The God of winter who knows for what he is destined is his enemy, and would be very pleased if he could devour him. And winter at present ruling is much stronger than the weak child. But his endeavour to get rid of his enemy comes to nought. Do you then want to know why he is so grim? He knows that he has only a short time. His might is already broken although we may be yet unaware of it. The year has already changed to spring. The child grows up in heaven; the days become longer, the light of the sun stronger. As soon as he is grown up he descends and overthrows his old enemy. ' Only trust in God without despair, spring must come ' " (" Schöpfung und Chaos," 889 *sq.*).

hinterland of Asia Minor that this is the case to such an extent as to make this idea one of the central points of religious belief. Even here it points back to a past time when the people concerned still had their dwelling-place along with the kindred Aryan tribes in a much more northerly locality.* Thus Mithras, the " Sol invictus " of the Romans, struggling victoriously through night and darkness, is a Sun hero, who must have found his way into Persia from the north. This is shown, amongst other things, by his birthday being celebrated on the 25th of December, the day of the winter solstice. Again, the birth of the infant Dionysus, who was so closely related to the season Gods of Nearer Asia, used to be celebrated as the feast of the new birth of the sun at about the same time, the God being then honoured as Liknites, as "the infant in the cradle " (the winnowing-fan). The Egyptians celebrated the birth of Osiris on the 6th of January, on which occasion the priests produced the figure of an infant from the sanctuary, and showed it to the people as a picture of the new-born God.† That the Phrygian Attis came thither with the Aryans who made their way from Thrace into Asia Minor, and must have had his home originally in Northern Europe, appears at once from the striking resemblance of the myth concerning him with that of the northern myth of Balder. There can be no doubt that the story in Herodotus of Atys, son of Crœsus, who while out boar hunting accidently met his death from the spear of his friend, only gives another version of the Attis myth. This story, however, so closely resembles that of the death of Balder, given in the Edda, that the theory of a connection between them is inevitably forced upon one's mind. In the Edda the wife of Balder is called Nanna. But Nanna (*i.e.*, " mother ") was accord-

* Dupuis has already pointed this out, *op. cit.*, 152.
† Macrobius, " Saturnal.," i. 18, i. 84–35.

ing to Arnobius * the name of the mother of the Phrygian Attis.

Now the Sun and Summer God Balder is only a form of Odin, the Father of Heaven, with summer attributes, and he too is said, like Attis, Adonis and Osiris, to have met his death through a wild boar. Just as anemones sprang from the blood of the slain Adonis and violets from that of Attis, so also the blood of the murdered Odin (Hackelbernd) is said to have been changed into spring flowers.† At the great feast of Attis in March a post or pine-tree trunk decked with violets, on which the picture of the God was hung, used to form the central point of the rite. This was a reminder of the way in which in ancient times the human representative of the God passed from life to death, in order by sacrifice to revive exhausted nature. According to the verses of the Eddic Havamal, Odin says of himself :—

> " I know that I hang on the wind-rocked tree
> Throughout nine nights,
> Wounded by the spear, dedicated to Odin,
> I myself to myself." ‡

---

* " Adversus Nationes," v. 6 and 13.

† Cf. Simrock, "Handbuch der deutschen Mythologie," 4th ed., 1874, 201 and 225.

‡ *Op. cit.*, 188. The transfixing of the victim with the holy lance, as we meet it in John xix. 34, appears to be a very old sacrificial custom, which is found among the most different races. For example, both among the Scythian tribes in Albania in the worship of Astarte (Strabo) and in Salamis, on the island of Cyprus, in that of Moloch (Eusebius," Praep. Evang.," iv. 16). " The lance thrust," says Ghillany, with reference to the Saviour's death, " was not given with the object of testing whether the sufferer was still alive, but was in order to correspond with the old method of sacrificing. The legs were not broken because the victim could not be mutilated. In the evening the corpse had to be taken down, just as Joshua only allowed the kings sacrificed to the sun to remain until evening upon the cross " (*op. cit.*, 558).

By this self-sacrifice and the agonies which he endured, the northern God, too, obtained new strength and life. For on this occasion he not only discovered the Runes of magic power, the knowledge of which made him lord over nature, but he obtained possession at the same time of the poetic mead which gave him immortality and raised the Nature God to be a God of spiritual creative power and of civilisation. This is obviously the same idea as is again found in the cult of Attis and in the belief in the death of the God. The relationship of all these different views seems still more probable in that a sacrificial rite lay at the root of the Balder myth also. This myth is only, so to speak, the text of a religious drama which was performed every year for the benefit of dying nature—a drama in which a man representing the God was delivered over to death.* As all this refers to the fate of a Sun God, who dies in winter to rise again in the spring, the same idea must have been associated originally with the worship of the Nearer Asiatic Gods of vegetation and fruitfulness, and this idea was only altered under changed climatic conditions into that of the death and resurrection of the plant world, without, however, losing in its new form its original connection with the sun and winter.

At the same time the myth of the Sun God does not take us to the very basis and the real kernel of the stories of the divine child's birth. The Persian religion was not so much a religion of Light and Sun as of Fire, the most important and remarkable manifestation of which was of course the sun. Dionysus too, like all Gods of the life-warmth, of the rising plant sap and of fruitfulness, was in his deepest nature a Fire God. In the Fire Religion, however, the birth of the God forms the centre of all

---

* Frazer, *op. cit.*, 345 *sq.* F. Kauffmann, "Balder Mythus u. Sage nach ihren dichterischen u. religiösen Elementen untersucht," 1902, 266 *sq.*

religious ideas ; and its form was more exactly fixed through the peculiar acts by means of which the priest rekindled the holy fire.

For the manner in which this occurred we have the oldest authentic testimony in the religious records of the Indian Aryans. Here Agni, as indeed his name (ignis, fire) betokens, passed for the divine representative of the Fire Element. His mystic birth was sung in numberless passages in the hymns of the Rigveda. At dawn, as soon as the brightening morning star in the east announced that the sun was rising, the priest called his assistants together and kindled the fire upon a mound of earth by rubbing together two sticks (aranî) in which the God was supposed to be hidden. As soon as the spark shone in the " maternal bosom," the soft underpart of the wood, it was treated as an " infant child." It was carefully placed upon a little heap of straw, which at once took fire from it. On one side lay the mystic " cow "—that is, the milk-pail and a vessel full of butter, as types of all animal nourishment—upon the other the holy Soma draught, representing the sap of plants, the symbol of life. A priest fanned it with a small fan shaped like a banner, thereby stirring up the fire. The " child " was then raised upon the altar. The priests turned up the fire with long-handled spoons, pouring upon the flames melted butter (ghrita) together with the Soma cup. From this time " Agni " was called " the anointed " (Akta). The fire flickered high. The God was unfolding his majesty. With his flames he scared away the dæmons of darkness, and lighted up the surrounding shadows. All creatures were invited to come and gaze upon the wonderful spectacle. Then with presents the Gods (kings) hastened from heaven and the herdsmen from the fields, cast themselves down in deep reverence before the new-born, praying to it and singing hymns in its praise. It grew visibly before their eyes. The new-born Agni already had become "the teacher" of all living creatures, "the wisest of the wise," opening to mankind the secrets of existence. Then, while everything around him grew bright and the sun rose over the horizon, the God, wreathed in a cloud of smoke, with the noise of darting flames, ascended to heaven, and was united there with the heavenly light.*

Thus in ancient India the holy fire was kindled anew each morning, and honoured with ritualistic observances (Agnihotra). This took place, however, with special ceremony at the time of the winter solstice, when the days began again to increase (Agnistoma). They then celebrated the end of the time "of darkness," the Pitryana, or time of the Manes, during which the worship of the Gods had been at a standstill. Then the Angiras, the priestly singers, summoned the Gods to be present, greeting with loud song the beginning of the "holy" season, the Devayana, with which the new light arose. Agni and the other Gods again returned to men, and the priests announced to the people the "joyful tidings" (Evangelium) that the Light God had been born again. As Hillebrand has shown, this festival also indicates the memory of an earlier home in the North whence the Aryan tribes had migrated, since in India, where the shortest and longest days only differ by about four hours, no reason exists for celebrating the "return" of the light.†
Indeed, it appears that we have to do here with a rite which reaches back into the very origins of all human civilisation, and preserves the memory of the discovery of fire in the midst of the horrors of the Stone Age.

There is no doubt that we have before us in the Vedic Agni Cult the original source of all the stories of the birth of the Fire-Gods and Sun-Gods. These Gods usually

---

* Rigv. v. 1, v. 2, iii. 1, vii. 12, i. 96, &c.
† Hillebrand, " Vedische Mythologie," 1891-1902, ii. 88 *sq.*

enter life in darkness and concealment. Thus the Cretan Zeus was born in a cavern, Mithras, Dionysus, and Hermes in a gloomy grotto, Horus in the " stable " (temple) of the holy cow (Isis)—Jesus, too, was born at dead of night in a lowly " stable " * at Bethlehem. The original ground for this consists in the fact that Agni, in the form of a spark, comes into existence in the dark hollow of the hole bored in the stick. The Hymns of the Rigveda often speak of this " secret birth " and of the " concealment " of Agni. They describe the Gods as they set out in order to seek the infant. They make the Angiras discover it " lying in concealment," and it grows up in hiding.† But the idea of the Fire-God being born in a " stable " is also foreshadowed in the Rigveda. For not only are the vessels of milk and butter ready for the anointing compared with cows, but Ushas, too, the Goddess of Dawn, who is present at the birth, is called a red milch-cow, and of men it is said that they flocked " like cows to a warm stable " to see Agni, whom his mother held lovingly upon her lap.‡

It is a common fundamental feature of all Nature religions that they distinguish between the particular and the general, between earthly and heavenly events, between human acts and natural occurrences as little as they do between the spiritual and natural. The Agni Cult shows, as does the Vedic religion in general, this interplay of the earthly and heavenly world, of the microcosmic individual and the macrocosm. The kind-

---

* According to early Christian writers, such as Justin and Origen, Jesus also came into the world in a cave, and Jerome complains (Epist. lviii.) that ¦in his time the heathens celebrated the feast of the birth of Tammuz at Bethlehem¦in the same cave in which Jesus was born.

† I. 72, 2 ; v. 11, 6 ; v. 2, 1 ; iii. 1, 14 ; i. 65, 1 ; x. 46, 2.

‡ III. 1, 7; iii. 9, 7; v. 1, 1; v. 2, 1, and 2; iii. 7, 2 ; x. 4, 2, and 3.

ling of the fire upon the earth at the same time betokened the rising of the great light of the skies, the sun. The fire upon the altar did not merely represent but actually was the sun, the earthly and the heavenly Agni were one. Thus it was that the nations of antiquity were able to think of transferring earthly events into heaven, and conversely were able to read earthly events in heavenly occurrences such as the relations of the stars to one another. It was on this that astrology rested. Even the ancient Fire Worship appears in very early times to have been transformed into astrology, and what was in the beginning a simple act of worship was generalised by the priests in a macrocosmic sense and was transferred to the starry heavens as a forecast. Thus the altar or place of sacrifice upon which the sacred fire was kindled was enlarged into the Vault of the Spheres or Grotto of the Planets. Through this the sun completed its annual journey among the twelve signs of the Zodiac, and in so doing assumed successively the form and fulfilled the functions of that constellation with which it entered into astronomical relations. The metaphorical name of "stable" for the place of sacrifice attains a new significance from the fact that the sun during a certain epoch of the world (something between 3000 and 800 B.C.) at the beginning of spring passed through the constellation of the Bull, and at the time of the winter solstice commenced its course between the Ox (Bull) and the Great Bear, which anciently was also called the Ass.* The birth of the God is said to have been in secret because it took place at night. His mother is a "virgin" since at midnight of the winter solstice the constellation of the

---

* Cf. Volney, "Die Ruinen," 1791 (Reclam), note 83 to chap. xiii. This is the reason why the infant Christ was represented in early Christian pictures lying in his mother's lap or in a cradle between an Ox and an Ass.

Virgin is on the eastern horizon.* Shortly afterwards Draco, the Dragon (the snake Pytho), rises up over Libra, the Balance, and seems to pursue the Virgin. From this comes the story of the Winter Dragon threatening Leto, or Apollo ; or, as it is also found in the Myth of Osiris and the Apocalypse of John, the story of the pursuit of the child of light by a hostile principle (Astyages, Herod, &c.).† Unknown and in concealment the child grows up. This refers to the course of the sun as it yet stands low in the heavens. Or like Sargon, Dionysus, or Moses it is cast in a basket upon the waters of some great stream or of the sea, since the sun in its wanderings through the Zodiac has next to pass through the so-called watery region, the signs of the Water-carrier and the Fishes, the rainy season of winter. Thus can the fate of the new-born be read in the sky. The priests (Magi) cast his horoscope like that of any other child. They greet his birth with loud rejoicings, bring him myrrh, incense and costly presents, while prophesying for him a glorious future. The earthly Agni is completely absorbed in the heavenly one ; and in the study of the great events which are portrayed in the sky, the simple act of sacrificial worship, which had originally furnished the opportunity for this whole range of ideas, gradually fell into oblivion.‡

---

* Jeremias, "Babylonisches im Neuen Testament," 85, note 1. Cf. Dupuis, *op. cit.*, 111 *sqq.*

† Dupuis, *op. cit.*, 143 *sq.*

‡ Cf. also Winckler, " Die babylonische Geisteskultur Wissenschaft u. Bildung," 1907. Jeremias, " Babylonisches im N.T.," 62 *sqq.* The astral references of the Christ myth are very beautifully shown in the " Thomakapelle " at Karlsruhe, where the Master has depicted in costly profusion and unconscious insight the chief points of the Gospel " history " in connection with the signs of the Zodiac and the stars—the riddle of the Christ story and its solution ! As is well known, the theological faculty in Heidelburg conferred an " honorary doctorate of theology " upon the Master.

It has been often maintained that Indian influences
have worked upon the development of the story of the
childhood of Jesus, and in this connection we are accustomed to think of Buddhism. Now, as a matter of fact,
the resemblances between the Christian and Buddhist
legends are so close that we can scarcely imagine it to be
a mere coincidence. Jesus and Buddha are both said to
have been born of a "pure virgin," honoured by heavenly
spirits at their birth, prayed to by kings and loaded with
presents. "Happy is the whole world," sing the Gods
under the form of young Brahmins at the birth of the
child—as we are told in the Lalita Vistara, the legendary
biography of Buddha, dating from before Christ, "for he
is indeed born who brings salvation and will establish the
world in blessedness. He is born who will darken sun
and moon by the splendour of his merits and will put all
darkness to flight. The blind see, the deaf hear, the
demented are restored to reason. No natural crimes
afflict us any longer, for upon the earth men have become
righteous. Gods and men can in future approach each
other without hostility, since he will be the guide of their
pilgrimage." * Just as the significance of Jesus was
announced beforehand by Simeon, in the same way
according to the Buddhist legend, the Seer Asita foresees
in his own mind the greatness of the child and bursts into
tears since he will not see him in the splendour of his
maturity and will have no part in his work of redemption.
Again, just as Jesus † even in his early youth astonished

---

* " Le Lalita Vistara, traduit du sanscrit en français," i. 76 *sqq.*

† Further in R. Seydel, "Die Buddhalegende u. das Leben Jesu,"
2nd ed., 1897, and in his "Das Evangelium von Jesus in seinem
Verhältnis zur Buddhasage u. Buddhalegende," 1882. Also Van
den Bergh van Eysinga, "Indische Einflüsse auf evang. Erzäh-
lungen," 2nd ed., 1909. Cf. also O. Pfleiderer, "Das Christusbild,"
23 *sqq.*

the learned by his wisdom, so Prince Siddharta (Buddha) put all his teachers at school to shame by his superior knowledge, and so on. The Buddhist legend itself, however, goes back to a still older form, which is the Vedic Agni Cult. All its various features are here preserved in their simplest form and in their original relation to the sacrificial worship of the Fire-God. This was the natural source of the Indian and Christian legends, and it was the original of those myths which the Evangelist worked up for his own purposes, which according to Pfleiderer belonged "to the common tribal property of the national sagas of Nearer Asia." * Again, it could the more easily reappear in the Evangelists' version of the story of the childhood of Jesus, since the sacrificial act had been re-interpreted mythologically, and the corresponding myths transformed into astrology, and, as it were, written with starry letters upon the sky, where they could be read without trouble by the most distant peoples of antiquity.

The myth of Krishna offers a characteristic example of the manner in which in India a sacrificial cult is changed into a myth. Like Astyages and Herod, in order to ward off the danger arising from his sister's son, of which he had been warned by an oracle, King Kansa caused his sister and her husband Vasudewa to be cast into prison. Here, in the darkness of a dungeon, Krishna comes into the world as Jesus did in the stable at Bethlehem. The nearer the hour of birth approaches the more beautiful the mother becomes. Soon the whole dungeon is filled with light. Rejoicing choirs sound in the air, the waters of the rivers and brooks make sweet music. The Gods come down from heaven and blessed spirits dance and sing for joy. At midnight his mother Dewaki (*i.e.*, the divine) brings the child into the world,

* "Urchristentum," i. 411 *sq.*

at the commencement of a new epoch. The parents themselves fall down before him and pray, but a voice from heaven admonishes them to convey him from the machinations of the tyrant to Gokala, the land of the cow, and to exchange him for the daughter of the herdsman Nanda. Immediately the chains fall from the father's hands, the dungeon doors are opened, and he passes out into freedom. Another Christopher, he bears the child upon his shoulders through the river Yamuna, the waters of which recede in reverence before the son of God, and he exchanges Krishna for the new-born daughter of Nanda. He then returns to the dungeon, where the chains again immediately fasten of their own accord upon his limbs. Kansa now makes his way into the dungeon. In vain Dewaki entreats her brother to leave her the child. He is on the point of tearing it forcibly from her hands when it disappears before his eyes, and Kansa gives the order that all newly-born children in his country under the age of two years shall be killed.

At Mathura in Gokala Krishna grew up unknown among poor herdsmen. While yet in his cradle he had betrayed his divine origin by strangling, like Hercules, a dreadful snake which crawled upon him. He causes astonishment to every one by his precosity and lofty wisdom. As he grows up he becomes the darling of the herdsmen and playmate of Gopias, the milkmaid; he performs the most astonishing miracles. When, however, the time had come he arose and slew Kansa. He then fought the frightful " Time Snake " Kaliyanaga, of the thousand heads (the Hydra in the myth of Hercules, the Python in that of Apollo), which poisoned the surrounding air with its pestilential breath ; and he busied himself in word and deed as a protector of the poor and proclaimer of the most perfect teaching. His greatest act, however, was his descent into the Under-world. Here he overpowered Yama, the dark God of death, obtained from him a recognition of his divine power, and led back the dead with him to a new life. Thus he was a benefactor of mankind by his heroic strength and miraculous power, leading the purest life, healing the sick, bringing the dead back to life, disclosing the secrets of the world, and withal humbly condescending to wash the feet of the Brahmins. Krishna finally died of an arrow wound which he sustained accidentally and in an unforeseen manner on his heel—the only vulnerable part of his body (cf. Achilles, Balder, Adonis, and Osiris). While dying he delivered the prophecy that thirty-six years after his death the fourth Epoch of the World, Caliyuga, the Iron Age, would begin, in which men would be both unhappy and wicked. But according to Brahmin teaching Krishna will return at the end of all time, when bodily and moral need will have reached its highest pitch upon the earth. In the clouds of heaven he will appear upon his white steed. With a comet in his right hand as a sword of flame he will destroy the old earth by fire, founding a new earth and a new heaven, and establishing a golden age of purity and perfection in which there will be nothing but pure joy and blessedness.

This reminds us strongly of the Persian Eschatology, of Mithras and Saoshyant, and of the Jewish Apocalyptics. But following the ancient sacred poem, the Barta Chastram, the former conception as well as the doctrine of a Messiah rest upon a prophecy according to which Vishnu Jesudu (!) was to be born a Brahmin in the city of Skambclam. He was to hold intercourse with men as a God, to purify the earth from sin, making it the abode of justice and truth, and to offer a sacrifice (self-sacrifice?). But still more striking are the resemblances of the Krishna myth with the Gospels. Does any connection between the two exist? The question is hard to answer because, owing to the uncertainty in all Indian citation of dates, the age of the story of Krishna cannot be settled. In the oldest Indian literature, the Vedas, Krishna appears to be the name of a Dæmon. In the Mahâbbhârata, the great Indian heroic epic, he plays indeed a prominent part, and is here on the point of assuming the place of the God Indra. The age of the poem, however, is debatable, although it is probably of pre-Buddhist origin. The chief source of the Krishna myth is the Puranas, especially the Bhagavat Purana and Vishnu Parana. But since the antiquity of these also is uncertain, and their most modern portions presumably belong only to the eighth or ninth century of the Christian era, a decision as to the date of the appearance of the Krishna myth can only be arrived at from internal evidence.

Now the Pantanjalis Mahâbhashya, *i.e.*, "Great Commentary," of the second century before Christ, shows that the story of Kansa's death at the hands of Krishna was at that time well known in India, and was even the subject of a religious drama. Thus the story of the birth at least of Krishna, who had already been raised to be a Cult God of the Hindoos, cannot have been unknown. The other portions of the myth, however, belong as a whole to the general circle of Indian ideas, and are in part only transferred from other Gods to Krishna. Thus, for example, the miraculous birth of the divine child in the darkness, his precosity, his up-bringing among the herdsmen, and his friendship with Gopias, remind us of Agni, the God of Fire and Herds-men, who also is described in the Rigveda as a "friend and lover of the maidens" (of the Cloud Women?). His combat with the Time Snake, on the other hand, is copied from the fight of Indra with the wicked dragon Vritra or Ahi. Again, in his capacity as purifier and deliverer of the world from evil and dæmons the God bears such a striking resemblance to Hercules, that Megasthenes, the ambassador of Seleucus at the court of the king at Pataliputra, in the third century before Christ, simply identified him with the latter. No impartial critic of the matter can now doubt that the Krishna myth was in existence and was popularised long before Christianity appeared in the world. The great importance, however, which the God possesses in present-day India may have been attained only during the Christian era, and the Puranas may have been composed only after the appearance of the Gospels; for their being written down later proves nothing against the antiquity of the matter they contain. It appears that even Buddhism did not obtain its corresponding legends direct from the Vedas, but through the channel of the Krishna myth. Since, however, Buddhism is certainly at least four hundred years older than Christianity, it must be assumed that it was the former which introduced the Krishna myth to Christianity, and not *vice versâ*, if we are not to consider the Babylonian - Mandaic religion as the intermediary between Krishna and Christ.*

For the rest the supposition of Indian influences in the Gospel story is not by any means an improbable one. It is pure theological prejudice, resting upon a complete ignorance of the conditions of national intercourse in ancient times, when it is denied, as, for example, by Clemen in his "Religionsgeschichtlichen Erklärung des Neuen Testaments" (1909), that the Gospels were influenced by Indian ideas, or when only a dependence the other way about is allowed; † and this although Buddha

* Robertson, "Christianity and Mythology," 1900, 129–302.

† *Op. cit.*, 25 *sqq.*, 289–244; cf., on the other hand, Paul W. Schmidt, "Die Geschichte Jesu erläutert," 1904, 16.

left to his disciples, as one of the highest precepts, the practice of missionary activity, and although as early as 400 B.C. mention is made in Indian sources of Buddhist missionaries in Bactria. Two hundred years later we read of Buddhist monasteries in Persia. Indeed, in the last century before the Christian era the Buddhist mission in Persia had made such progress that Alexander Polyhistor actually speaks of a period during which Buddhism flourished in that country, and bears witness to the spread of the Mendicant Orders in the western parts of Persia. Buddhism also reached Syria and Egypt at that time with the trade caravans ; as we have to suppose a frequent exchange of wares and ideas between India and the countries of the Eastern Mediterranean, especially after the campaigns of Alexander. Communication took place, not only overland by way of Persia, but by sea as well. Indian thought made advances in the Near East, where Alexandria, the London and Antwerp of antiquity, and a headquarters of Jewish syncretism, favoured the exchange of ideas. With the rediscovery of the South-west Monsoon at the beginning of the first century after Christ the intercourse by sea between India and the Western world assumed still greater dimensions. Thus Pliny speaks of great trading fleets setting out annually for India and of numerous Indian merchants who had their fixed abode in Alexandria. Indian embassies came to Rome as early as the reign of Augustus. The renown of Indian piety caused the author of the Peregrinus Proteus to choose the Indian Calanus as an example of holiness. Indeed, so lively was the Western world's interest in the intellectual life of India, that the library at Alexandria, as early as the time of the geographer Eratosthenes under Ptolemy Euergetes (246 B.C.), was administered with special regard to Indian studies. The monastic organisation of the Essenes in Palestine also very probably points to Buddhist influence. Again, although the Rigveda, which contains the groundwork of all Indian religions, may have been unknown in Nearer Asia, yet the Fire Worship of the Mazda religion at any rate reaches back to the time before the division between the Indian and Persian Aryans. Certain fundamental ideas, therefore, of the Fire Religion may through Persian influences on Nearer Asia have been known to the surrounding peoples.*

As a matter of fact, the Mandaic religions contains much that is Indian. This is the less strange considering that the headquarters and centre of Mandaism was in Southern Babylonia; and the ancient settlements of the Mandæi, close to the Persian Gulf, were easily reached by sea from India. Moreover, from ancient times Babylonian trade went down to India and Ceylon.† Consequently it is by no means improbable that the many remarkable resemblances between the Babylonian and Indian religions rest upon mutual influences. Indeed, in one case the borrowing of a Mandaic idea from India can be looked upon as quite certain. The Lalita Vistara begins with a description of Buddha's ante-natal life in heaven. He teaches the Gods the "law," the eternal truth of salvation, and announces to them his intention of descending into the bosom of an earthly woman in order to bring redemption to mankind. In vain the Gods endeavour to hold him back and cling weeping to his feet : " Noble man, if thou remainest here no longer, this abode of heaven will be bright no more." He leaves them, however, a successor, and consecrates him solemnly

---

* Cf. also Seydel, " Evangelium von Jesus," 305 *sqq.*; " Buddha-Legende," 46 *sqq.* Also Émile Burnouf, " La Science des Religions," 4th ed., 1885, 105.

† R. Kessler, " Realenz. f. prot. Theol. u. Kirche," xii. 163.

to be the possessor of the future dignity of Buddha:
" Noble man, thou art he who will be endowed after me
with the perfect intelligence of a Buddha." *   " Man "
(Purusha) is thus here the usual name for the divine
nature of Buddha destined for individual incarnations.
It is also called the "great man " (Mahapurusha) or the
" victorious lord " (Cakravartin).   Here we have the
original of the Mandaic " son of man," whom we meet
with in the Jewish Apocalyptics (Daniel, Enoch, Ezra),
a figure which plays so great a part in the primitive
Gospel records of Christianity, and has called forth so
many explanations.   And the Elcesaitic Gnostics teach
a like doctrine when they imagine the " son of man," or
Christ, as a heavenly spirit and king of the world to come
who became incarnate first in Adam, then in Enoch,
Noah, Abraham, Isaac, Jacob and so on, in order finally
to appear by a supernatural virgin-birth in the person of
Jesus, and to illumine the dark earth by his true message
of salvation.†

Of all the Gods of the Rigveda Agni bears the closest
relationship to the Perso-Jewish Messiah, and it is he
also who stands closest to man's soul.   He is rightly
called king of the universe, as God of Gods, who created
the world and called into life all beings that are upon it.
He is the lord of the heavenly hosts, the guardian of the
cosmic order and judge of the world, who is present as an
invisible witness of all human acts, who as a " knower of
nature " works in every living thing, and as a party to all
earthly secrets illuminates the unknown.   Sent down by
his father, the Sky-God or Sun-God, he appears as the
" light of the world."   He releases this world from the
Powers of Darkness and returns to his father with the
" Banner of Smoke " in his hand as a token of victory.

* Foucaux, " Le Lalita Vistara," i. 40.
† Hippolytus, op. cit., 9, 10 ; Epiphanius, op. cit., 30, 53.

Agni blazes forth in the lightning flash from out of the watercloud, the "sea of the sky," in order to annihilate the Dæmons of Darkness and to release oppressed humanity from the fear of its tormentors. Thus, according to Isaiah xi., 4, the Messiah too will burn his enemies with the fiery breath of his mouth; and in this he is clearly a Fire-God. Again, in the Apocalypse of Esdras (chap. xiii.) the Seer beholds the "Son of Man" (Purusha) rise up from out of the sea, fly upon the clouds of heaven, destroy the hostile forces by the stream of fire which proceeded from his mouth, free the scattered Israelites from their captivity and lead them back into their country.* But this "first-born" son of the Sun-God and the Sky-God is at the same time the father and ancestor of men, the first man (Purusha), the head of the community of mankind, the guardian of the house and of the domestic flock, who keeps from the threshold the evil spirits and the enemies who lurk in the darkness. Agni enters the dwellings of men as guest, friend (Mitra), companion, brother and consoler of those who honour him. He is the messenger between this world and the beyond, communicating the wishes of men to the Gods above, and announcing to men the will of the Gods. He is a mediator between God and men who makes a report to the Gods of everything of which he becomes aware among mankind. Although indeed he takes revenge for the men's faults yet he is a gracious God, disposed to forgive, in his capacity of an expiatory, propitiatory and redeeming power, atoning for their sins and bringing them the divine grace. Finally, he is also the guide of souls—he conducts the Gods down to the sacrifices offered by man and makes ready for men the path upon which he leads them up to God. And when their time has come he, as the purifying fire, consumes

* Cf. Pfleiderer, "Christusbild," 14 *sq.*

their bodies and carries that which is immortal to heaven.*

Agni's father is, as has been said, the sky, or rather the light, the sun, the source of all warmth and life upon the earth. He bears the name of Savitar, which means " creator " or " mover," is called " the lord of creation," " the father of all life," " the living one," or " the heavenly father " simply.† At the same time Tvashtar also passes as the father of Agni. His name characterises him simply as modeller (world-modeller) or work-master, divine artist, skilful smith, or " carpenter," in which capacity he sharpens Brihaspati's axe, and, indeed, is himself represented with a hatchet in his hand.‡ He appears to have attained this rôle as being the discoverer of the artificial kindling of fire, by means of which any fashioning (welding), any art in the higher sense of the word became possible, as being the preparer of the apparatus for obtaining fire by friction or rotation—" the fire cradle "—which consisted of carefully chosen wood of a specified form and kind. Finally, the production of fire is ascribed to Matariçvan also, the God of the Wind identical with Vayu, because fire cannot burn without air, and it is the motion of the breeze which fans the glimmering spark.§ All of these different figures are identical with one another, and can mutually take the place one of another, for they are all only different mani-

* Cf. also Max Müller, " Natural Religion "; Bergaigne, " La religion védique d'après les hymnes du Rigveda," 1878–83; Holtzmann, " Agni nach den Vorstellungen des Mahâbbhârata," 1878.

† Rgv. iii. 1, 9, 10.

‡ Id. ii. 23 ; i. 7; xcv. 2, 5; x. 2, 7; viii. 29, 3.

§ Id. iii. 5, 10; i. 148, 1. Cf. also Adalb. Kuhn, " Die Herabkunft des Feuers und des Göttertrankes," 2nd ed., 1886–9. In Mazdeism also the light is indissolubly connected with the air, passing as this does as its bearer. Cf. F. Cumont, " Textes et monuments," i. 228, ii. 87 sq., and his " Mystères de Mithra."

festations of warmth. It is this which reveals itself as well in the lightning of the sky and motion of the air, as in the glimmering of the fire, and not only as the principle of life, but also as that of thought and of knowledge or the " word " (Vâc, Veda), appearing on the one side as the productive, life-giving, and fructifying power of nature, on the other as the creative, inspiring spirit. This is the reason why, among the ancients, the God of life and fertility was in his essential nature a Fire-God, and why the three figures of the divine " father," " son," and " spirit," in spite of the differences of their functions, could be looked upon without inconsistency as one and the same being.

As is well known, Jesus, too, had three fathers, namely, his heavenly father, Jahwe, the Holy Spirit, and also his earthly father, Joseph. The latter is also a work-master, artizan, or " carpenter," as the word " tekton " indicates. Similarly, Kinyras, the father of Adonis, is said to have been some kind of artizan, a smith or carpenter. That is to say, he is supposed to have invented the hammer and the lever and roofing as well as mining. In Homer he appears as the maker of the ingenious coat of mail which Agamemnon received from him as a guest-friend.* The father of Hermes also is an artizan. Now Hermes closely resembles Agni as well as Jesus. He is the " good messenger," the Euangelos ; that is, the proclaimer of the joyful message of the redemption of souls from the power of death. He is the God of sacrifices, and as such " mediator " between heaven and earth. He is the " guide of souls " (Psychopompos) and "bridegroom of souls " (beloved of Psyche). He is also a God of fertility, a guardian of the flocks, who is represented in art as the " good shepherd," the bearer of the ram, a

---

* Il., xi. 20 ; cf. Movers, *op. cit.*, 242 *sq.*

guide upon the roads of earth, a God of the door-hinge (Strophaios) and guardian of the door,* a god of healing as well as of speech, the model of all human reason, in which capacity he was identified by the Stoics with the Logos that dwelt within the world.† Just as in the Rigveda Tvashtar stands with Savitar, the divine father of Agni, and Joseph the "carpenter" with Jahwe, as father of the divine mediator, so the divine artificer, Hephaistos, whose connection with Tvashtar is obvious, is looked upon together with Zeus, the father of heaven, as the begetter of Hermes.‡

Now if Joseph, as we have already seen, was originally a God, Mary, the mother of Jesus, was a Goddess. Under the name of Maya she is the mother of Agni, i.e., the principle of motherhood and creation simply, as which she is in the Rigveda at one time represented by the fire-producing wood, the soft pith, in which the fire-stick was whirled; at another as the earth, with which the sky has mated. She appears under the same name as the mother of Buddha as well as of the Greek Hermes. She is identical with Maira (Maera) as, according to Pausanias, viii. 12, 48, the Pleiad Maia, wife of Hephaistos, was called. She appears among the Persians as the "virgin" mother of Mithras. As Myrrha she is the mother of the Syrian Adonis; as Semiramis, mother of the Babylonian Ninus (Marduk). In the Arabic legend she appears under the name of Mirzam as mother of the mythical saviour Joshua, while the Old Testament gives this name to

* Cf. John x. 3, 7, 9.

† O. Gruppe, "Griech. Mythologie," 1900, ii. 1328, note 10.

‡ Id., op. cit., 1307. According to the Arabian legend Father Abraham, also, who here plays the part of a saviour and redeemer, was under the name of Thare, a skilful master workman, understanding how to cut arrows from any wood, and being specially occupied with the preparation of idols (Sepp, "Das Heidentum und dessen Bedeutung für das Christentum," 1853, iii. 82).

the virgin sister of that Joshua who was so closely
related to Moses; and, according to Eusebius,* Merris
was the name of the Egyptian princess who found Moses
in a basket and became his foster-mother.

After all this it seems rather naïve to believe that the
parents of the "historical" Jesus were called Joseph and
Mary, and that his father was a carpenter. In reality the
whole of the family and home life of the Messiah, Jesus,
took place in heaven among the Gods. It was only
reduced to that of a human being in lowly circumstances
by the fact that Paul described the descent of the Messiah
upon the earth as an assumption of poverty and a relin-
quishment of his heavenly splendour.† Hence, when the
myth was transformed into history, Christ was turned
into a "poor" man in the economic sense of the word,
while Joseph, the divine artificer and father of the sun,
became an ordinary carpenter.

Now it is a feature which recurs in all the religions of
Nearer Asia that the "son" of the divine "virgin"
mother is at the same time the "beloved" of this
Goddess in the sexual sense of the word. This is the
case not only with Semiramis and Ninus, Istar and
Tammuz, Atargatis (Aphrodite) and Adonis, Cybele and
Attis, but also with Aphrodite (Maia) and Hermes,‡ Maia
and Iasios, one of the Cabiri, identical with Hermes or
Cadmus, who was slain by his father, Zeus, with a
lightning stroke, but was raised again and placed in
the sky as a constellation.§ We may conclude from the
connection between Iasios and Joshua that a similar
relationship existed between the latter and his mother
Mirzam. Indeed, a glimmer of this possibly appears

* "Praep. Evang.," ix. 27.
† 2 Cor. viii. 9.
‡ Gruppe, *op. cit.*, 1322, 1331.
§ Preller, "Griech. Mythol.," 1894, 775 *sq.*, 855.

even in the Gospels in the relationship of the various
Maries to Jesus, although, of course, in accordance with
the character of these writings, they are transferred into
quite a different sphere and given other emotional
connections.*

Now in Hebrew the word "spirit" (ruach) is of
feminine gender. As a consequence of this the Holy
Ghost was looked upon by the Nassenes and the earliest
Christians as the "mother" of Jesus. Indeed, it appears
that in their view the birth of the divine son was only
consummated by the baptism and the descent of the
Spirit. According to the Gospels which we possess, on
the occasion of the baptism in the Jordan a voice from
above uttered these words : " Thou art my beloved son ;
in thee I am well pleased." †   On the other hand, in an
older reading of the passage in question in Luke, which
was in use as late as the middle of the fourth century,
it runs, in agreement with Psalm ii. 7 : "Thou art my
son, this day have I begotten thee." In this case the
spirit who speaks these words is regarded as a female
being. This is shown by the dove which descends from
heaven, for this was the holy bird, the symbol of the
Mother Goddess of Nearer Asia.‡ But it was not the
Nassenes alone (Ophites) who called the Holy Spirit
" the first word " and " the mother of all living things:"§

* Robertson, "Christianity and Mythology," 322.
† Matt. iii. 17 ; Mark i. 11 ; Luke iii. 22.
‡ Phereda or Pheredet, the dove, is the Chaldaic root of the name
Aphrodite, as the Goddess in the car drawn by two doves was called
among the Greeks.   In the whole of Nearer Asia the cult of doves
was connected with that of the Mother Goddess.   As is well known,
the dove as a symbol of innocence or purity is also the bird of the
Virgin Mary, who is often compared to one. Indeed, in the Protevan-
gelium of James she is actually called a dove which nested in the
temple, a plain reference to the dove cult of the Syrian Aphrodite or
Atargatis (Astarte, Astaroth).
§ Irenæus, i. 28.

other Gnostic sects, such as the Valentinians, regarded
the Spirit which descended in the shape of a dove as the
" word of the mother from above, of wisdom." * Viewed
in this sense, baptism also passed in the Mysteries as
a new birth. Indeed, its Greek name, phōtisma or
phōtismós (*i.e.*, illumination), clearly indicates its origin
in fire-worship. Thus, when Justin † too speaks of a
flame appearing at the baptism of Jesus, he alludes
thereby to the connection between that solemn act
and the birth of a Fire-God.‡ Ephrem, the Syrian
composer of hymns, makes the Baptist say to Jesus :
" A tongue of fire in the air awaits thee beyond the
Jordan. If thou followest it and wilt be baptized, then
undertake to purify thyself, for who can seize a burning
fire with his hands ? Thou who art all fire have mercy
upon me." § In Luke iii. 16 and Matt. iii. 11 it is said
in the same sense : " I indeed baptize you with water ;
but there cometh he that is mightier than I. . . . He
shall baptize you with the Holy Ghost and with fire."

---

* Hippolytus iv. 85. This brings to mind that, according to
Persian ideas also, besides the Trinity of Heaven (Ahuramazda),
Sun, Fire (Mithras), and Air (Spirit, "word," Honover, Spenta
Armaiti), the earth stood as a fourth principle (Anahita, Anaitis,
Tanit). This stood in the same relation to Mithras as Istar to
Tammuz, Cybele to Attis, Atargatis to Adonis, Maya to Agni,
Aphrodite to Hermes, Mary to Jesus, &c., becoming identical,
however, usually with the "word" of God, the holy spirit
(Cumont, *op. cit.*, ii. 87 *sq.*).

† " Dialog.," 88.

‡ One cannot therefore say, as is usual, that Mark, in whom the
story of the birth given in Matthew and Luke is not found, knew
nothing of a supernatural birth of Christ. For the narrative of the
baptism is the history of his birth, while the corresponding narrative
of the other Evangelists only came into existence later, when the
original sense of the story of the baptism in Mark was no longer
understood.

§ Quoted in Usener, " Religionsgesch. Untersuchungen," 1889, i. 64.

And in Luke xii. 49 *sq.* we read the words: "I came to cast fire upon the earth : and what will I, if it is already kindled? But I have a baptism to be baptized with." Here is a reference to fire falling upon the eyes and being made to blaze up by "baptism," that is, the pouring on of a nourishing liquid, as we have seen in the worship of Agni.*

Just as John, who was closely related to the Essenes, baptized the penitents in the Jordan in the open air, so also the Mandæi, whose connection with the Essenes is extremely probable, used to perform baptisms in flowing water only, on which account they were also called "the Christians of John" in later times. This custom among them was obviously connected with the fact that Hibil Ziwâ, who was venerated by them as a Redeemer, was a form of Marduk, and the latter was a son of the great Water-God, Ea ; he thus incorporated the healing and cleansing powers of water in himself. On the other hand, as has been already said, the "anointing" of the God in the Agni Cult with milk, melted butter, and the fluid Soma, served to strengthen the vital powers of the divine child and to bring the sparks slumbering in the fire-wood to a blaze. There is no doubt that this idea was also present in the baptism as it was usually practised in the mystic cults. By baptism the newly admitted member was inwardly "enlightened." Often enough, too, for example, in the Mysteries of Mithras, with the ceremony there was also associated the actual flashing forth of a light, the production of the Cult God himself

---

* Thus Mithras also was said to have been born on the bank of a river, just as Jesus received baptism in or near the Jordan. On this account "the Rock-born" was usually represented with a torch in his left and a sword or knife in his right hand (Cumont, "Myst. d. Mithra," 97). This recalls to mind the words of Jesus in Matt. x. 34 : "I came not to send peace, but a sword."

manifested in light.* By this means the faithful were "born again," in the same way as Agni was "baptized" at his birth, and thereby enabled to shine forth brightly and to reveal the disorder of the world hidden in the darkness.

> "The world was swallowed up, veiled in darkness,
> Light appeared, when Agni was born." †

> "Shining brightly, Agni flashes forth far and wide,
> He makes everything plain in splendour." ‡

A complete understanding of the baptism in the Jordan can only be attained if here, too, we take into consideration the translation of the baptism into astrological terms. In other words, it appears that John the Baptist, as we meet him in the Gospels, was not an historical personage. Apart from the Gospels he is mentioned by Josephus only,§ and this passage, although it was known to Origen ‖ in early days, is exposed to a strong suspicion of being a forgery by some Christian hand.¶ Again, the account in

* Cf. Wobbermin, "Religionsgesch. Studien zur Frage der Beeinflussung des Urchristentums durch das antike Mysterienwesen," 1896, 154 *sqq.* The Christian Church also surrounded the act of baptism with an unusual splendour of lights and candles. Not only was the House of God lit up on this occasion in a festive manner, but each individual to be baptized had to carry a burning candle. The sermons which have come down to us delivered on the feast of the Epiphany, the feast of the birth and baptism of the Saviour which in earlier days fell together (!), excel in the description of the splendour of the lights ; indeed, the day of the feast itself was actually called "the day of lights " or " the lights " (phōta).

† Rgv. x. 88, 2.

‡ *Id.* v. 2, 9.

§ "Antiq.," xviii. 5, 2.

‖ "Contra Celsum," i. 47.

¶ Graetz calls it "a shameless interpolation" ("Gesch. d. Juden," 1888, iii. 278). Cf. J. Chr. K. v. Hofmann, "Die heiligen Schriften des N.T.," vii. Tl. 3, 1876, 4 ; Schürer, "Gesch. des jüdischen Volkes im Zeitalter Jesu," i. 438, note.

the Gospels of the relations between John and Jesus is full of obscurities and contradictions, as has been pointed out by Strauss. These, however, disappear as soon as we recognise that under the name John, which in Hebrew means "pleasing to God," is concealed the Babylonian Water-God, Oannes (Ea). Baptism is connected with his worship, and the baptism of Jesus in the Jordan represents the reflection upon earth of what originally took place among the stars. That is to say, the sun begins its yearly course with a baptism, entering as it does, immediately after its birth, the constellations of the Water-carrier and the Fishes. But this celestial Water Kingdom, in which each year the day-star is purified and born again, is the Eridanus, the heavenly Jordan or Year-Stream (Egyptian, iaro or iero, the river), wherein the original baptism of the divine Saviour of the world takes place.* On this account it is said in the hymn of Ephrem on the Epiphany of the divine Son : " John stepped forward and adored the Son, whose form was enveloped in a strange light," and " when Jesus had received the baptism he immediately ascended, and his light shone over the world." † In the Syrian Baptismal Liturgy, preserved to us under the name of Severus, we read the words : " I, he said, baptize with water, but he who comes, with Fire and Spirit, that spirit, namely, which descended from on high upon his head in the shape of a dove, who has been baptized and has arisen from the midst of the waters, whose light has gone up over the earth." According to the Fourth Gospel, John was not himself the light; but he gave testimony of the light, " that true light which lighteth every man coming into the world," by whom the world was made and of whose fulness we have all received grace.‡ In this the refer-

---

* Cf. Sepp., *op. cit.*, i. 168 *sqq.*   † Cf. Usener, *op. cit.*, 62.
‡ I. 8, 9, 10, 16 ; cf. Matt. iv. 16.

ence to the sun is unmistakable, while the story of John's birth * is copied from that of the Sun-Gods Isaac † and Samson.‡ In John, the Baptist himself is called by Jesus " a burning and shining lamp," § and he himself remarks, when he hears of the numerous following of Jesus, "he must increase but I must decrease," ‖ a speech which probably at first referred to the summer solstice, when the sun, having reached the highest point in its course, enters the winter hemisphere and loses strength day by day. John is said to have been born six months before Jesus.¶ This, too, points to the fact that both are essentially identical, that they are only the different halves of the year, representing the sun as rising and setting, these two phases being related to one another as Caleb and Joshua, Nergal and Tammuz, &c. John the Baptist is represented as wearing a cloak of camel-hair, with a leathern girdle about his loins.** This brings to mind the garb of the prophet Elijah,†† to whom Jesus himself likened him.‡‡ But Elijah, who passed among the Jews for a forerunner of the Messiah, is a form of Sun-God transferred to history. In other words, he is the same as the Greek Helios, the German Heljas, and Ossetic Ilia, with whom he coincides in most important points, or at any rate characteristics of this God have been transferred to the figure of the prophet.§§

---

* Luke i. 5 *sqq.*	† Gen. xvii. 16 *sqq.*	‡ Judges, xiii. 2 *sqq.*
§ John v. 35.	‖ *Id.* iii. 30.	¶ Luke i. 26.
** Matt. iii. 4.	†† 2 Kings i. 8.	‡‡ Matt. xi. 14.

§§ Cf. Nork, " Realwörterbuch," i. 451 *sqq.* The Baptist John in the Gospels also appears as the " forerunner," announcer, herald, and preparer of the way for Jesus, and it appears that the position of Aaron in regard to Moses, he being given the latter as a mouthpiece or herald, has helped in the invention of the Baptist's figure. A similar position is taken in the Old Testament by the " Angel of the Countenance," the messenger, mediator, ambassador, and " Beginning of the way of God," the rabbinic Metatron, whom we saw earlier

According to Babylonian ideas corresponding to the
"baptism of water" at the commencement of the efficacious power of the sun, was the "baptism of fire,"
was identical with Joshua (see above, p. 56 *sq.*). In the Syro-
Phœnician and the Greek Mysteries Cadmus, Kadmilos, or Kadmiel,
a form of the divine messenger and mediator Hermes, also called
Iasios (Joshua), corresponded to him, his name literally meaning
"he who goes before God" or prophesies of him, the announcer,
herald, or forerunner of the coming God (cf. Schelling, "Die Gott-
heiten von Samothrake Ww.," i. 8, 358, 392 *sqq*). Ezra ii. 40, 39, and
Nehem. vii. 43, call Kadmiel a Levite, he being always named together
with the High Priest Joshua. It is probably only another name of
the latter himself, and characterises him as servant and herald of
God. Now Kadmiel is the discoverer of writing and the establisher
of civilisation, and in so far identical with Oannes, the Babylonian
"Water-man" and Baptism-God (Movers, *op. cit.*, 518 *sqq.*). Can
Oannes (Johannes) the Baptist in this way have become Kadmiel, the
"forerunner" and preparer of the way of Jesus, who announced his
near arrival, and the God Jesus, in consequence of this, have divided
into two different figures, that of Joshua-Kadmiel (Johannes) and the
Messiah Jesus? In this regard it is certainly not without significance
that the figure of the High Priest Joshua in Zechariah wavers
between the Messiah (Zemah) and a mere forerunner of the latter.
John's question to Jesus, "Art thou he that cometh, or look we for
another?" (Matt. xi. 3) is exactly the question which strikes the
reader in reading the corresponding passage of Zechariah. Possibly
the presence of the dove at the baptism in the Jordan obtains in this
way a still closer explanation, for Semiramis, the Dove Goddess, is
the spouse of Oannes (Ninus); John and the dove accordingly are the
parents, who are present at the "birth" of the divine son. But
the violent death of John at Herod's command and the head of the
prophet upon the dish have prototypes in the myth of Cadmus.
For the head of the latter is supposed to have been cut off by his
brother and to have been buried upon a brazen shield, a cult story
which plays a part especially in the Mysteries of the Cabiri Gods, to
whom Cadmus belongs (cf. Creuzer, "Symbolik und Mythologie
der alten Völker," 1820, ii. 333). According to Josephus (*op. cit.*)
John was put to death because Herod feared political disorders from
his appearance, while Matthew makes him fall a victim to Herod's
revenge, the latter having been censured by John for his criminal
marriage with the wife of his brother. Moreover, the prophet Elijah,
who accuses Ahab of having yielded to his wife Jezebel and of having

when it was at the height of its annual course, at the
time of the summer solstice, and its passage was again
inclined downwards.* This idea, too, is found in the

murdered Naboth (1 Kings xxi.), as well as the prophet Nathan, who
reproaches David for having killed Uriah and having married his
wife (2 Sam. xii., cf. also Esther v. 7, 2), are also prototypes.
According to this a religious movement or sect must, in the minds
of posterity, have been condensed into the figure of John the Baptist.
Its followers, who closely resembled the Essenes, in view of the
imminent nearness of the kingdom of heaven, exhorted men to a
conversion of mind, looked upon the Messiah in the sense of Daniel
essentially as the God appointed (" awakened ") judge over the living
and the dead, and sought by baptism to apply to the penitents the
magic effects which should flow from the name of their Cult God
Johannes (Oannes), the Babylonian-Mandiac Baptism and Water-
God. The stern and gloomy character of this sect may have been
reflected in the character sketch of the John in the Gospels, and
between it and the sect of Jesus many collisions, disagreements, and
conversions appear to have taken place (Matt. xi. 1 *sq.* ; Luke vii. 18
sqq. ; John i. 37). Possibly the sect of Jesus was originally only
an excrescence from, and a development of, the conception which the
disciples of John had of the Messiah, as is indicated by the supposed
blood relationship between Jesus and John. At any rate, the adherents
of the former in their belief in the sufferings, death, and resurrection
of the Messiah felt that their point of view was higher and more
perfect as compared with that of John's disciples, who do not appear
to have risen essentially above the general ideas of the Jewish
Apocalyptics. According to Matthew iii. 13 Jesus came out of
Galilee, the " Galilee of the Heathens," to the baptism of John.
Herein the original heathenish origin of the faith of Jesus was pointed
to. " The people which sat in darkness have seen a great light. To
them which sat in the region and shadow of death, to them did light
spring up " (Matt. iv. 16 ; cf. Smith, *op. cit.*, 95). The opposition of
the two different sects was, at any rate, so great that John's disciples
needed a further instruction and a new baptism " in the name of the
Lord Jesus " to receive the Holy Ghost, in order to be received into
the Christian community. For example, the twelve at Ephesus, who
had simply received the baptism of John, as well as the eloquent and
literary Alexandrian, Apollo, who none the less proclaimed the message
of salvation (τὰ περὶ τοῦ Ἰησοῦ) (Acts xviii. 24 *sqq.*, xix. 1–7).

* Cf., Sepp, " Heidentum," i. 170 *sq.*, 190 *sq.* ; Winckler, " Die babylonische Geisteskultur," 89, 100 *sq.* By this reference of the Gospel

Gospels, in the story of the transfiguration of Jesus upon the mountain.* It takes precisely the same place in the context of his life-year, as depicted by the Evangelists, as the Sun's "baptism of fire" in the Babylonian world system, since it too marks the highest and turning-point in the life of the Christian Saviour. On this occasion Moses and Elijah appeared with the Saviour, who shone like a pillar of fire, " and his garments became glistening, exceeding white, like unto snow, so as no fuller on earth can whiten them." And there came a cloud which overshadowed the three disciples whom Jesus had taken with him on to the mountain. And a voice came from the cloud, saying, " This is my beloved Son, hear ye him." As at the baptism, so here, too, was Jesus proclaimed by a heavenly voice as the Son or beloved of God, or rather of the Holy Spirit. As the latter is in Hebrew of the feminine gender, it consequently appears that in this passage we have before us a parallel to the baptism of Jesus in the Jordan. The incident is generally looked upon as though by it was emphasised the higher significance of Jesus in comparison with the two chief representatives of the old order, and as though Jesus was extolled before Moses and Elijah by the transfiguration. Here too, however, the Sun-God, Helios, is obviously concealed beneath the form of the Israelite Elijah. On this account Christianity changed the old places of worship of Zeus and Helios upon eminences into chapels of Elijah; and Moses is no other than the Moon-God, the Mēn of Asia Minor. And he has been

story to the sun's course it appears that the activity of Jesus from his baptism in the Jordan to his death, according to the account of the Synoptics, only covered a year. It is the mythological year of the sun's course through the Watery Region in January and February until the complete exhaustion of its strength in December.

* Mark ix. 2-7.

introduced into the story because the divine lawgivers in almost all mythologies are the same as the moon, the measurer of time and regulator of all that happens (cf. Manu among the Indians, Minos among the Greeks, Men (Min) among the Egyptians).* According to Justin,† David is supposed to have made the prophecy that Christ would be born " before the sun and the moon." The sun and moon often appear upon the pictures of the Nearer Asiatic Redeemer, God (*e.g.*, Mithras), paling before the splendour of the young Light-God, as we have seen in the case of Buddha,‡ and as, according to the narrative of the Rigveda, also happened at the birth of the Child Agni. Accordingly we have before us in the story of the transfiguration in the Gospels only another view of the story of the birth of the Light-God or Fire-God, such as lies at the root of the story of the baptism of the Christian Saviour.§ And with the thought of the new birth of the Saviour is associated that of the baptism of Jesus, and particularly that of the fire-baptism, of which the sun partakes at the height of its power.‖

* The horns (crescent) which he also shares with Jahwe, as the Syrian Hadah shows (Winckler, " Gesch. Israels," ii. 94), recalls to mind the Moon nature of Moses. Moses is, as regards his name, the " Water-drawer." The moon is, however, according to antique views, merely the water-star, the dispenser of the dew and rain, and the root ma (mo), which, in the name of Moses, refers to water, is also contained in the various expressions for the moon.

† " Contra Tryph.," xlvi.

‡ Cf. above, 112.

§ Burnouf, *op. cit.*, 195 *sq.*

‖ That in the closer description of this occurrence Old Testament ideas have had their part has already been advanced by others. Thus in the transfiguration of Jesus the transfiguration of Moses upon Sinai without doubt passed before the mind of the narrator. And just as Jesus took with him his three chief disciples on to the mount of transfiguration, so Moses took his three trusted followers, Aaron, Nadab, and Abihu, to partake in the vision of Jahwe (Strauss, " Leben Jesu," ii. 269 *sqq.*).

VI

THE SELF-OFFERING OF THE MESSIAH. THE SUPPER

LIKE Baptism, the sacrament of the "Supper," the partaking of the sacred host and wine (in place of which among certain sects water is also found), has its precedent in the most ancient fire-worship. When the sacred fire had been kindled upon the altar, the faithful were accustomed, as the Rigveda shows, to sit down in order to partake of the sacred cake prepared from meal and butter, the symbol of all solid food, and of the Soma cup, the symbol of all liquid nourishment. It was thought that Agni dwelt invisible within these substances: in the meal as though in the concentrated heat of the sun, in the Soma, since the drink in its fiery nature and invigorating power disclosed the nature of the God of Fire and Life. Participation therein opened to the faithful communion with Agni. Thereby they were incorporated with the God. They felt themselves transformed into him, raised above the actuality of every day, and as members of a common body, as though of one heart and one soul, inflamed by the same feeling of interdependence and brotherhood. Then some such hymn as follows would mount towards heaven from their breasts overflowing with thankfulness:—

> "Oh great Agni, true-minded
> Thou dost indeed unite all.
> Enkindled on the place of worship
> Bring us all that is good.

Unitedly come, unitedly speak,
And let your hearts be one,
Just as the old Gods
For their part are of one mind.

Like are their designs, like their assembly,
Like their disposition, united their thoughts.
So pray I also to you with like prayer,
And sacrifice unto you with like sacrifice.
The like design you have indeed,
And your hearts are united.
Let your thoughts be in unison,
That you may be happily joined together." *

While the faithful by partaking of the sacred cake and the fiery Soma cup united themselves with the God and were filled with his "spirit," the sacrificial gifts which had been brought to him burnt upon the altars. These consisted likewise of Soma and Sacred Cake, and caused the sacred banquet to be of such a kind that it was partaken of by Agni and men together. The God was at and present in the banquet dedicated to him. He consumed the gifts, transformed them into flame, and in sweet-smelling smoke bore them with him up to heaven. Here they were partaken of by the other divine beings and finally by the Father of Heaven himself. Thus Agni became not merely an agent at the sacrifice, a mystic sacrificial priest, but, since the sacrificial gifts simply contained him in material form, a sacrificer, who offered his own body in sacrifice.† While man sacrificed God, God at the same time sacrificed himself. Indeed, this sacrifice was one in which God was not only the subject but also the object, both sacrificer and sacrificed. "It was a common mode of thinking among the Indians," says Max Müller, "to look upon the fire on the altar as at the same time subject and object of the sacrifice. The fire burnt the offering and was accord-

* Rgv. x. 191 ; cf. i. 72, 5.   † *Id.* iii. 28, vi. 11.

ingly the priest as it were. The fire bore the offering to the Gods and was accordingly a mediator between God and men. But the fire also represented something divine. It was a God, and if honour was paid to this God, the fire was at once subject and object of the sacrifice. Out of this arose the first idea, that Agni sacrificed to himself, that is, that he brought his own offering to himself, then, that he brought himself as a victim—out of which the later legends grew." [*] The sacrifice of the God is a sacrificing of the God. The genitive in this sentence is in one case to be understood in an objective, in the other in a subjective sense. In other words, the sacrifice which man offers to the God is a sacrifice which the God brings, and this sacrifice of the God is at the same time one in which the God offers himself as victim.

In the Rigveda Agni, as God of Priests and Sacrifices, also bears the name of Viçvakarman, *i.e.*, " Consummator of All." Hymn x., 81 also describes him as the creator of the world, who called the world into existence, and in so doing gave his own body in sacrifice. Hence, then, the world, according to x. 82, represents nothing existing exterior to him, but the very manifestation of Viçvakarman, in which at the creation he as it were appeared. On the other hand, Purusha, the first man, is represented as he out of whose body the world was formed.[†] But Purusha is, as we have seen, the prototype of the Mandaic and apocalyptic " son of man." Herein lies the confirmation of the fact that the " son of man " is none other than Agni, the most human of the Vedic Gods. In the Mazda religion the first mortals were called Meshia and Meshiane, the ancestors of fallen mankind,

[*] Max Müller, " Einleitung in die vergl. Religionswissenschaft," note to p. 219.

[†] Rigv. x. 90.

who expect their redemption at the hands of another Meshia. This meaning of the word Messiah was not strange to the Jews too, when they placed the latter as the "new Adam" in the middle of the ages. Adam, however, also means man.* The Messiah accordingly, as the new Adam, was for them too only a renewal of the first man in a loftier and better form. This idea, that mankind needed to be renewed by another typical representative of itself, goes back in the last resort to India, where, after the dismemberment of Purusha, a man arose in the person of Manu or Manus. He was to be the just king, the first lawgiver and establisher of civilisation, descending after his death to rule as judge in the under-world (cf. the Cretan Minos). But Manu, whose name again meant no more than man or human being (Manusha), passed as son of Agni. Indeed, he was even completely identified with him, since life, spirit, and fire to the mind of primitive man are interchangeable ideas, although it is spirit and intelligence which are expressed under the name of Manu (Man = to measure, to examine).†

* The Rigveda describes Purusha as a gigantic being (cf. the Eddic Ymir) who covers the earth upon all sides and stretches ten fingers beyond. The Talmud, too (Chagiga, xii. 1), ascribes to the first man Adam a gigantic size, reaching as he did with his head to heaven and with his feet to the end of the world. Indeed, according to Epiphanius ("Haeres." xix. 4), the Essenes made the size of Christ too, the "second Adam," stretch an immeasurable distance.

† In Hebrew Messiah means "the anointed." But Agni too as God of Sacrifices bears the name of the anointed, akta (above, p. 99). Indeed, it appears as though the Greek Christ, as a translation of Messiah, stands in relation to Agni. For the God over whom at his birth was poured milk or the holy Soma cup and sacrificial butter, bore the surname of Hari among the members of the cult. The word signified originally the brightness produced by anointing with fat and oil. It appears in the Greek Charis, an epithet of Aphrodite, and is contained in the verb chrio, to anoint, of which Christos is the participial form (cf. Cox, "Mythology of the Aryan Nations," 1903, 27, 254).

We thus also obtain a new reason for the fact that the divine Redeemer is a human being. We also understand not only why the "first-born son of God" was, according to the ideas of the whole of Nearer Asiatic syncretism, the principle of the creation of the world, but also why the redemption which he brought man could be for this reason looked upon as a divine self-sacrifice.*

The sacrifice of the God on the part of mankind is a sacrifice of the God himself—it is only by this means that the community between God and man was completed. The God offers sacrifice for man, while man offers sacrifice for God. Indeed, more than this, he offers himself for mankind, he gives his own body that man may reap the fruit of his sacrifice. The divine "son" offers himself as

---

* The Bhagavadgîta shows that the idea of a self-sacrifice was associated with Krishna also, whom we have already learnt to recognise as a form of Agni, and that his becoming man was regarded as such a sacrifice. It (ii. 16) runs: "I am the act of sacrifice, the sacrifice of God and of man. I am the sap of the plant, the words, the sacrificial butter and fire, and at the same time the victim." And in viii. 4 Krishna says of himself: "My presence in nature is my transitory being, my presence in the Gods is Purusha (i.e., my existence as Purusha), my presence in the sacrifices is myself incorporated in this body." But Mithras too offers himself for mankind. For the bull whose death at the hands of the God takes the central position in all the representations of Mithras was originally none other than the God himself—the sun in the constellation of the Bull, at the spring equinox—the sacrifice of the bull accordingly being also a symbol of the God who gives his own life, in order by his death to bring a new, richer and better life. Mithras, too, performs this self-sacrifice, although his heart struggles against it, at the command of the God of Heaven, which is brought to him by a raven, the messenger of the God of Gods. (cf. Cumont, op. cit., 98 sqq.). And just as according to Vedic ideas Purusha was torn in pieces by the Gods and Dæmons and the world made out of his parts, so too according to Persian views the World Bull Abudad or the Bull Man Gayomart at the beginning of creation is supposed to have shed his blood for the world, to live again as Mithras (Sepp., op. cit., i. 330, ii. 6 sq.).

a victim. Sent down by the "father" upon the earth in the form of light and warmth, he enters men as the "quickening and life-giving spirit" under the appearance of bread and wine. He consumes himself in the fire and unites man with the father above, in that by his disposal of his own personality he removes the separation and difference between them. Thus Agni extinguishes the hostility between God and man, thus he consumes their sins in the glow of his fiery nature, spiritualising and illuminating them inwardly. Through the invigorating power of the "fire-water" he raises men above the actuality of every day to the source of their existence and by his own sacrifice obtains for them a life of blessedness in heaven. In the sacrifice, too, God and man are identified. Therein God descends to man and man is raised to God. That is the common thought which had already found expression in the Rigveda, which later formed the special "mystery" of the secret cults and religious unions of Nearer Asia, which lay at the root of the sacrament of "the Supper," which guaranteed to man the certainty of a blessed life in the beyond, and reconciled him to the thought of bodily death.* Agni is accordingly nothing else than the bodily warmth in individuals, and as such the subject of their motions and thoughts, the principle of life, their soul. When the body grows cold in death the warmth of life leaves it, the eyes of the dead go up to the sun, his breath into the wind; his soul, however, ascends towards heaven where the "fathers" dwell, into the kingdom of everlasting light and life.† Indeed, so great is the power of Agni, the divine physician and saviour of the soul,‡ that he, as the God of all creative power, can, by merely laying on his hands, even call the dead back to life.§

* Cumont, "Myst. de Mithra," 101. † Rgv. x. 16.
‡ Id. x. 16, 6. § Id. lx.; cf. also Burnouf, op. cit., 176 sqq.

Even in the Old Testament we meet with the idea of a. sacramental meal. This is pointed to in Genesis xiv. 18 *sqq.*, when Melchisedek, the prince of peace ("King of Salem"), the priest of "God Most High," prepares for Abraham a meal of bread and wine, and at it imparts to him the blessing of the Lord God. For Melchisedek, the ruler of Salem, the city of peace, " the King of Justice," as he is called in the Epistle to the Hebrews, is even in this book plainly described as an ancient God: "without father, without mother, without genealogy, having neither beginning of days nor end of life, but made like unto the Son of God, he abideth a priest continually." * So also the Prophet Jeremiah speaks of holy feasts, consisting of cake and wine, of nightly sacrifices of burnt-offerings and liquids, which were offered to the Queen of Heaven (*i.e.*, the Moon) and other Divinities.† Isaiah, too, is indignant against those who prepare a drinking-feast for God and make liquid offerings to Meni.‡ Now Meni is none other than Mēn, the Moon-God of Asia Minor, and as such is identical with Selene-Mēne, the Goddess of the Moon in the Orphic hymns. Like her he is a being of a dual sex, at once Queen and King of Heaven. Consequently a liquid sacrifice appears to have been offered by all the people of Nearer Asia in honour of the Moon. As Moon-God (Deus Lunus) and as related to Meni, in whose worship a sacramental meal also plays the chief part, Agni appears in the Vedas under the name of Manu, Manus, or Soma. He too is a being of dual sex. Of this we are again reminded when Philo, the Rabbinic speculation of

* *Op. cit.*, vii. 8. He is Jahwe, the King of Jeru-Salem itself (Josephus, " Ant.," x. 2), and corresponds to the Phœnician Moloch (Melech) Sidyk, who offered his only born son, Jehud, to the people as an expiation. Cf. *supra*, p. 77.

† *Op. cit.*, xix. 18, xxxii. 29, xliv. 17, xviii. 25.

‡ *Op. cit.*, lxv. 11.

the Kabbala, as well as the Gnostics ascribe to the first man (Adam Kadmon) two faces and the form of a man and woman, until God separated the two sexes from one another.* According to this we should probably look upon the fire-worship in Asia Minor also as the foundation of the sacramental meal.

Obviously we have to do with a meal of this kind in the bringing in of the so-called shew-bread. Every Sabbath twelve cakes were laid by the priests "upon the pure table before the Lord," "and it shall be for Aaron and his sons, and they shall eat it in a holy place, for it is most holy unto him of the offerings of the Lord, by a perpetual statute." †

It appears, then, that this meal, presided over by the High Priest as representative of Aaron, was partaken of by twelve other priests, and Robertson rightly sees herein the Jewish prototype of the Christian Supper and of the number of apostles—the Twelve—present at it. But the High Priest Aaron is a personification of the Jewish Ark of the Covenant, that is, of the visible expression of the Covenant between God and man, one of the chief prototypes of the Messiah. And if the self-offering of the Messiah, as we have seen above (p. 78), has its precedent in the self-offering of Aaron, so also the great solemnity of the Aaronic sacrificial meal would not be wanting in the story of the Christian Redeemer.

As is well known, Joshua too, the Jesus of the Old Testament, whom we have learnt to recognise as an ancient Ephraimitic God of the Sun and Fruitfulness, was accompanied in his passage of the Jordan by twelve assistants, one from each tribe. And he is said after circumcising the people to have celebrated the Paschal

---

* As is well known, the Germanic first man, Mannus, according to Tacitus, was a son of the hermaphrodite Thuisto.

† Lev. xxiv. 5–9.

Feast on the other bank.* Hence, taking into account
what has been said above concerning Joshua, we are
probably justified in drawing the conclusion that his
name was permanently connected with the partaking of
the Easter lamb.† In any case the so-called " Supper "
of Christianity did not only later take its place as the
central point of religious activity, but from the beginning
it held this central position in the cults of those sects out
of which Christianity was developed. It was the point of
crystallisation, the highest point, of the other ritualistic
acts, in a way the germ cell out of which in association
with the idea of the death and resurrection of the God
Redeemer the Christian outlook upon the world has
grown. Just as in the Vedic Agni Cult the sacrifice
offered by men to their God was a self-sacrifice of this
God as well in a subjective as in an objective sense ; just
as the participating in common of the sacrificial gifts
served the purpose of rendering the sacrifice in an inward
sense their very own, and thereby making them immediate participators in its efficacy, so, too, the Christian
partakes in the bread of the body of his God and in the
wine drinks his blood in order to become as it were him-

---

* Jos. iv. 1 *sqq.* ; ch. v.

† Thus Helios also, the Greek Sun-God, the heavenly physician
and saviour, annually prepared the " Sun's Table " in nature, causing
the fruit to ripen, the healing herbs to grow, and inviting mortals to
the life-giving feast. " This Table of the Sun was always spread in
the land of the happy and long-living Ethiopians ; even the twelve
Gods journeyed thither each year with Zeus for twelve days, *i.e.*, in
the last Octave of the old and new year, as though to the feast of
Agape " (Sepp., *op. cit.*, i. 275). For the rest the number twelve had
throughout the whole of antiquity in connection with such ceremonial
feasts a typical signification. For example, among the Athenians,
whose common religious feasts were celebrated annually on the
occasion of the spring sacrifices ; also among the Jews at least twelve
persons had to be assembled round the table of the Easter Lamb
(Sepp., *op. cit.*, ii. 313 *sqq.*).

self God. The Evangelists make the Supper coincide with the Feast of the Pasch, because originally a man was immolated on this occasion; and he, as the first-born and most valuable of sacrificial gifts, took the place of the God who offered himself in sacrifice.*

The celebration of sacramental feasts was very widespread throughout the whole of antiquity. They were among the most important acts of worship in the Mystic religions, above all in connection with the idea of the Saviour (Soter) and God of Sacrifices, who gave his life for the world. Thus Mithras, the Persian Agni, is said to have celebrated in a last meal with Helios and the other companions of his toils the end of their common struggle. Those initiated into the Mysteries of Mithras also celebrated this occurrence by common feasts in which they strove to unite themselves in a mystic manner with the God. Saos (Saon or Samon), the son of Zeus or Hermes, the God of Healing, and a nymph, reminds us of the name of Mithras, rejuvenated and risen again, of Saoshyant or Sosiosh. He is said to have founded the Mysteries in Samothrace, and appears to be identical with the mythical Sabus, who is supposed to have given his name to the Sabines, to have founded Italian civilization, and to have invented wine.† His name characterises him as the "sacrificer" (Scr., Savana, sacrifice); and he appears to be a Western form of Agni, the God of Sacrifices and preparer of the Soma, since Dionysus also bore the surname of Saos or Saotes and, as distributor of the wine, is supposed to have shed his blood for the salvation of the world, to have died and to have risen again, and thus has a prototype in the Vedic Agni. With Saos are connected Iasios (Jasion), the son and beloved of Demeter or Aphrodite (Maia), and of Zeus

* Ghillany, *op. cit.*, 510 *sqq.*
† Preller, "Griech. Mythol.," 398, 850, and his "Röm. Mythol.," 275.

or the divine " artificer " Hephaistos (Tvashtar). Just as
Saos established the worship of the Cabiri, Iasios is said to
have established the worship of Demeter in Samothrace.
In this connection he is identified with Hermes–Cadmus,
the divine sacrificial priest (Kadmilos, *i.e.*, Servant of
God) of the Samothracian religion (cf. Adam–Kadmon
of the Kabbala and the Gnostics, who is connected both
with Agni-Manu and Jesus). According to Usener his
name is connected with the Greek "iasthein," to cure,
and consequently characterises its bearer as " saviour."
But this is also the real meaning of the name Jason,
whose bearer, a form of the patron of physicians,
Asclepios (Helios), wanders about as a physician,
exorciser of demons and founder of holy rites, and was
venerated as God of Healing in the whole of Nearer
Asia and Greece.* The myth also connects him with
the establishment of the worship of the twelve Gods.†

Now, Iasios (Jason) is only a Greek form of the name
Joshua (Jesus). Just as Joshua crossed the Jordan with
twelve assistants and celebrated the Pasch (lamb) on the
further bank, just as Jesus in his capacity of divine
physician and wonder-worker wanders through Galilee
(the district of Galil !) with twelve disciples, and goes to
Jerusalem at the Pasch in order to eat the Easter lamb
there with the Twelve, so does Jason set out with twelve
companions in order to fetch the golden fleece of the
lamb from Colchis.‡ And just as Jason, after overcoming innumerable dangers, successfully leads his companions to their goal and back again to the homes they
so longed for, so does Joshua lead the people of Israel

---

* Strabo, xi. 2 ; Justin, xlii. 3.
† Preller, " Griech. Mytholog.," 110.
‡ It is worth while to observe that the High Priest Joshua
returned to Jerusalem at the head of twelve elders (Ezra ii. 2 ;
Nehem. vii. 7. Cf. Stade, "Gesch. d. V. Israel," ii. 102).

into the promised land "where milk and honey flow," and so Jesus shows his followers the way to their true home, the kingdom of heaven, the land of their "fathers," whence the soul originally came and whither after the completion of its journey through life it returns. It can scarcely be doubted that in all of these cases we have to do with one and the same myth—the myth of the Saving Sun and Rejoicer of the peoples, as it was spread among all the peoples of antiquity, but especially in Nearer Asia. We can scarcely doubt that the stories in question originally referred to the annual journey of the sun through the twelve signs of the Zodiac. Even the names (Iasios, Jason, Joshua, Jesus; cf. also Vishnu Jesudu, see above) agree, and their common root is contained also in the name Jao (Jahwe), from which Joshua is derived. Jao or Jehu, however, was a mystical name of Dionysos among the Greeks, and he, like Vishnu Jesudu (Krishna), Joshua, and Jesus, roamed about in his capacity of travelling physician and redeemer of the world.* Of all of these wandering Healers, Physicians, and Deliverers it is true that they were honoured in the Mysteries by sacramental meals and offered the faithful both the chalice of corporal and spiritual healing and the "bread of life."

* Cf. Movers, *op. cit.*, 539 *sqq.*; Sepp., "Heidentum," 271, 421.

VII

SYMBOLS OF THE MESSIAH: THE LAMB AND THE CROSS

OF a great number of modes of expression and images in the New Testament we know that they originated from the common treasury of the languages of the secret sects of the Orient, having their source above all in Mandaism and the Mithraic religion. Thus "the rock," "the water," "the bread," "the book," or "the light of life,"[*] "the second death," "the vine," "the good shepherd," &c., are simply expressions which in part are known also by the Rigveda and there belong to the ideas grouped about Agni, the God of Fire, Life, and Shepherds. Of the latter, too, as of Jesus, it is said that he loses not a single one of the flock entrusted to his care,[†] for Pushan, to whom the hymn in this connection is addressed, is only a form of Agni. In its symbols also the earliest Christianity coincides with Indian thought in such a striking manner that it can scarcely be explained as chance. Thus the horse,[‡] the hare, and the peacock, which play so great a part in symbolic pictures of the catacombs, point to an ultimately Vedic origin, where they all stand in connection with the nature of Agni. Again, the Fish was already to be found in the

[*] Cf. Jeremias, "Babyl. im N.T.," 69–80.
[†] Rgv. vi. 54.
[‡] Cf. "The Hymns to Dadhikra," iv. 38–40

Indian Fire Worship and appears to have here originally represented Agni swimming in the water of the clouds, the ocean of heaven.* In the hymn of the Rigveda

* Cf. Burnouf, *op. cit.*, 196. The connection between the Fire-God and water is of extreme antiquity. As is well known, in the Edda Loki seeks to escape the pursuit of the Gods in the shape of a salmon; Hephaistos, too, after being cast forth from heaven remains concealed in the sea until Dionysus brings him out; in Rome on the 22nd of August fish from the Tiber used to be sacrificed to Vulcan, being cast living into the fire in representation of the souls of men (Preller, " Röm. Mythol.," ii. 151). It is uncertain whether or to what degree the relations of the sun to the constellation of the Fishes have influenced these images. As regards Babylon, where astrology underwent the most accurate development, this can indeed be looked upon as certain. Here Ea (Oannes), the God of Water and of Life, the father of the Redeemer God Marduk, was represented under the form of a fish. Again, it was not only to the Philistinian Dagon that fish as well as doves were sacred (above, p. 118), but also to the Syrian Atargatis, the latter having borne, as was said, the "Ichthus," or fish, and the worship of fish being connected with devotion to her (Robertson Smith, "Religion of the Semites," 174 *sqq.*). In Egypt Horus was the "divine fish," being represented with a fish-tail and holding a cross in the hand. But the Joshua of the Old Testament, in whom we believe we see the Israelite original of the Christian Saviour, was also called a "Son of the Fish" (Nun, Ninus, a form of Marduk, whose spouse or beloved, Semiramis, is also a Fish Divinity and is the same as Derketo (Atargatis), the Syrian Mother Goddess. The Rabbinists called the Messiah son of Joseph (see above, p. 80 *sq.*), Dag (Dagon) the Fish, and made him to be born of a fish; that is, they expected his birth under the constellation of the Fishes, on which account the Jews were long accustomed to immolate a fish on expiatory feasts. Finally, the fish is also Vishnu's symbol, in whose worship baptism of water takes an important place. Again, the God is said in the form of a fish to have come to the rescue of the pious Manu, the only just man of his time, the Indian Noah, and to have steered the Ark through the flood, thus ensuring to mankind its continuation. It is not difficult to suppose that this idea as well influenced the symbols of Christianity through Mandaic (Gnostic) channels. At any rate, it cannot be admitted at all that the symbol of the fish first arose out of a mere play on letters so far as the formula " Jesous Christos Theou Huios Soter " represents in five

itself Agni is often invoked as "the Bull." This was probably originally a simple nature symbol, the Bull as image of the strength of the God; then the Fire-God and Sun-God, in his capacity of preparer of the Soma cup, was identified with the moon (Manu), whose crescents were taken as the horns of a bull. Later, however, the image of the Bull was driven out by that of the Ram. As early as in the Rigveda there is frequent mention of the God's "banner of smoke." Thus he was accustomed to be represented leading a ram with a banner in his hand or simply with a banner in his hand with the picture of a ram upon it, just as Christ is portrayed under the shape of a ram or lamb bearing a banner like a cross.

About the year 800 B.C. the sun, the heavenly Agni, which had hitherto been at the commencement of spring in the constellation of the Bull, entered (as a consequence of the advance of equality between day and night) that of the Ram. Thus it became, according to astrological modes of thought, itself a ram.* While it had formerly, in the shape of a bull, opened the spring and released the world from the power of winter—an image which was still retained in the Mithras Cult—these functions were now transferred to the ram, and this became a symbol of the God and the beast offered in expiatory sacrifices. Now the constellation of the Ram was described by the Persians in a word which could also mean lamb. In other cases also the lamb often took the place of the ram in the sacrificial worship of Nearer Asia; for example, among the Jews, who were accustomed to consume the Paschal lamb at the beginning of the year in spring. This is the explanation of the mystical lamb in the

words the expression of the quintessence of the Christian faith (cf. van den Bergh van Eysinga, "Ztschr. d. Deutchen Morgenländ. Gesellschaft B.," ix., 1906, 210 *sqq.*).

* Cf. Iamblichus, "De Symbol. Aegyptiorum," ii.,7.

Revelation of John (which is scarcely an original Christian work, but shows signs of a pre-Christian Cult of Jesus*), being depicted by seven horns or rays in a way which rather implies the idea of a ram.

The fifth chapter of Revelation describes the lamb in its quality of heavenly victim of expiation. No one can open the book with the seven seals, which God holds in his right hand, in which the fate of the world appears to be written, but the lamb alone succeeds in so doing— "In the midst of the four-and-twenty elders who, clad in white garments and with crowns on their heads, sit around the divine throne, and in the midst of the four beasts who sit around it, the lamb, suddenly and without anything happening, stands as though it had been slain, having seven horns and seven eyes which are the seven spirits of God, sent forth into all the earth. And when he had taken the book the four living creatures and the four-and-twenty elders fell down before the lamb, having each one a harp, and golden bowls full of incense, which are the prayers of the saints. And they sing a new song saying, Worthy art thou to take the book and to open the seals thereof, for thou wast slain and didst purchase unto God with thy blood men of every tribe, and tongue, and people, and nation, and madest them to be unto our God a kingdom and priests; and they reign upon the earth."†

The scene recalls to mind the self-offering of Agni in the midst of the Gods, Priests, and victims, and the ascension of the God which then took place. Just as the sacrifice of the lamb in Revelation refers to the entrance of the sun into the constellation of the Ram, and the victory of light over wintry darkness and the beginning of a new life which it heralds, so were mystic

* Gunkel, *op. cit.*, 32. *sq.*; Robertson, " Pagan Christs," 135 *sq.*
† *Op. cit.*, v. 6 *sq.*

sacrifices of bulls and rams in the other Sun Cults of Nearer Asia, especially in those of Attis and Mithras, very customary for purposes of expiation or new birth. On these occasions the beast was immolated while tanding, and the blood which poured in streams from the victim was looked upon as a means of cleansing and of life-giving. In any case, throughout Revelation the lamb plays the part of the heavenly fire revealing God's illuminatory nature, unfolding his wisdom and enlightening the world. As it is said of the heavenly Jerusalem : " And the city needed no sun and no moon to shine upon her, for the glory of God illumined her, and her light is the lamb."*

Again, in the Church of the first century, at Easter, a lamb was solemnly slaughtered upon an altar and its blood collected in a chalice.† Accordingly in the early days of Christianity the comparison of Christ with the light and the lamb was a very favourite one. Above all the Gospel of John makes the widest use of it. As had already been done in the Vedic Cult of Agni, here too were identified with Christ the creative word of God that had existed before the world—the life, the light, and the lamb. And he was also called " the light of the world " that came to light up the darkness ruling upon the earth, as well as " the Lamb of God, who bore the sins of the world."‡ And indeed the Latin expression for lamb (agnus) also expresses its relation to the ancient Fire-God and its sanctity as a sacrificial animal. For its root is connected with ignis (Scr. agni, the purifying fire, and yagna, victim), and also, according to Festus Pompeius, with the Greek " hagnos," pure,

* Rev. xxi. 23.

† Hatch, "The Influence of Greek Ideas and Usages upon the Christian Church," Hibbert Lectures, 1888, 300.

‡ John i. 7, 12; ix. 5; xii. 36, 46.

consecrated, and "hagnistes," the expiator.* In this sense "Agnus Dei," the Lamb of God, as Christ is very frequently called, is in fact nothing else than "Agni Deus," since Agnus stands in a certain measure as the Latin translation for Agni.† But in India at the so-called Hulfeast, at the spring equinox, a ram (lamb) used to be solemnly burnt as an expiatory victim representing Agni. The "crucifixion" of Jesus, as will likewise appear, is in a certain sense only the symbol of the burning of the divine lamb, which by its death redeems man from sin. In both cases the lamb refers to the lamb of the Zodiac, the constellation of the Ram, into which the sun enters at the time of the spring equinox, and with which consequently, in accordance with the astrological way of looking at things, it is blended, and which is as though burnt up by it. Thus were completed the victory of the Sun Fire (Agni) over the night of winter and the resurrection of nature to a new life, this cosmic process finding its reflection in the sacrifice upon earth of a lamb (agnus).

During the first century after Christ the lamb in association with light and fire was among the most popular images in ecclesiastical language and symbolism. The heathen Romans used to hang "bullæ" round the necks of their children as amulets. The Christians used consecrated waxen lambs, which were manufactured out of the remains of the Easter candles of the preceding year and distributed during Easter week. The belief then attached itself to these "Agnus Dei's," that if they were preserved in a house they gave protection against lightning and fire. Above all the lamps offered a convenient opportunity for symbolising Christ as a light, and thus making use of the image of the lamb.‡ The *motif*

---

* Sepp., i. 853. † Burnouf, *op. cit.*, 186 *sq.*
Cf., for example, F. X. Kraus, "Geschichte d. christl. Kunst," i. 105.

of the lamb with the cross is also found very frequently in old Christian art upon glass bowls, sarcophagi, and articles of use of all kinds. And indeed in such cases the cross is sometimes found upon the head or shoulder, sometimes at the side of the lamb or even behind him, while a nimbus in the shape of a disc of sunlight surrounds his head and points to the "light" nature of the lamb. The nimbus, too, is an old Indian symbol, and thus indicates that the whole conception was borrowed from the circle of Indian ideas. Later the lamb is also found upon the cross itself, and indeed at the point of intersection of the two arms surrounded by the disc of sunlight. This seems to point to the Saviour's death upon the cross, the cross here appearing to be understood as the gibbet. But is it really certain that the cross in the world of Christian thought possessed this significance from the beginning as the instrument by means of which Jesus was put to death?

In the whole of Christendom it passes as a settled matter that Jesus "died upon the cross"; but this has the shape, as it is usually represented among painters, of the so-called Latin cross, in which the horizontal cross-piece is shorter than the vertical beam. On what then does the opinion rest that the cross is the gibbet? The Evangelists themselves give us no information on this point. The Jews described the instrument which they made use of in executions by the expression "wood" or "tree." Under this description it often occurs in the Greek translation of the Old Testament, in which the gibbet is rendered by xúlon, the same expression being also found in the Gospels. Usually, however, the gibbet is described as staurós (*i.e.*, stake), so much so that staurós and xúlon pass for synonyms. The Latin translation of both these words is crux. By this the Romans understood any apparatus for the execution of men generally, without thinking, however, as a rule of anything else than a stake or gallows (patibulum, stipes) upon which, as Livy tells us, the delinquent was bound with chains or ropes and so delivered over to death.* That the method of execution in Palestine differed in any way from this is not in any way shown. Among the Jews also the condemned used to be hanged upon a simple stake or beam, and exposed to a lingering death from heat, hunger, and thirst, as well as from the natural tension of his muscles. "To fasten to the cross" (stauroun, afigere cruci) accordingly does not mean either in East or West to crucify in our sense, but at first simply "to torture" or "martyr," and later "to hang upon a stake or gallows." And in this connection it appears that the piercing of hands and feet with nails, at least at the time at which the execution of Jesus is supposed to have occurred, was something quite unusual, if it was ever employed at all. The expressions *prospassaleuein* and *proséloun*, moreover, usually signify only to "fasten," "to hang upon a nail," but not at all "to nail to" in the special sense required.†

There is not then the least occasion for assuming that according to original Christian views an exception to this mode of proceeding was made at the execution of Jesus. The only place in the Gospels where there is any mention of the "marks of the nails" (viz., John xx. 25) belongs, as does the whole Gospel, to a relatively later time, and appears, as does so much in John, as a mere strengthening and exaggeration of the original story. For example, Luke xxiv. 39, upon which John is based, does not speak at all of nail-marks, but merely of the marks of the wounds which the condemned must naturally have received as a consequence of being fastened to the

---

* "Hist. Rom.," i. 26.

† Cf. Zöckler, "Das Kreuz Christi," 1875, 62 *sqq.*; Hochart, "Études d'histoire religieuse," 1890, chap. x., "La crucifix."

stake. Accordingly the idea that Christ was "nailed" to the cross was in the earliest Christianity by no means the ruling one. Ambrose, for example, only speaks of the "cords" of the "cross" and the "ligatures of the passion" ("usque ad crucis laqueos ac retia passionis"), * and consequently knew nothing of nails having been used in this case.† If we consider that the "crucifixion" of Jesus corresponds to the hanging of Attis, Osiris, and so forth, and that the idea of the gibbeted gods of Nearer Asia called forth and fixed the Christian view; if we remember that Haman, the prototype of Jesus at the Purim feast, was also hanged upon a gallows,‡ then it becomes doubly improbable that our present ideas on the matter correspond to the views of the early Christians. For although we have no direct picture of the hanging of those Gods, yet we possess representations of the execution of Marsyas by Apollo, in which the God has his rival hauled up on to a tree by ropes round his wrists, which have been bound together.§ But Marsyas, the inventor of the flute, the friend and guide of Cybele in the search for the lost Attis, is no other than the latter himself, or at any rate a personality very near akin to Attis.‖ It is not difficult to conclude that Attis too, or the man who represented him in the rites, was hung in the same manner to the stake or tree-trunk and thus put to death. Thus it seems that originally the manner of death of the Jewish Messiah was imagined in the same way, and so the

---

* Aringhi, " Roma subterranea," vi. ch. 23, " De Cervo."
† Cf. on the other hand Justin, " Apol.," i. 35.
‡ Esther v. 14, vii. 10.
§ Cf. the picture of Marsyas hanging upon a tree-trunk in the collection of antiquities at Karlsruhe ; also the illustrations in P. Schmidt, " Die Geschichte Jesu, erläutert," 1904.
‖ Movers, *op. cit.*, 687 ; Nork, " Reallexikon," ii. 122 *sq.* ; Frazer, "Adonis, Attis, Osiris," 185 *sq.*

heathens too called the new God in scorn " the Hanged One."

How, then, did the idea come into existence that Jesus did not die upon a simple gallows, but rather upon wood having the well-known form of the cross? It arose out of a misunderstanding, from considering as the same and mingling two ideas which were originally distinct but described by the same word wood, tree, xúlon, lignum, arbor. This word signifies, as we have already said, on the one hand indeed the stake or gallows (staurós, crux) upon which the criminal was executed; but the same word, corresponding to the Hebrew text of the Old Testament, also referred to the " wood," " the tree of life," which was supposed to stand in Paradise. According to the Revelation of John it was to serve as food for the holy in the new Paradise to come,* and it was honoured by the Christians as the " seal " and guarantee of their salvation under the form of the mystic cross or Tau.

In all private religious associations and secret cults of later antiquity the members made use of a secret sign of recognition or union. This they carried about in the form, in some cases, of wooden, bronze, or silver amulets hung round the neck or concealed beneath the clothes, in others woven in their garments, or tattooed upon the forehead, neck, breast, hands, &c. Among these signs was the cross, and it was usually described under the name " Tau," after the letter of the old Phœnician alphabet. Such an application of the cross to mystic or religious ends reaches back into grey antiquity. From of old the cross was in use in the cult of the Egyptian Gods, especially of Isis and Horus. It was also found among the Assyrians and Persians, serving, as the pictures show, in part as the mark and ornament of distinguished persons, such as priests and

* Rev. ii. 7, xxii. 2.

kings, in part also as a religious attribute in the hands of the Gods and their worshippers. According to some it was the sign which Jahwe ordered the Israelites to paint upon their doors with the blood of the lamb when he sent the angel of death to destroy the first-born of their Egyptian oppressors. It played a similar part also in Isaiah* and Ezekiel,† when it was a question of separating the god-fearing Israelites from the crowd of other men whom Jahwe purposed to destroy. When the Israelites were pressed in battle by the Amalekites Moses is said to have been helped by Aaron and Hur to stretch out his arms in the shape of that magic sign, and thus to have rendered possible a victory for his people over their enemies.‡ Among the other nations of antiquity also—the Greeks, Thracians, the Gaulish Druids, and so on—the Tau was applied in a similar manner to ritualistic and mystic ends. It appears as an ornament on the images of the most different divinities and heroes—*e.g.*, Apollo, Dionysus, Demeter, Diana (the Phœnician Astarte). It is also found upon innumerable Greek, Roman, Egyptian, and Phœnician coins, upon vases, pictures, jewellery, &c. In Alexandria the Christians found it chiselled upon the stone when the temple of Serapis was destroyed, in 391. In this temple Serapis himself was represented of superhuman size, with arms outstretched in the form of a cross, as though embracing the universe. In Rome the Vestal virgins wore the cross upon a ribbon round the neck. Indeed, it even served as an ornament upon the weapons of the Roman legions and upon the standards of the cavalry long before Constantine, by his well-known "vision," gave occasion for its being expressly introduced under the form of the so-called "Monogram of

* lxvi. 19.　　　　　† ix. 3, 4.

‡ Exod. xvii. 10 *sqq.*

Christ" into the army as a military sign.* But in the North also we find the cross, not only in the shape of the hooked-cross and the three-armed cross (Triskele), but also in the form of Thor's hammer, upon runic, stones, weapons, utensils, ornaments, amulets, &c. And when the heathens of the North, as Snorre informs us, marked themselves in the hour of death with a spear, they scratched upon their bodies one of the sacred signs that has been mentioned, in doing which they dedicated themselves to God.†

That here we have to do with a sun symbol is easily recognised wherever the simple, equally-armed cross appears duplicated with an oblique cross having the same point of intersection with it, ✳, or where it has the shape of a perpendicular which is cut symmetrically by two other lines crossing one another, ✳. And as a matter of fact this symbol of a sun shedding its rays is found upon numberless coins and illustrations, in which it is obvious that a reference to the sun is intended— *e.g.*, upon the coins of the Egyptian Ptolemies, of the city Gods of Rome, of Augustus and the Flavian Cæsars. Here the Sun sign appears to have been adopted as a consequence of the fusing of the Sun Cult of later antiquity with the cult of the Emperor. Much more frequent, however, is the simple Tau, sometimes, indeed, in a shape with equal limbs (Greek cross), +, sometimes with the upright below lengthened (Latin cross), †, sometimes upright, sometimes oblique (St. Andrew's cross), ✕,

---

* For particulars see Zöckler, *op. cit.*, 7 *sqq.*; also Hochart, *op. cit.*, chap. viii., "Le symbole de la croix"; G. de Mortillet, "Le signe de la croix avant le christianisme," 1866; Mourant Brock, "La croix payenne et chrétienne," 1881; Goblet d'Alviella, "La migration des symboles," 1891.

† Henry Petersen, "Über den Gottesdienst u. den Götterglauben des Nordens während der Heidenzeit," 1882, 39 *sqq.* 95 *sqq.*

sometimes, again, like the Greek letter Tau, T, sometimes in the shape of the so-called mirror of Venus, ♀, in which the ring plainly refers to the sun, sometimes in that of the Svastika, or hooked cross, ⊹, sometimes with, sometimes without a circle, and so on. A form made up of the oblique and the ring cross of the Egyptians (so-called Key of the Nile) is the cross known under the description of the "Monogram of Christ," ☧. According to the legend it was first employed by Constantine on account of his "vision"; and ecclesiastical writers, especially on the Catholic side, try even to-day to support this view, in spite of all facts. For this form of the cross also is clearly of pre-Christian origin, and had its prototype in the ancient Bactrian Labarum cross, as is found, for example, upon the coins of the Bactrian king Hippostratos (about 130 B.C.), of the Egyptian Ptolemies, of Mithridates, upon Attic Tetradrachma, &c.*

After the careful investigations on this subject which have been undertaken by French savants especially, there can be no doubt that we have before us in this so-called "seal" of the Gods and religious personalities a symbol of the creative force of nature, of the resurrection and the new life, a pledge of divine protection in this world and of everlasting blessedness after. As such it appears upon heathen sarcophagi and tombstones; and on this account in some cases their Christian character is too quickly assumed. Moreover, the cross has been preserved in present-day musical notation as the sign of the raising of a note,† while its use in the Mysteries and private Cult associations is authority for the statement that precisely in these the thought of a new-birth and resurrection in company with the hero of the association or God of the

---

* Zöckler, *op. cit.*, 21 *sqq.*
† Winckler, "Die babyl. Geisteskultur," 82.

union stood as a central point of faith. One understands the painful feeling of the Christians at the fact that the private sign used by them and their special sacraments were in use among all the secret cults of antiquity. They could explain this to themselves only as the work of spiteful dæmons and an evil imitation of Christian usages on the heathens' part.* In reality the symbol of the cross is much older than Christianity; and, indeed, the sign of the cross is found associated in a special manner with the cult of divinities of nature or life with its alternations of birth, blossoming, and decay, representatives of the fertility and creative force of nature, the Light-Gods and Sun-Gods subjected to death and triumphing victoriously over it. It is only as such, as Gods who died and rose again, that they were divinities of the soul and so of the Mysteries and pious fraternities. The idea of the soul, however, is found everywhere in nature religion considered as being connected with the warmth of life and with fire, just as the sun was honoured as the highest divinity and, so to speak, as the visible manifestation of the world-soul solely on account of its fiery nature. Should not, then, the symbol of life, which in its developed form plainly refers to the sun, in its simplest and original shape point to the fire, this "earliest phenomenon" of all religious worship?

Naturally, indeed, different views can be held as to what the various forms of the cross betoken. Thus, for example, according to Burnouf, Schliemann, and others, the Svastika represents the "fire's cradle," *i.e.*, the pith of the wood, from which in oldest times in the point of intersection of the two arms the fire was produced by whirling round an inserted stick.† On the other hand, according to the view most widespread at the present

---

* Tertullian, " Contra Haereses," 40.
† Burnouf, *op. cit.*, 240.

day, it simply symbolises the twirling movement when making the fire, and on this, too, rests its application as symbol of the 'sun's course.* Hochart considers the cross in the shape of the Greek Tau as the inserted stick (pramantha) of the Vedic priests.† Very likely, however, this form arose simply through the identity of sound between the Greek and Phœnician letter, the Greeks having interchanged the like-sounding foreign letter with their own Tau. That the cross generally speaking, however, is connected with the Fire Cult, and that both parts of the sign originally contained a reference to the pieces of wood (aranî) of which in most ancient times use was made to produce fire, has been placed beyond doubt by the investigations into the matter. This is confirmed *inter alia* by the use of the symbol in the worship of the Vestals, the Roman fire-priestesses. This is the explanation of the wide extent of the symbol of the cross. Not only among the peoples of antiquity and in Europe, but also in Asia among the Indians and Chinese, it is in use from ancient times. In America, too, among the Mexicans and Incas, it played a part in worship long before the arrival of Europeans. In the same way is explained the close association of that symbol with the priestly office and kingly dignity, which was itself often connected with that office; similarly the intimate relations between the sign of the cross and the Gods of Fertility, Vegetation, and Seasons. For all of these were, as representatives of the warmth of life and the soul's breath, in their deepest nature, Fire-Gods special aspects, closer characterisations and connections of that one divinity, of whom the oldest form known to us is in the Vedic Agni, and in whose service the priests of all

* Goblet d'Alviella, *op. cit.*, 61. *sqq.* Cf. also Ludw. Müller, "Det saakaldte Hagekors Anvendelse og Betydning i Oldtiden," 1877.

† *Op. cit.*, 296.

peoples and times grew to their overwhelming strength.* Julius Firmicus Maternus was thus quite right when he declared that Mithras, whose followers bore the sign of the cross upon their foreheads and at their communion-meal had the cross, imprinted upon the holy loaf, before their eyes, was an ancient Fire-God.† But if the cross is the symbol of fire and also of the Mediator God, who brings earth and heaven into connection, then the reason can be found why Plato in the "Timæus" makes the World Soul in the form of a Chi, *i.e.*, an oblique cross, stretched between heaven and earth.‡ Then, indeed, it is not strange that the Christians of the first century regarded as an inspiration of the devil Plato's doctrine of the mediatory office of the "double-natured" World Soul, which, according to that philosopher, was formed from a mixture of ideal and sensible matter. It is not strange that a Justin, "the most foolish of the Christian fathers" (Robertson), could actually assert that Plato borrowed the idea, as well as that of a world-conflagration, from —Moses.§

In the Old Testament also, as was shown above, we meet the cross. Here it served as a mark of recognition and distinction of the God-fearing Israelites from the heathen, and as a magic sign. With a similar signifi-cance we meet it again in the New Testament. In the Revelation of John it appears as "the seal (sphragís) of the living God." By it here, too, are the chosen ones of Israel marked off from the rest of mankind whom judgment has overtaken. At the same time, it is said that this sign

---

* One feels the words of Revelation quoted above brought to his mind: " And madest them to be unto our God a kingdom and priests ; and they reign upon the earth ! "

† " De errore profanae religionis," i. 5.

‡ *Op cit.*, § 48.

§ " Apolog.," i. ch. 60.

is imprinted upon the foreheads of the inhabitants of the true Jerusalem.* In the Epistles to the Galatians and Ephesians it is said of the believers in Christ that they were " sealed " before God by the mystic sign upon their foreheads, hands, or feet. The sign thus serves them as a pledge of redemption.† Again, in the Epistle of Barnabas ix. 8, the cross contained in the letter T is expressly interpreted as (charis) " grace." Under the form of the Greek Tau the cross appears during the first century of the Christian era, especially among the Christians in Egypt, and according to many was a symbol of Adonis or Tammuz.‡ Now since the expressions xýlon and staurós, lignum and crux, were of double significance and denoted both the " seal " of religious salvation and the gibbet, it is possible that the two different significations became of themselves identical in the minds of the faithful.§ This was possible so much the more easily since the biblical account placed by the side of the " tree of life " in Paradise a "tree of death," the fateful " tree of the knowledge of good and evil," which was supposed to have been accountable for the death of Adam and so of the whole of mankind, and as such made the comparison possible with

* III. 12, vii. 3 *sqq.*, ix. 4, xiv. 1, xx. 4, xxii. 4.
† Gal. vi. 17 ; Ephes. i. 13 *sq.*
‡ Mourant Brock, *op. cit.*, 177 *sqq.*, 178 *sqq.*
§ So also in Tertullian when, with reference to the passage of Ezekiel above quoted (ix. 5), he describes the Greek letter Tau as "our [the Christians'] kind of cross " (*nostra species crucis*), not because it had the shape of the gibbet upon which Jesus is supposed to have died, but because it represented the seal or sign upon the inhabitants of the New Jerusalem (" Contra Marcionem," iii. 22). And when in the same work (iii. 18) he explains the horns of the " unicorn " (ox ?) mentioned in the Blessing of Moses (Deut. xxxiii, 17) as the two arms of the cross, this happens only for the reason that the sign of union and uplifting and the gibbet became commingled in his fancy into the one and the same form (cf. also " Adv. Judaeos," 10, and Justin, " Dial.," 91 ; also Hochart, *op, cit.*, 365–369).

the wood upon which Jesus died. We meet again with a special form of the cross in the old Assyrian or Babylonian so-called "mystical tree of mystery," which was also a symbol of life. Among the Persians it appears to have had some reference to the holy Haoma tree; and here, too, as well as in India, where it was connected with the Bodhi tree, under which Sakyamuni by his devout humility rose to be a Buddha, it was represented in the artificial shape of a many-armed cross.*

One and the same word, then (xúlon, crux), betokens both the gibbet and the pledge of life. Christ himself appears as the true "Tree of Life," as the original of that miraculous tree the sight of which gave life to the first man in Paradise, which will be the food of the blessed in the world to come, and is represented symbolically by the mystical cross. It was easy to unite the ideas connected with those expressions, to look upon the "seal" of Christ (*to semeion tou staurou, signum crucis*) as the cross upon which he suffered, and *vice-versâ*, and to ascribe to the "wood" upon which Jesus is supposed to have died, the shape of the mystic sign, the Tau, or cross. The heathens had been accustomed to regard the stake upon which their Gods were hanged both as the representative of the God in question and the symbol of life and fruitfulness. For example, the stake furnished with four oblique sticks (like a telegraph post), which went by the name of the tatu, tat, dad, or ded and was planted at the feast of Osiris in Egypt, often had a rough picture of the God painted upon it, as also the pine-tree trunk of Attis, in which connection the idea that the seed contained in the cones of the rock-pine from of old had served men as food, while the sap found in them was prepared into an intoxicating drink

* Zöckler, *op. cit.*, 14 *sq.*

(Soma), played its part.* We are reminded also of the Germanic custom of the planting of the may-tree. This was not only a symbol of the Spring God, but also represented the life bestowed by him. In the same way the cross did not appear to the Christians originally as the form of the gibbet upon which God died, but as " the tree of life," the symbol of the new birth and redemption. Since, however, the word for the mystical sign was identical with the expression for the gibbet, the double meaning led to the gibbet of Jesus being looked upon as the symbol of life and redemption, and the idea of the gibbet was mingled with that of the cross, the shape of the latter being imagined for the former. As Justin in his conversation with the Jew Trypho informs us, the Jews used to run a spit lengthwise through the whole body of the Paschal lamb and another cross-wise through its breast, upon which the forefeet were fastened, so that the two spits made the shape of a cross. This was to them obviously not a symbol of execution but rather the sign of reconcilement with Jahwe and of the new life thereon depending. For the Christians, however, who compared their Saviour with the Paschal lamb, this may have been an additional cause for the above-mentioned commingling of ideas, and this may have strengthened them in the conception that their God died upon the " cross." The Phrygians, moreover, according to Firmicus Maternus, at the Spring Feast of Attis, used to fasten a ram or lamb at the foot of the fig-tree trunk on which the image of their God was hung.†

---

* Frazer, " Adonis, Attis, Osiris," 174 *sq*., 276 *sqq*.

† Cf. on the whole subject Hochart, *op. cit.*, 359 *sqq*. ; P. Schmidt, " Gesch. Jesu," 386–394. In spite of all his efforts Zöckler has not succeeded in proving that Jesus was nailed to a piece of wood having the form of a four-armed cross. The assertion that this form of gibbet was borrowed by the Romans from the Carthaginians, and was the

In agreement with this view is the fact that the earliest representations of Christ in connection with the cross had for their subject not the suffering and crucified, but the miraculous Saviour triumphing over sickness and death. He appeared as a youthful God with the Book of the Law, the Gospel, in his hand, the lamb at his feet, the cross upon his head or in his right hand, just as the heathen Gods, a Jupiter, or some crowned ruler, used to be depicted with a cross-shaped sceptre. Or Jesus' head was placed before the cross, and this in the orb of the sun—and exactly at the point of intersection of the arms of the cross, thus at the place where one otherwise finds the lamb. Even the Church, probably with a right feeling of the identity of Agnus and Agni, and in order to remove the connection of ideas therein contained, in the year 692, by the Quini-sext Synod (in Trullo), forbade the pictures of the lamb and required the representation to be of the Saviour's human shape. In spite of this even then they did not represent " the Crucified " in the present-day sense of the word, but portrayed Christ in the form of one standing before the cross praying with outstretched arms. Or he was shown risen from the grave, or standing upon the Gospels at the foot of the cross, out of this arising later the support for the feet in the pictures of him crucified. Here he was represented with open eyes, with his head encircled by the sun's orb. In all of these different representations accordingly the cross only brought again before the eyes in symbolical form what was at the same time expressed by the figure of Christ standing at the cross,

usual one in late pre-Christian days, is simply a figment of the imagination. All passages usually brought forward in support of this traditional view either prove nothing, as the appeal to Luke xxiv. 39, John xx. 20 and 25, or they refer to the symbol, not to the gibbet of the cross, and consequently cannot serve to support the usual view of the matter (Zöckler, *op. cit.*, especially 78 ; 431 *sqq.*).

just as at the feasts of Osiris or Attis the God was doubly represented, both in his true shape (as image or puppet) and in the symbolical form of the Jatu or pine-tree trunk. This mode of depicting Christ lasted a long while, even though as early as the fifth or sixth century mention is made of crucifixion, and in arbitrary interpretation of Psa. xxii. 17 he was depicted with the marks of the nails. For, as has been said, "crux" betokens both the gibbet and the mystical sign, and the marks of the nails served to symbolise the Saviour's triumph over pain and death. An ivory plate in the British Museum in London, mentioned and copied by Kraus,* is considered the oldest representation of a crucifixion in our present sense. It is said to be of fifth-century origin. This assignment of date is, however, just as uncertain as the other, according to which the miniature from the Syrian Gospel manuscript of the monk Rabula of the monastery of Zagba in Mesopotamia, which also has the crucifixion for subject and is to be found in the Bibliotheca Laurenziana at Florence, is assigned to the year 586. In any case, as a general rule until the eleventh century it was not the dead but the living Christ who was depicted before or on the cross. Consequently an illustration in the Bibliotheca Laurenziana of about the date 1060 is considered as the first certain example of a dead crucified Christ.†

The conception of Christ being put to death upon the cross is, comparatively speaking, a late one. The connection of Christ with the cross was originally not a reproduction of the manner of his death. It rather symbolises, as in the ancient Mysteries, precisely the reverse—the victory of the Christian Cult-God over death —the idea of resurrection and life. Hence it is obvious

* " Geschichte der christlichen Kunst," 174.
† Cf. Detzel, " Christl. Ikonographie," 1894, 392 *sqq.* ; Hochart, *op. cit.,* 378 *sqq.*

that the above-mentioned juxtaposition of the cross and lamb must have expressed the same idea. Here, too, the cross was originally only the symbol of fire and life. The lamb encircled by the sun's orb refers to the ceremonial burning of the lamb at the spring equinox as an expiatory sacrifice and as a pledge of a new life. It appears the more plainly to be a figure of Agni (Agnus), since it is usually placed exactly at the point of intersection of the two arms—that is, at the place whence the divine spark first issued at the kindling of the fire with the two arani.*

* Moreover, the so-called Flabellum, the fan, which in the early Christian pictures of the birth of Christ a servant holds before the child, shows the connection of the Christ Cult and that of Agni. This fan, which was in use in divine service of the Western Church as late as the fourteenth century, cannot be for the driving away of insects or for cooling purposes, as is usually considered, for this would obviously be in contradiction to the " winter " birth of the Saviour. It refers to the fanning of the divine spark in the ancient Indian fire-worship. In this sense it has been retained until the present day in the Greek and Armenian rites, in which during the Mass the fan is waved to and fro over the altar. A synopsis of all the facts and illustrations bearing on the matter are to be found in A. Malvert's " Wissenschaft und Religion," 1904.

THE CHRISTIAN JESUS

I

THE PAULINE JESUS

THE faith in a Jesus had been for a long time in existence among innumerable Mandaic sects in Asia Minor, which differed in many ways from each other, before this faith obtained a definite shape in the religion of Jesus, and its adherents became conscious of their religious peculiarities and their divergence from the official Jewish religion. The first evidence of such a consciousness, and also the first brilliant outline of a new religion developed with Jesus as its central idea, lies in the epistles of the tent-maker of Tarsus, the pilgrim-apostle Paul.

Of the epistles in his name which have been handed down to us, that to the Hebrews is quite certainly not Paul's. But also the two epistles to the Thessalonians, that to the Ephesians, as well as the so-called pastoral epistles (to Timothy, Titus, and Philemon), are considered by the overwhelming majority of theologians to be forgeries; and also the authenticity of the epistles to the Colossians and Philippians is negatived by considerations of great weight. But with all the more certainty modern critical theologians believe that Paul was the writer of the four great didactic epistles—one to the Galatians, two to the Corinthians, and one to the Romans; and they are wont to set aside all suspicion of these epistles as a " grave error " of historical hypercriticism.

In opposition to this view the authenticity of even these epistles is contested, apart from Bruno Bauer, especially by Dutch theologians, by Pierson, Loman, von Mauen, Meyboom, Matthes, and others ; and, in addition, recently the Bern theologian R. Steck, and B. W. Smith, Professor of Mathematics in the Tulane University of New Orleans, with whom the late Pastor Albert Kalthoff of Bremen was associated, have contested the traditional view with objections that deserve consideration. They have attempted to prove the Pauline epistles, as a literary product, to be the work of a whole school of second-century theologians, authors who either simultaneously or successively wrote for the growing Church.

This much is certain—a conclusive proof that Paul was really the author of the epistles current in his name cannot be given. With regard to this it must always remain a ground for doubt that Luke, who accompanied Paul on his missionary travels, was completely silent as to such literary activity of the apostle ; and this, although he devoted the greatest portion of his account in the Acts to Paul's activities.[*] Also the proof given by Smith, that the Pauline epistles were as yet completely unknown in the first century A.D., that· in particular the existence of the Epistle to the Romans is not testified to before the

[*] Of course the " Acts of the Apostles " is, and remains in spite of all modern attempts at vindication (Harnack), a very untrustworthy historical document, and the information it gives as to Paul's life is for the most part mere fiction. We need not go so far as Jensen, who disputes the existence at any time of an historical Paul ("Moses, Jesus, Paulus. Drei Sagenvarianten des babylonischen Gottmenschen Gilgamesch," 2 Aufl., 1909), but will nevertheless not be able to avoid the view that the description of Paul, as Bruno Bauer has already shown, represents an original, in any case very much worked over, and in the opinion of many only a copy of the original, which preceded it in the portrayal of the " chief of the apostles," Peter (cf., on the historical value of the Acts, also E. Zeller, " Die Apg. nach ihrem Inhalt und Ursprung kritisch untersucht," 1854).

middle of the second century, must speak seriously against Paul's authorship, and is evidence that those epistles cannot be accepted as the primary source of the Pauline doctrines. For this reason it can in no way be asserted that the critical theology of last century has " scientifically and beyond question established " * the authenticity of the Pauline writings.

It is well known that the ancient world was not as yet in possession of the idea of literary individuality in our sense of the word. At that time innumerable works were circulated bearing famous names, whose authors had neither at the time nor probably at any time anything to do with the men who bore those names. Many such productions were circulated among the members of Sects of antiquity, which passed, for example, under the names of Orpheus, of Pythagoras, of Zoroaster, &c., and thereby sought to procure the canonical acceptance of their contents ! Of the works of the Old Testament neither the Psalms, nor the Proverbs, nor the so-called Preacher, nor the Book of Wisdom, can be connected with the historical kings David and Solomon, whose names they bear; and the prophet Daniel is just such a fictitious personality as the Enoch and the Ezra of the Apocalypses known under their names. Even the so-called Five Books of Moses are the literary product of an age much later than the one in which Moses is supposed to have lived, while Joshua is the name of an old Israelite God after whom the book in question is called.† There has never anywhere

---

* Cf. H. Jordan, " Jesus und die modernen Jesusbilder. Bibl. Zeit-u-Streitfragen," 1909, 36.

† " To create authors who have never written a letter, to forge whole series of books, to date the most recent production back into grey antiquity, to cause the well-known philosophers to utter opinions diametrically opposed to their real views, these and similar things were quite common during the last century before and the first after Christ. People cared little at that time about the author of a work, if

been such a Moses as the one described in the Old Testament.

The possibility of the so-called Pauline epistles having been the work of later theologians, and of having been christened in the name of Paul, the apostle of the Gentiles, only to increase their authority in the community, is therefore by no means excluded; especially when we consider how exuberantly literary falsifications and " pious frauds " flourished in the first century, and at other times also, in the interests of the Christian Church. Indeed, at that time they even dared, as is shown by Christian documents of the second century, to alter the very text of the Old Testament, and thereby, as they used to say, to " elucidate " it. Already in the middle of the second century Marcion, the Gnostic, reproached the Church with possessing the Pauline epistles only in a garbled form, and who can say whether it was a false accusation? He himself undertook to restore the correct text by excisions and completions.*

But let us leave completely on one side the question of the authenticity of the Pauline epistles, a question absolute agreement on which will probably never be

---

only its contents were in harmony with the taste and needs of the age " (E. Zeller, " Vorträge u. Abhdlg.," 1865, 298 *sq.*). " It was at that time a favourite practice to write letters for famous men. A collection of not less than 148 letters was attributed to the tyrant Phalaris, who ruled Agrigentum in the sixth century B.C. Beyschlag has proved that they were ascribed to him in the time of Antoninus. Similarly the letters attributed to Plato, to Euripides and others, are spurious. It would have been indeed strange if this custom of the age had not gained an influence over the growing Christian literature, for such forgery would be produced most easily in the religious sphere, since it was here not a question of producing particular thoughts, but of being an organ of the common religious spirit working in the individual " (Steck, *op. cit.*, 384 *sq.* ; cf. also Holtzmann, " Einl. in das N.T.," 2 Aufl., 223 *sqq.*).

* E. Vischer, " Die Paulusbriefe, Rel. Volksb.," 1904, 69 *sq.*

attained, for the simple reason that we lack any certain basis for its decision. Instead of this let us turn rather to what we learn from these epistles concerning the historical Jesus.

There we meet in the first place with the fact, testified to by Paul himself, that the Saviour revealed himself in person to him, and at the same time caused him to enter his service (Gal. i. 12). It was, as is stated in the Acts, on the way to Damascus that suddenly there shone round about him a light out of heaven, while a voice summoned him to cease his former persecution of the community of the Messiah, and revealed itself to him as Jesus.* There is no need to doubt the fact itself; but to see in it a proof of the historical Jesus is reserved for those theologians who have discovered the splendid conception of an "objective vision," basing the objective reality of the vision in question on Paul's life in the desert. It was obviously only an "inner vision," which the "visionary" and "epileptic" Paul attributed to Jesus; and for this reason it proves nothing as to the existence of an historical Jesus when he asks, 1 Cor. ix. 1, "Have I not seen our Lord Jesus?" and remarks, 1 Cor. xv. 9, "Last of all he appeared to me also."

It only proves the dilemma of theologians on the whole question that they have recently asserted that Paul, notwithstanding his own protestations (Gal. i.), must have had a personal knowledge of the historical Jesus, as otherwise on the occasion at Damascus he could not have recognised the features and voice of the transfigured Jesus, not being already acquainted with them from some other quarter! With equal justice we might assert that the heathens also, who had visions of their Gods, must previously have known them personally, as otherwise they could not have known that Zeus or Athene or

* *Op. cit.*, ix. 8 *sqq.*

any other definite God had appeared to them. In the Acts we read only of an apparition of light which Paul saw, and of a voice which called to him, "Saul, why persecutest thou me?" Is the supposition referred to necessary to account for the fact that Paul, the persecutor of Jesus, referred the voice and the vision to Jesus?

The case is similar with Paul's testimony as to those who, like him, saw the Saviour after his death.* It is possible that the people concerned saw something, that they saw a Jesus "risen up" in heavenly transfiguration; but that this was the Jesus of the so-called historical theology, whose existence is hereby established, even its supporters would not in all probability insist upon; for in their view the historical Jesus had in no way risen from the dead: but here also there would only be question of a purely subjective vision of the ecstatically excited disciples. Moreover, the passage of the Epistle to the Corinthians in question (5–11) seems clearly to be one at least very much interpolated, if it is not entirely an after-insertion. Thus, the Risen Jesus is said to have been seen by "more than five hundred Brethren at once." But of this the four Gospels know nothing; and also, according to xv. 5, that "the twelve" had the vision, would lead us to suspect that it was first inserted in the text at a much later date.†

Paul himself never disguised the fact that he had seen Jesus, not with mortal eyes, but only with those of the Spirit, as an inner revelation. "It has pleased God," he says (Gal. i. 16), "to reveal his Son within me." ‡ He

* 1 Cor. xv. 5 sqq.

† Cf. W. Seufert, "Der Ursprung und die Bedeutung des Apostolates in der christlichen Kirche der ersten Jahrhunderte," 1887, 46, 157.

‡ An attempt is now being made to prove the contrary, citing 2 Cor. v. 16, which runs: "Wherefore we henceforth know no man after the flesh: even though we have known Christ after the flesh, yet now we know him so no more." The passage has been most differently explained. According to Baur the "Christ after the

confesses that the Gospel preached by him was not " of men," that he neither received nor learnt it from any man, but that he had obtained it direct from the heavenly Christ and was inspired by the Holy Ghost.* He seems also to have had no interest at all in giving accurate information as to the personality of Jesus, as to his fortunes and teachings. When three years after his conversion he first returns to Jerusalem, he visits only Peter and makes the acquaintance of James during the fourteen days of his stay there, troubling himself about none of the other apostles.† But when, fourteen years after, he meets with the " First Apostles " in the so-called Council of the Apostles in Jerusalem, he does not set about learning from them, but teaching them and pro-

flesh " refers to the Jewish Messiah, the expected king and earthly Saviour of the Jews from political and social distress, in whom even Paul believed at an earlier date ; and the meaning of the passage quoted is that this sensuous and earthly conception of the Messiah had given place in him to the spiritual conception (" Die Christuspartei in der kor. Gemeinde Tüb. Ztschr.," 1831, 4 Heft, 90). According to Heinrici the " even though we have known " is not a positive assertion of a point of view which had once determined his judgment of Christ, but a hypothetical instance, which excludes a false point of view without asserting anything as to its actuality (" Komment," 289). According to Beyschlag the passage is to be understood as asserting that Paul had seen Jesus at Jerusalem during his life on earth. But with Paul there is no talk of a mere seeing, but rather of a knowing. Lütgert disproves all these different hypotheses with the argument that the words " after the flesh " refer not to Christ but to the verb. " The apostle no longer knows any one ' after the flesh,' and so he no longer knows Jesus thus. At an earlier stage his knowledge of Christ was ' after the flesh.' At that time he did not have the spirit of God which made him able to see in Jesus the Son of God. Paul then is not protecting himself from the Jews, who denied him a personal knowledge of Jesus, but from the Pneumatics, who denied him a pneumatic knowledge of Jesus " (" Freiheitspredigt und Schwarmgeister in Korinth," 1908, 55–58).

* Gal. i. 11, 12; 1 Cor. ii. 10 ; 2 Cor. iv. 6.
† Gal. i. 17–19.

curing from them recognition of his own missionary
activity; and he himself declares that he spoke with
them only on the method of proclaiming the Gospel, but
not on its religious content or on the personality of the
historic Jesus.*

Certainly that James whose acquaintance Paul made in
Jerusalem is designated by him as the "Brother of the
Lord"; † and from this it seems to follow that Jesus
must have been an historical person. The expression
"Brother," however, is possibly in this case, as so often
in the Gospels,‡ only a general expression to designate a
follower of Jesus, as the members of a religious society
in antiquity frequently called each other "Brother" and
"Sister" among themselves. 1 Cor. ix. 5 runs: "Have
we [i.e., Paul and Barnabas] not also right to take about
with us a wife that is a sister, even as the other Apostles
and Brothers of the Lord and Cephas?" There it is
evident that the expression by no means necessarily refers
to bodily relationship, but that "Brother" serves only
to designate the followers of the religion of Jesus.§
Accordingly Jerome seems to have hit the truth exactly
when, commenting on Gal. i. 19, he writes: "James was
called the Brother of the Lord on account of his great
character [though the Pauline epistles certainly show the

* Gal. ii. 1 sqq.
† Id. i. 19.
‡ Matt. xxviii. 10; Mark xiii. 33 sqq.; John xx. 17.
§ In the opinion of the Dutch school of theologians, whom
Schläger follows in his essay, "Das Wort kürios (Herr) in Seiner
Bezichung auf Gott oder Jesus Christus" ("Theol. Tijdschrift," 33,
1899, Part I.), this mention of the "Brother of the Lord" does not
come from Paul; as according to Schläger, all the passages in 1 Cor.,
which speak of Jesus under the title "Kurios," are interpolated.
"Missionary travels of Brothers of Jesus are unknown to us from any
other quarter, and are also in themselves improbable" (op. cit., 46;
cf. also Steck, op. cit., 272 sq.).

opposite of this], of his incomparable faith and extraordinary wisdom. The other Apostles were as a matter of fact also called Brothers, but he was specially so called, because the Lord at his death had confided to him the sons of his mother " (*i.e.*, the members of the community at Jerusalem).* And how then should Paul have met with a physical brother of that very Jesus whom, as will be shown, he could only treat as a myth in other respects? The thing is, considered now purely psychologically, so improbable that no conclusion can in any case be drawn from the expression concerning James as the Brother of the Lord as to the historical existence of Jesus; especially in view of the fact that theologians from the second century to the present day have been unable to come to an agreement as to the true blood-relationship between James and Jesus.† Moreover, if we consider how the glorification of James came into fashion in anti-Pauline circles of the second century, and how customary it was to connect the chief of the Jewish Christians at Jerusalem as closely as possible with Jesus himself (*e.g.*, Hegesippus, in the so-called Epistles of Clement, in the Gospel of the Nazarenes, &c.), the

* Similarly Origen, " Contra Celsum," i. 35; cf. Smith, *op. cit.*, 18 *sq.*

† Cf. as to this Sieffert in " Realenzyklop. f. prot. Theol. und Kirche " under " James." In Ezr. ii. 2 and 9 there is also mention of " Brothers " of the High Priest Joshua, by which only the priests subordinate to him seem to be meant; and in Justin (" Dial c. Tryph.," 106) the apostles are collectively spoken of as " Brothers of Jesus." Similarly in Rev. xii. 17, those " who keep the word of God and bear testimony to Jesus Christ " are spoken of as children of the heavenly woman and also as Brothers and Sisters of the Divine Redeemer, whom the dragon attempts to swallow up together with his mother. As Revelation owes its origin to a pre-Christian Jesus-cult, the designation of pious brothers of a community as physical brothers of Jesus seems also to have been customary in that cult, antecedent to the Pauline epistles and the Gospels."

suspicion forces itself on us that the Pauline mention of James as " the Brother of the Lord " is perhaps only an after-insertion in the Epistle to the Galatians in order thereby to have the bodily relationship between James and Jesus confirmed by Paul himself.* Jesus' parents are not historical personalities (see above, 117 ff.) ; and it is probably the same with his brothers and sisters. Also Paul never refers to the testimony of the brothers or of the disciples of Jesus concerning their Master; though this would have been most reasonable had they really known any more of Jesus than he himself did. " He bases," as Kalthoff justly objects, "not a single one of his most incisive polemical arguments against the adherents of the law on the ground that he had the historical Jesus on his side ; but he gives his own detailed theological ideas without mentioning an historical Jesus, he gives a gospel of Christ, not the gospel which he had heard at first, second, or third hand concerning a human individual Jesus." †

From Paul, therefore, there is nothing of a detailed nature to be learnt about the historical Jesus. The apostle does indeed occasionally refer to the words and opinions of the " Lord," as with regard to the prohibition of divorce,‡ or to the right of the apostles to be fed by the community.§ But as the exact words are not given there is no express reference to an historical individual of the name of Jesus ; and so we are persuaded that we here have to do with mere rules of a community such as were current and had canonical significance everywhere in the religious unions as " Words of the Master," i.e., of

---

* This is actually the view of the Dutch school of theologians.

† A. Kalthoff, " Was wissen wir von Jesus ? Eine Abrechnung mit Prof. D. Bousset," 1904, 17.

‡ 1 Cor. vii. 10.

§ Id. ix. 14.

the patrons and celebrities of the community (cf. the " αὐτὸς ἔφα : he himself, viz., the Master, has said it " of the Pythagoreans). Only once, 1 Cor. xi. 23 *sq*., where Paul quotes the words at the Last Supper, does the apostle apparently refer to an experience of the " historical " Jesus : " The Lord Jesus, in the night in which he was betrayed, took bread," &c.* Unfortunately here we have to do with what is clearly a later insertion. The passage is obscure throughout (vers. 23–32), and through its violent and confusing interruption of the Pauline line of thought may be recognised as an after-insertion in the original text, as is even acknowledged by many on the theological side.† Paul says that he had obtained these things from the " Lord " himself. Does this mean that they were directly " revealed " to him by the transfigured Jesus? It seems much more reasonable to believe that he took them from a religion already existing. This could indeed refer at most only to the words of the Last

---

* 1 Cor. xi. 23.

† Cf. Brandt, "Die evangel. Geschichte u. d. Ursprung d. Christentums," 1893, 296. Schläger also agrees with the Dutch school, and produces telling arguments in favour of the view that 1 Cor. xi. 23–32 is an interpolation. "In our opinion," he says, "the opening words, 'For I received of the Lord,' betray the same attempt as can be seen in vii. 10 and ix. 14—and probably the attempt of one and the same interpolator—to trace back Church institutions and regulations to the authority of the Lord, of the Kurios. In the three cases in which the latter is mentioned he is called 'the Lord,' which is a fact well worthy of consideration in view of the usual designation." Schläger also shows that verse 32 is a very appropriate conclusion to verse 22 ; while as they stand now the logical connection is broken in a forcible manner by the interpolation of the account of the Last Supper. Another proof of the interpolation of 23–32 is to be found, Schläger thinks, in the fact that in verse 33 as in verse 22 the Corinthians are addressed in the second person, while in verses 31 and 32 the first person plural is used (*op. cit.*, 41 *sq.*). In view of these notorious facts we can hardly understand how German theologians can with such decision

Supper in themselves. On the other hand, the words "in the night in which he was betrayed" are certainly an addition. They will do neither in the connection of a "revelation" nor of an existing religion, but stand there completely by themselves as a reference to a real event in the life of Jesus; and so, for this alone, they form much too small a basis for testimony as to its historical truth.*

All expressions concerning Jesus which are found in Paul are accordingly of no consequence for the hypothesis of an historical person of that name. The so-called "words of the Lord" quoted by him refer to quite unimportant points in the teachings of Jesus. And, on the other hand, Paul is just as silent on those points in which modern critical theology finds the particular greatness and importance of this teaching; as, *e.g.*, on

adhere to the authenticity of the passage, reproaching those who contest it with "faults in method." As against this view of theirs Schläger justly objects that "References to words and events from the life of Jesus are so isolated in the Pauline writings that we are entitled to and forced to raise the question as to each such reference, whether it is not the reflection of a later age, of an age which already placed confidence in the Gospel literature, that brought Jesus' authority into the text" (Schläger, *op. cit.*, 36). And the critical theologians are convinced that the writings of the New Testament are worked over to a great extent, rectified to accord with the Church, and in many places interpolated. But when some one else brings this to publicity, and dares to doubt the authenticity of a passage, they immediately raise a great outcry, and accuse him of wilfully misrepresenting the text; as if there were even one single such passage on which the views of critics are not divergent!

* M. Brückner's opinion also is "that the Pauline account of the scene at the Last Supper is in all probability not a purely historical one, but is a dogmatic representation of the festival." And he adds: "In any case just on account of its religious importance this scene cannot be cited to prove Paul's acquaintance with the details of Jesus' life" ("Die Entstehung der paulinischen Christologie," 1903, 44). Cf. also Robertson, "Christianity and Mythology," 388 *sq.*

Jesus' confidence in the divine goodness of the Father, his command of the love of our neighbours as the fulfilment of the Law, his sermon about humility and charity, his warning against the over-esteem of worldly goods, &c., as on Jesus' personality, his trust in God, and his activity among his people.*

* Holtzmann has, as a matter of fact, in an essay in the " Christliche Welt " (No. 7, 1910) recently attempted to prove the contrary, citing from Paul a number of moral exhortations, &c., which are in accord with Jesus' words in the Gospels. But in this argument there is a presupposition, which should surely be previously proved, that the Gospels received their corresponding content from Jesus and not, on the contrary, from Paul's epistles. It is admitted that they were in many other respects influenced by Pauline ideas. Moreover, all the moral maxims cited have their parallels in contemporary Rabbinical literature, so that they need not necessarily be referred back to an historical Jesus ; also, such is their nature, that they might be advanced by any one, *i.e.*, they are mere ethical commonplaces without any individual colouring. Thus we find the Rabbis in agreement with Rom. xiii. 8 *sq.* and Gal. v. 14, which Holtzmann traces back to Matt. vii. 12 : " Bring not on thy neighbour that which displeases thee ; this is our whole doctrine." Rom. xiii. 7 has its parallel not only in Matt. xxii. 21, but also in the Talmud, which runs : " Every one is bound to fulfil his obligations to God with the like exactness as those to men. Give to God his due ; for all that thou hast is from him." Rom. xii. 21 runs in the Sanhedrin : " It is better to be persecuted than to persecute, better to be calumniated by another than to slander." So that the remark need not necessarily be based on Matt. v. 39 ; in fact, the last-named passage is not found at all in the standard MSS., in the Codex Sinaiticus and Vaticanus. The phrase, " to remove mountains " (1 Cor. xiii. 2), is a general Rabbinical one for extolling the power of a teacher's diction, and so could easily be transferred to the power of faith. So also the phrase, Mark ix. 50, " Have salt in yourselves, and be at peace one with another "— which Rom. xii. 18 is supposed to resemble—is a well-known Rabbinical expression. Matt. v. 39 *sq.*, which is supposed to accord with 1 Cor. vi. 7, runs in the Talmud : " If any one desires thy donkey, give him also the saddle." Matt. vii. 1–5, on which Rom. ii. 1 and xiv. 4 are supposed to be based, equally recalls the Talmud : " Who thinks favourably of his neighbour brings it about that fair judgments are also made of him." " Let your judgment of

Paul did not give himself the least trouble to bring the Saviour as a man nearer to his readers. He seems to know nothing of any miraculous power in Jesus. He says nothing of his sympathy with the poor and oppressed, though surely just this would have been specially adapted

your neighbour be completely good." "Even as one measures, with the same measure shall it also be measured unto him." Rom. xiv. 13 and 1 Cor. viii. 7–13 need not necessarily be an allusion to Jesus' tender consideration for those who are ruined by scandal, as we find in the Talmud: "It would have been better that the evil-minded had been born blind, so that they would not have brought evil into the world (cf. also Nork, "Rabbinische Quellen und Parallelen zu neutestamentlichen Schriftstellen," 1839). And does Paul's usual phrase of greeting, "from God our Father and the Lord Jesus Christ," really contain the avowal of the "Father-God" preached by Christ? For the connection of the divine Son and bearer of salvation with the "Father-God" is a general mythological formula which occurs in all the different religions—witness the relation between Marduk and ¡Ea, Heracles and Zeus, Mithras and Ormuzd, Balder and Odin. What then does it mean when Paul speaks of the "meekness and humility of Christ," who lived not for his own pleasure, who made no fame for himself, but was "submissive," assumed the form of a servant, and was "obedient" to the will of his "father," even to the death of the cross? All these traits are reproduced directly from the description of the suffering servant of God in Isaiah, which we know had a great part in shaping the personality of Jesus. Meekness, humility, charitableness, and obedience are the specific virtues of the pious of Paul's time. It was a matter of course for Christ also, the ideal prototype of good and pious men, to be endowed with these characteristics. Abraham was obedient when he sacrificed his son Isaac; and so was the latter to his father, being also submissive in himself bringing the wood to the altar and giving himself up willingly to the sacrificial knife. And we know what a significant rôle the story of Isaac's sacrifice has always played in the religious ideas of the Jews. Moreover, the heathen redeemer deities—Marduk, of the Mandaic Hibil Ziwâ, Mithras and Heracles—were also obedient in coming down upon earth at the bidding of their heavenly father, burst the gates of death, and gave themselves up, in the case of Mithras, even to be sacrificed; and Heracles served mankind in the position of a servant, fought with the monsters and horrors of hell, and assumed the hardest tasks at the will of others.

to turn the hearts of men towards his Jesus and to make an impression on the multitude that sought for miracles. All the moral-religious precepts and exhortations of Jesus are neither employed by Paul as a means of proselytising for him, nor in any way used to place his individuality in opposition to his prophetic precursors in a right light, as is the case in the Christian literature of the present day. " Thus, just those thoughts, which Protestant theologians claim as the particular domain of their historical Jesus, appear in the epistles independently of this Jesus, as individual moral effusions of the apostolic consciousness ; while Christian social rules, which the same theologians consider additions to the story, are introduced directly as rules of the Lord. For this reason the Christ of the Pauline epistles may rather be cited as a case against critical theologians than serve as a proof for the historical Jesus in their sense." *   Even so zealous a champion of this theology as Wernle must admit : " We learn from Paul least of all concerning the person and life of Jesus. Were all his epistles lost we should know not much less of Jesus than at present." Immediately after this, however, this very author consoles himself with the consideration that in a certain sense Paul gave us even more than the most exact and the most copious records could give. " We learn from him that a man (?) Jesus, in spite of his death on the cross, was able to develop such a power after his death, that Paul knew himself to be mastered, redeemed, and blessed by him ; and this in so marked a way that he separated his own life and the whole world into two parts : without Jesus, with Jesus. This is a fact which, explain it as we may, purely as a fact excites our wonder (!) and compels us to think highly of Jesus." †

* Kalthoff, " Die Entstehung d. Christentums," 1904, 15.

† P. Wernle, " Die Quellen des Lebens Jesu, Religionsgesch. Volks-bücher," 2 Aufl., 4.

What *does* excite our wonder is this style of historical "demonstration." And then how peculiar it is to read, from the silence of an author like Paul concerning the historical Jesus, an argument in its favour! As if it does not rather prove the unimportance of such a personality for the genesis of Christianity! As if the fact that Paul erected a religious-metaphysical thought construction of undoubted magnificence must necessarily be based on the "overwhelming impression of the person of Jesus," of the same Jesus of whom Paul had no personal knowledge at all! The disciples—who are supposed to have been in touch with Jesus for many years—Paul strenuously avoided, and of the existence of this Jesus no other signs are to be found in his epistles but such as may have quite a different meaning. Or did Paul, as historical theology says, reveal more of Jesus in his sermons than he did in the epistles? Surely that could only be maintained after it was first established that in his account Paul had in view any historical Jesus at all.

This seems to be completely problematic. The "humanity" of Jesus stands as the central point of the Pauline idea. And yet the Jesus painted by Paul is not a man, but a purely divine personality, a heavenly spirit without flesh and blood, an unindividual superhuman phantom. He is the "Son of God" made manifest in Paul; the Messiah foretold by the Jewish Apocalyptics; the pre-existing "Son of Man" of Daniel and his followers; the spiritual "ideal man" as he appeared in the minds of the Jews influenced by Platonic ideas; whom also Philo knew as the metaphysical prototype of ordinary sensual humanity and thought he had found typified to in Gen. i. 27. He is the "great man" of the Indian legends, who was supposed to have appeared also in Buddha and in other Redeemer figures—the Purusha of the Vedic Brahmans, the Mandâ de hajjê and Hibil Ziwâ of the Mandaic religion influenced by Indian ideas, the tribe-God of syncretised Judaism. The knowledge which Paul has of this Being is for this reason not an ordinary acquaintance from teachings, but a Gnosis, an immediate consciousness, a "knowledge inspired"; and all the statements which he makes concerning it fall within the sphere of theosophy, of religious speculation or metaphysics, but not of history. As we have stated, the belief in such a Jesus had been for a long time the property of Jewish sects, when Paul succeeded, on the ground of his astounding personal experiences, in drawing it into the light from the privacy of religious arcana, and setting it up as the central point of a new religion distinct from Judaism.

"There was already in their minds a faith in a divine revealer, a divine-human activity, in salvation to be obtained through sacraments." * Among the neighbouring heathen peoples for a very long time, and in Jewish circles at least since the days of the prophets, there had existed a belief in a divine mediator, a " Son of God," a " First-born of all creation," in whom was made all that exists, who came down upon earth, humbled himself in taking on a human form, suffered for mankind a shameful death, but rose again victorious, and in his elevation and transfiguration simultaneously renewed and spiritualised the whole earth.† Then Paul appeared—in an age which

---

* Gunkel, *op. cit.*, 93.

† Gunkel also takes the view " that before Jesus there was a belief in Christ's death and resurrection current in Jewish syncretic circles (*op. cit.*, 82). Now we have already seen (p. 57) that the term " Christ " is of very similar significance to " Jesus." So that it is not at all necessary to believe, as Gunkel asserted in the Darmstadt discussion, that Paul in speaking of " Jesus " testifies to an historical figure, because Jesus is the name of a person. " Jesus Christ " is simply a double expression for one and the same idea—that is, for the idea of the Messiah, Saviour, Physician, and Redeemer; and it is not

was permeated as no other with a longing for redemption; which, overwhelmed by the gloom of its external relations, was possessed with the fear of evil powers; which, penetrated with terror of the imminent end of the world, was anxiously awaiting this event and had lost faith in the saving power of the old religion—then he gave such an expression to that belief as made it appear the only means of escape from the confusion of present existence. Can the assumption of an historical Jesus in the sense of the traditional conception really be necessary, in order to account for the fact that men fled impetuously to this new religion of Paul's? Is it even probable that the intelligent populations of the sea-ports of Asia Minor and Greece, among whom in particular Paul preached the Gospel of Jesus, would have turned towards Christianity for the reason that at some time or other, ten or twenty years before, an itinerant preacher of the name of Jesus had made an "overpowering" impression on ignorant fisher-folk and workmen in Galilee or Jerusalem by his personal bearing and his teachings, and had been believed by them to be the expected Messiah, the renowned divine mediator and redeemer of the world? Paul did not preach the man Jesus, but the heavenly spiritual being, Christ.* The public to which Paul turned consisted for the most part of Gentiles; and to these the conception of a spiritual being presented no difficulties. It could have no strengthening, no guarantee, of its truth, through proof of the manhood of Jesus. If the Christians of the

---

at all improbable, as Smith supposes, that the contradictions in the conception of the Messiah in two different sects or spheres of thought found their settlement in the juxtaposition of the two names.

* "Not the teacher, not the miracle-worker, not the friend of the publicans and sinners, not the opponent of the Pharisees, is of importance for Paul. It is the crucified and risen Son of God alone" (Wernle, *op. cit.*, 5).

beginning of our own historical epoch had only been able to gain faith in the God Christ through the Man Jesus, Paul would have turned his attention from that which, to him, particularly mattered; he would have obscured the individual meaning of his Gospel and brought his whole religious speculation into a false position, by substituting a man Jesus for the God-man Jesus as he understood him.*

Paul is said to have been born in the Greek city of Tarsus in Cilicia, the son of Jewish parents. At that time Tarsus was, like Alexandria, an important seat of Greek learning.

Here flourished the school of the younger Stoics, with its mixture of old Stoic, Orphic, and Platonic ideas. Here the ethical principles of that school were preached in a popular form, in street and market-place, by orators of the people. It was not at all necessary for Paul, brought up in the austerity of the Jewish religion of the Law, to visit the lecture-rooms of the Stoic teachers in

* " Indeed, the historical Jesus in the sense of the Ritschlian school would have been for Paul an absurdity. The Pauline theology has to do rather with the experiences of a heavenly being, which have, and will yet have, extraordinary significance for humanity " (M. Brückner, " Die Entstehung der paulinischen Christologie," 1903, 12). Brückner also considers it settled " that Jesus' life on earth had no interest at all for Paul " (op. cit., 46). " Paul did not trouble himself about Jesus' life on earth, and what he may here and there have learnt concerning it, with few exceptions, remained indifferent to him " (42). Brückner also shows that the passages which are cited to contradict this prove nothing as to Paul's more detailed acquaintance with Jesus' life on earth (41 sqq.). He claims " to have given the historical demonstration " in his work " that the Christian religion is at bottom independent of ' uncertain historical truths ' " (Preface). And in spite of this he cannot as a theologian free himself from the conception of an historical Jesus even with regard to Paul, though he is, nevertheless, not in a position to show where and to what extent the historical Jesus had a really decided influence over Paul.

order to gain a knowledge of Stoic views, for in Tarsus it was as though the air was filled with that doctrine. Paul was certainly acquainted with it. It sank so deeply into his mind, perhaps unknown to himself, that his epistles are full of the expressions and ideas of the Stoic philosopher Seneca, and to this are due the efforts which have been made to make Seneca a pupil of Paul's, or the reverse, to make Paul a pupil of Seneca's. A correspondence exists, which is admittedly a forgery, pretending to have passed between the two.

Tarsus, in spite of its Eastern character, was a city saturated with Greek learning and ways of thought, but not these alone. The religious ideas and motives of the time found also a fruitful soil there. In Tarsus the Hittite Sandan (Sardanapal) was worshipped, a human being upon whom Dionysus had bestowed the godhead of life and fecundity, who was identified by the Greeks either with Zeus, or with Heracles, the divine " Son " of the " Father " Zeus. He passed as the founder of the city, and was represented as a bearded man with bunches of grapes and ears of corn, with a double-headed axe in his right hand, standing on a lion or a funeral pyre ; and every year it was the custom for a human representative of the God, or in later times his effigy, to be ceremoniously burnt on a pyre.* But Tarsus was also at the same time a centre for the mystery-religions of the East. The worship of Mithras, in particular, flourished there, with its doctrine of the mystic death and re-birth of those received into the communion, who were thereby purified from the guilt of their past life and won a new immortal life in the " Spirit " ; with its sacred feast, at which the believers entered into a communion of life with Mithra by partaking of the consecrated bread and

---

* Movers, *op. cit.*, 438 *sqq.*; Fraser, " Adonis, Attis, Osiris," 42, 43, 47, 60, 79 *sq.*

chalice; with its conception of the magic effect of the victim's blood, which washed away all sins; and with its ardent desire for redemption, purification, and sanctification of the soul.* Paul was not unaffected by these and similar ideas. His conception of the mystic significance of Christ's death shows that; in which conception the whole of this type of religious thought is expressed, although in a new setting. Indeed, the expression (Gal. iii. 27), in which the baptized are said to have " put on " Christ, seems to be borrowed directly from the Mithraic Mysteries. For in these, according to a primitive animistic custom, the initiated of different degrees used to be present in the masks of beasts, representing God's existence under diverse attributes; that is, they used to " put on " the Lord in order to place themselves in innermost communion with him. Again, the Pauline expression, that the consecrated chalice and bread at the Lord's Supper are the " communion of the blood and body of Christ," † reminds us too forcibly of the method of expression in the Mysteries for this agreement to be purely a coincidence.‡

If in such circumstances Paul, the citizen of Tarsus, heard of a Jewish God of the name of Jesus, the ideas which were connected with him were in no way quite new and unaccustomed. Nearer Asia was, indeed, as we have seen, filled with the idea of a young and beautiful God, who reanimated Nature by his death; with popular legends connected with his violent end and glorious resurrection : and not merely in Tarsus, but also in Cyprus and in countless other places of the Western Asiatic civilised world, there was the yearly celebration in most impressive fashion of the feast of this God, who was

---

* Cumont, " Textes et monuments," &c., i. 240 ; Pfleiderer, " Urchristentum," i. 29 *sqq.*

† 1 Cor. x. 16.   ‡ Pfleiderer, *op. cit.*, 45.

called Tammuz, Adonis, Attis, Dionysus, Osiris, &c. Nowhere, perhaps, was the celebration more magnificent than at Antioch, the Syrian capital. But at Antioch, if we may believe the Acts * on this point, the Gospel of Jesus had been preached even before Paul. Men of Cyprus and Cyrene are said to have spoken there the Word of the dead and risen Christ, not only to the Jews but also to the Greeks, and they are said to have converted many of the heathens to the new "Lord." The Acts tells us this after it has recounted the persecution of the community of the Messiah at Jerusalem ; representing the spreading of the Gospel as a consequence of the dispersion of the community that followed the persecution. It seems, however, that Cyprus—where Adonis was particularly worshipped, at Paphos—and Cyrene were very early centres from which missionaries carried abroad the faith in Christ.† Consequently the Gospel was in origin nothing but a Judaised and spiritualised Adonis cult. ‡ Those earliest missionaries of whom we hear would not have attacked the faith of the Syrian heathens : they would have declared that Christ, the Messiah, the God of the Jewish religions, was Adonis : Christ is the "Lord"! They would only have attempted to draw the old native religion of Adonis into the Jewish sphere of thought, and by this means to carry on the Jewish propaganda which they could find everywhere at work, and which developed an efficacy about the beginning of our epoch such as it had never before possessed. They would carry on the propaganda, not in the sense of the strict standpoint of the Law, but of the Jewish Apocalypses and their religious teachings.§

* xi. 19 *sqq.*　　　　　　　　† Smith, *op. cit.,* 21 *sq.*
‡ Cf. Zimmern, "Zum Streit um die Christusmythe," 23.
§ "I am the A and the O, the beginning and the end," the Revelation of John makes the Messiah say (i. 8.). Is there not at the same

Such a man as Paul, who had been educated in the school of Gamaliel as a teacher of the Law of the strict Pharasaical sort, could not indeed calmly look on while the heathen belief in Adonis, which he must surely, even in his native city of Tarsus, have despised as a blasphemous superstition, was uniting itself, in the new religious sects, with the Jewish conceptions. " Cursed is he who is hung upon the tree," so it stood written in the Law ; * and the ceremony of the purification—at which one criminal was hung, amid the insults of the people, as the scapegoat of the old year, while another was set free as Mordecai, and driven with regal honours through the city, being revered as representative of the new year— must have been in his eyes only another proof of the disgrace of the tree, and of the blasphemous character of a belief that honoured in the hanged man the divine Saviour of the world, the Messiah expected by the Jews. Then on a sudden there came over him as it were enlightenment. What if the festivals of the Syrian Adonis, of the Phrygian Attis, and so on, really treated of the self-sacri-

---

time in this a concealed reference to Adonis ? The Alpha and the Omega, the first and last letters of the Greek alphabet, form together the name of Adonis—Ao (Aoos) as the old Dorians called the God, whence Cilicia is also called Aoa. A son of Adonis and Aphrodite (Maia) is said (" Schol. Theocr.," 15, 100) to have been called Golgos. His name is connected with the phallic cones (Greek, golgoi), as they were erected on heights in honour of the mother divinities of Western Asia, who were themselves, probably on this account, called Golgoi and golgōn anássa (Queens of the Golgoi), and is the same as the Hebraic plural Golgotha (Sepp, " Heidentum," i. 157 *sq*.). Finally, was the " place of skulls " an old Jebusite place of worship of Adonis under the name of Golgos, and was the cone of rock, on which statue of Venus was erected in the time of Hadrian, selected for the place of execution of the Christian Saviour because it was connected with the remembrance of the real sacrifice of a man in the rôle of Adonis (Tammuz) ?

* Deut. xxi. 23.

fice of a God who laid down his life for the world? The guiltless martyrdom of an upright man as expiatory means to the justification of his people was also not unknown to the adherents of the Law since the days of the Maccabean martyrs. The " suffering servant of God," as Isaiah had portrayed him, suggests as quite probable the idea that, just as among the heathen peoples, in Israel also an individual might renew the life of all others by his voluntary sacrifice. Might it not be true, as the adherents of the Jesus-religions maintained, that the Messiah was really a " servant of God," and had already accomplished the work of redemption by his own voluntary death? According to the heathen view, the people were atoned for by the vicarious sacrifice of their God, and that " justification " of all in the sight of the Godhead took place which the pious Pharisee expected from the strict fulfilment of the Jewish Law. And yet, when Paul compared the " righteousness " actually achieved by himself and others with the ideal of righteousness for which they strove, as it was required in the Law, then terror at the greatness of the contrast between the ideal and the reality must have seized him; and at the same time he might well have despaired of the divine righteousness, which required of the people the fulfilment of the Law, which weighed the people down with the thought of the imminent end of the world, and which, through the very nature of its commands, excluded the possibility of the Messiah meeting on his arrival, as he should have done, with a " righteous " people. Were those who expected the sanctification of humanity not from the fulfilment of the Law, but immediately, through an infusion of God himself, really so much in the wrong? It was not unusual among the heathen peoples for a man to be sacrificed, in the place of the Diety, as a symbolical representative; although already at the time of Paul it was the custom to represent the self-sacrificing God only by an effigy, instead of a real man. The important point, however, was not this, but the idea which lay at the foundation of this divine self-sacrifice. And this was not affected by the victim's being a criminal, who was killed in the rôle of the guiltless and upright man, and by the voluntariness of his death being completely fictitious. Might it not also be, as the believers in Jesus asserted, that the Messiah was not still to be expected, and that only on the ground of human righteousness; but that rather he had already appeared, and had already accomplished the righteousness unattainable by the individual through his shameful death and his glorious resurrection?

The moment in which this idea flashed through Paul's mind was the moment of the birth of Christianity as Paul's religion. The form in which he grasped that conception was that of an Incarnation of God; and at the same time this form was such that he introduced with it quite a new impulse into the former mode of thought. According to the heathen conception a God did indeed sacrifice himself for his people, without thereby ceasing to be God; and here the man sacrificed in the place of God was considered merely as a chance representative of the self-sacrificing God. According to the old view of the Jewish faith it was really the " Son of Man," a being of human nature, who was to come down from heaven and effect the work of redemption, without, however, being a real man and without suffering and dying in human form. With Paul, on the contrary, the stress lay just on this, that the Redeemer should be himself really a man, and that the man sacrificed in God's place should be equally the God appearing in human form : the man was not merely a representation of God's as a celestial and supernatural being, but God himself appearing in human form. God himself becomes man, and thereby a man is exalted to the Deity, and, as expiatory representative for his people, can unite mankind with God.* The man who is sacrificed for his people represents on the one hand his people in the eyes of God, but on the other hand the God sacrificing himself for mankind in the eyes of this people. And thereby, in the idea of the representative expiatory victim, the separation between God and Man is blotted out, and both fuse directly in the conception of the " God-man." God becomes man, and by this means mankind is enabled to become God. The man is sacrificed as well in the place of God as in that of mankind, and so unites both contradictories in a unity within himself.

It is evident that in reality it was merely a new setting to the old conception of the representative self-sacrifice of God—in which the genitive is to be taken both in its subjective and objective sense. No historical personality, who should, so to say, have lived as an example of the God-man, was in any way necessary to produce that Pauline development of the religion of Jesus. For the chance personalities of the men representing the God came under consideration just as little for Paul as for the heathens; and when he also, with the other Jews, designated the Messiah Jesus as the bodily descendant of David " according to the flesh," † *i.e.*, as a man ; when he treated him as " born of woman," he thought not at all of any concrete individuality, which had at a certain time embodied the divinity within itself, but purely of the idea of a Messiah in the flesh ; just as the suffering

* We notice that already in these distinctions the germs of those endless and absurd disputes concerning the " nature " of the God-man lie concealed, which later, in the first century A.D., tore Christendom into countless sects and " heresies," and which gave the occasion for the rise of the Christian dogma.

† Rom. i. 3.

servant of God of Isaiah, even in spite of the connection of this idea with an actually accomplished human sacrifice, had possessed only an ideal imaginary or typical significance. The objection is always being raised that Paul must have conceived of Jesus as an historical individual because he · designates him as the bodily descendant of David, and makes him " born of woman " (Gal. iv. 4). But how else could he have been born ? (Cf. Job xiv. 1.) The bringing into prominence the birth from woman, as well as the general emphasis laid by the Apostle on the humanity of Jesus, is directed against the Gnostics in the Corinthian community, but proves nothing whatsoever as to the historical Jesus. And the descent from David was part of the traditional characteristics of the Messiah ; so that Paul could say it of Jesus without referring to a real descendant of David. But even less is proved by Paul's, in Gal. iii. 1, reproaching the Galatians with having seen the crucified Christ " set forth openly " ; we would then have to declare also that there was an actual devil and a hell, because these are set forth to the faithful by the " caretakers of their souls " when preaching. Here then lies the explanation for the fact that the "man" Jesus remained an intangible phantom to Paul, and that he can speak of Christ as a man, without thinking of an historical personality in the sense of the liberal theology of the present day. The ideal man, as Paul represented Jesus to himself— the essence of all human existence—the human race considered as a person, who represented humanity to God, just as the man sacrificed in his rôle had represented the Deity to the people—the " Man " on whom alone redemption depended—is and remains a metaphysical Being—just as the Idea of Plato or the Logos of Philo are none the less metaphysical existences because of their descent into the world of the senses and of their assuming in it a definite individual corporality. And what Paul teaches concerning the "man" Jesus is only a detailed development and deepening of what the Mandæi believed of their Mandä de hajjê or Hibil Ziwâ, and of what the Jewish religions under the influence of the Apocalypses involved in their mysterious doctrines of the Messiah. For Paul the descent, death, and resurrection of Jesus represented an eternal but not an actual story in time; and so to search Paul for the signs of an historical Jesus is to misunderstand the chief point in his religious view of the world.

God, the "father" of our "Lord" Jesus Christ, "awakened" his son and sent him down upon the earth for the redemption of mankind. Although originally one with God, and for that reason himself a divine being, Christ nevertheless renounced his original supernatural existence. In contradiction to his real Being he changed his spiritual nature for "the likeness of sinful flesh," gave up his heavenly kingdom for the poverty and misery of human existence, and came to mankind in the form of a servant, "being found in fashion as a man," in order to bring redemption.* For man is unable to obtain religious salvation through himself alone. In him the spirit is bound to the flesh, his divine supersensible Being is bound down to the material of sensible actuality, and for that reason he is subject "by nature" to misfortune and sin. All flesh is necessarily "sinful flesh." Man is compelled to sin just in so far as he is a being of the flesh. Adam, moreover, is the originator of all human sin only for the reason that he was "in the flesh"—that is, a finite Being imprisoned in corporality. Probably God gave the Law unto mankind, in order to show them the right path in their obscurity; and thereby opened the possibility of being declared righteous or "justified" before his court,

* Rom. viii. 3; 2 Cor. viii. 9; Phil. ii. 7 *sq.*

through the fulfilment of his commands; but it is impossible to keep the commandments in their full severity.

And yet only the ceaseless fulfilment of the whole Law can save mankind from justice. We are all sinners.* So the Law indeed awakened the knowledge of guilt, and brought sin to light through its violation; but it has at the same time increased the guilt.† It has shown itself to be a strict teacher and taskmaster in righteousness, without, however, itself leading to righteousness. So little has it proved to be the desired means of salvation, that it may equally be said of it that it was given by God not for the purpose of saving mankind, but only to make it still more miserable. Consequently Paul would rather attribute the mediation of the Law of Moses not to God himself but to his angels, in order to relieve God of the guilt of the Law.‡ This circumstance is of so much the more consequence for mankind, because the sin aroused by the Law unresistingly drew death in its train; and that deprived them also of the last possibility of becoming equal to their higher spiritual nature. So is man placed midway between light and darkness—a pitiable Being. His spirit, that is kin with God, draws him upwards; and the evil spirit and dæmons drag him downwards, the evil spirits who rule this world and who lure him into sin—and who are at bottom nothing but mythical personifications of man's sinful and fleshly desires.

Christ now enters this world of darkness and of sin. As a man among men, he enters the sphere over which the flesh and sin have power, and must die as other men. But for the incarnate God death is not what it is in the ordinary sense. For him it is only the liberation from

* Gal. iii. 10 *sqq.*; Rom. iii. 9.
† Rom. iii. 20, iv. 15, v. 20, vii., *sqq.*
‡ Gal. iii. 19 *sqq.*

the incongruous condition of the flesh. When Christ dies, he merely strips off the fetters of the flesh and leaves the prison of the body, leaves the sphere over which sin, death, and evil spirits hold their sway. He, the God-man, dies to the sin, which was once unknown to him, once and for all. By prevailing over the power of death in his resurrection, the Son regains, by means of death, his original individual existence, perpetual life in and with the Father.* Thus also does he attain mastery over the Law, for this rules only in so far as there are fleshly men of earth, and ceases to hold good for him at the moment when Christ raises himself above the flesh and returns to his pure spiritual nature. Were there the possibility for mankind of similarly dying to their flesh, then would they be redeemed, as Christ was, from sin, death, and the Law.

There is, in fact, such a possibility. It lies in this: even Christ himself is nothing but the idea of the human race conceived as a personality, the Platonic idea of Humanity personified, the ideal man as a metaphysical essence; and so in his fate the fate of all mankind is fulfilled. In this sense the saying holds, "If one has died for all, then have they all died."† In order to become partakers of the fruit of this Jesus' death, it is certainly necessary that the individual man become really one with Christ; that he enter into an inner unity with the representative, with the divine type of the human race, not merely subjectively, but objectively and actually; and this takes place, according to Paul, by means of "faith." Faith, as Paul understands it, is not a purely external belief in the actuality of Jesus' death as a victim and of his resurrection, but the turning of the whole man to Jesus, the spiritual unification with him and the divine disposition produced thereby, from which the corre-

* Rom. vi. 9 *sq.*   † *Id.* v. 14.

sponding moral action proceeds of itself. It is only in this sense that Paul sets faith above works as demanded by the Law. An action that does not proceed from faith, from the deepest conviction of the divine, has no religious value, be it ever so conformable to the letter of the Law. That is a view which Paul completely shared with the Stoic philosophy of his age, and which was at that time being brought more and more to the front in the more advanced circles of the old civilisation. Man is justified not through the Law, not through works, but through faith; faith, even without works, is reckoned as righteousness.* It is only another expression for the same thought when Paul says that God justifies man, not according to his merit and actions, but "gratuitously," "of his grace." In the conception of the Jewish religion of the Law the idea of justification has a purely juridical significance. Reward here answers exactly to merit. Justification is nothing but an "obligation" according to an irrevocable standard. In Paul's new conception it is, on the contrary, a natural product of God's mercy. But mercy consists finally in this, that God of his own accord sacrificed his Son, so that mankind may share in the effects of his work of redemption by "faith" in him, and by the unity with him thus brought about. But faith is only one way of becoming one with Christ; and real unity with him must also be externally effected. Baptism and the Lord's Supper must be added to faith. There Paul directly follows the Mysteries and their sacramental conception of man's unification with the deity; and shows the connection of his own doctrines with those of the heathen religions. By his baptism, his immersion and disappearance in the depths of the water, man is "buried in death" with Christ. In that he rises once more from the water, the resurrection with Christ to a

* Rom. iv. 3 *sqq.*

new life is fulfilled, not merely in a symbolic but also in a magical mystic fashion.* And Christ is as it were "put on"† through Baptism, so that henceforth the baptized is, no longer potentially but actually, one with Christ; Christ is in him, and he is in Christ. The Lord's Supper is indeed on one hand a feast of fraternal love and recollection, in memory of the Saviour; just as the adherents of Mithras used to hold their love-feasts (Agape) in memory of their God's parting feast with his own people.‡ But on the other hand it is a mystic communion of the blood and body of Christ, through the drinking of the sacramental chalice and the eating of the sacramental bread—a mystic communion in no other sense than that in which the heathens thought they entered into inner connection with their Gods through sacrificial feasts, and in which savages generally even to-day believe that through the eating of another's flesh, be it beast's or man's, and through the drinking of his blood, they become partakers of the power residing in him.§ Even for Paul baptism and the Lord's Supper are to such an extent purely natural processes or magic practices, that he does not object to the heathen custom of baptizing, by proxy, living Christians for dead ones; and in his opinion unworthy eating and drinking of the Lord's Supper produce sickness and death.‖ In this respect, consequently, there can be no talk of a "transcending of the naturalism of the heathen mysteries" in Paul; and to attribute to him a much higher or more spiritual conception of the sacrament than the heathens had seems difficult to reconcile with his express statements.¶

Now Christ, as already stated, is for Paul only a

---

* Rom. vi. 3 *sqq.*   † Gal. iii. 27.
‡ Cf. above, p. 137.   § 1 Cor. x. 16 *sqq.*, xi. 23–27.
‖ 1 Cor. x. 3 *sqq.*, 16–21.   ¶ Cf., *e.g.*, Pfleiderer, *op. cit.*, 333.

comprehensive expression for the ideal totality of men, which is therein represented as an individual personal being. It is clearly the Platonic idea of humanity, and nothing else ; just as Philo personified the divine intelligence and made this coalesce with the " ideal man," with the idea of humanity.* As in the Platonic view the union of man with the ideal takes place through love, through immediate intellectual perception on the basis of ideal knowledge, and the contradiction between the world of sense and the world of ideas is overcome by the same means ; as also thereby man is raised to membership in the cosmos of ideas ; in just such a manner, according to Paul, Christians unite together by means of faith and the sacraments into constitutive moments of the ideal humanity. Thus they realise the idea of humanity, and enter into a mystic communion with Jesus, who himself, as we have already said, represents this idea in its united compass. The consequence of this is, that all that is fulfilled in Christ is equally experienced along with him, in mysterious fashion, by those men who are united with him. Consequently they can now be termed " members of the one body of Christ," who is its " head " or " Soul " ; and this indeed in the same sense as with Plato the different ideas form but members and moments of the one world of ideas, and their plurality is destroyed in the unity of the comprehensive and determining idea of the One or the Good.

Just what an elevation of the spirit to the world of ideas is for Plato, the union of mankind with Christ is for Paul. What the man actually in possession of knowledge, the " wise man," is for the former, " Christ " is for the latter. What is there called Eros—the mediator of the unity between the world of ideas and the sense-

* Cf. above, p. 49 *sqq.*

world, of Being and Conscious Being, of objective and
subjective thought, and at the same time the very
essence of all objective thought—is here called Christ.
Eros is called by Plato the son of riches and poverty,
who bears the "nature and signs" of both : "He is
quite poor, runs around barefoot and homeless, and
must sleep on the naked earth without a roof, in the
open air, at the doors and on the streets, in conformity
with his mother's nature." "As, however, he is neither
mortal nor immortal, at one moment he is flourishing
and full of life, at another he is weary and dies away,
and all that often on the self-same day ; but ever he rises
up again in life in conformity with his father's nature." *
So also the Pauline Christ contains all the fulness of
the Godhead† and is himself the "Son of God"; yet
nevertheless Christ debases himself, takes on the form
of a servant, becomes Man, and dies, thereby placing
himself in direct opposition to his real nature, but
only to rise again continually in each individual man
and allow mankind to participate in his own life.
And as Christ (in 1 Tim. ii. 5) is the "mediator"
between God and men, so also the Platonic Eros
"is midway between the immortal and the mortal."
"Eros, O Socrates, is a daimon, a great daimon, and
everything of this nature is intermediate between God
and man. The daimon transfers to the Gods what
comes from man, and to man what comes from the
Gods; from the one prayer and sacrifice, from the
other the orders and rewards for the sacrifice. Midway,
he fills the gap between the immortal and the mortal,
and everything is through him bound into one whole.
By his mediation is disseminated every prophecy and
the religious skill which has reference to sacrifice,
sanctification, sacred maxims, and each prediction and

* Plato, "Symposium," c. 22.   † Col. ii. 9.

magic spell. God himself does not mix with mankind, but all intercourse and all speech between God and man, as well in waking as in sleep, takes place in the way mentioned. Whoever has experienced this, in him is the daimon." In this connection we recall to our minds that Eros appears in the " Timæus " under the name of the " world-soul," and this is supposed by Plato to have the form of an oblique cross.*

The Platonic Eros is the mythical personification of the conception that the contemplation of Being (obj. gen.) as such is at the same time a contemplation of Being's (sub. gen.); or that in the contemplation of the Ideas the subjective thought of the Philosopher and the objective ideal Reality as it were meet each other from two sides and fuse directly into a unity.† It is thus only the scientific and theoretical formulation of the fundamental idea of the old Aryan Fire Cult. According to this the sacrifice of Agni—that is, the victim which man offers to God—is as such equally Agni's sacrifice, the victim which God offers, and in which he sacrifices himself for humanity. It is in agreement with this that according to Paul the death and resurrection of Christ, as they take place in the consciousness of the believer, represent a death and resurrection of Christ as a divine personality : man dies and lives again with Christ, and God and man are completely fused together in the believer. As mankind by this means becomes a " member " of the " Body of Christ," so in the Vedic conception the partaker of the Fire-God's sacrifice, by the tasting of the blood and the eating of the sacred bread, is associated with a mystic body, and is infused with the one Spirit of God, which destroys his sins in its

---

* *Op. cit.*, 80.

† Cf. my work, " Plotin und der Untergang der antiken Welt-anschauung," 1907.

sacred fire, and flows through him with new life-power. In India, from the cult of the Fire-God and the complete unity of God and man thereby attained, Brahmanism was developed, and gained an influence over all the Indian peoples. In Plato intellectual contemplation formed the basis of cognition. He placed the wise man at the head of the social organism, and regarded the philosopher as the only man fitted for the government of the world. And the future development of the Church as a " Communion of Saints " appears already in the Pauline conception of the faithful as the " Body of Christ," in which the Idea of the human race (Christ) is realised, as the kingdom of God upon earth, as the true humanity, as the material appearance of the divine ideal man, to belong to which is mankind's duty, and without which it is impossible for man to live in his real ideal nature.

Ancient philosophy had attempted until now in vain to overcome the contradiction between the sense-world and the world of ideas, and to destroy the uncertainty of human thought and life which results from this contradiction. From the time of Plato it had worked at the problem of uniting, without contradiction, Nature and Spirit, whose contradictory nature had first been brought to notice by the founder of metaphysical idealism. Religion, particularly in the Mystery Cults, had tried to solve in a practical way the problem that seemed insoluble by abstract means, and had sought to secure for man a new basis and resting-place by means of devotion and " revelation "—a mystic sinking into the depths of God. But Paul's Christianity first gave a form to all this obscure desire, a form which united the thrills and joy of mystic ecstasy with the certainty of a comprehensive religious view of the world, and enlightened men as to the deepest meaning of their emotional impulse towards

certainty: man obtains unity with God and certainty as
to the true reality, not by an abstract dialectic, as Plato
supposed; not by logical insight into the cosmos in the
sense of an abstract knowledge attainable only by the
few, but through faith, through the divine act of
redemption. To adopt this internally, thereby to live with
it directly—this alone can give man the possibility of
emerging from the uncertainty and darkness of corporeal
existence into the clear light of the spiritual. All
certainty of the true or essential being is consequently
a certainty of faith, and there is no higher certainty than
that which is given to men in faith and piety. As
Christ died and was thereby freed from the bonds of the
body and of the world, so also must man die in the spirit.
He must lay aside the burden of this body, the real cause
of all his ethical and intellectual shortcomings. He
must inwardly rise with Christ and be born again, thereby
taking part in his spiritual certitude and gaining together
with the "Life in the Spirit" salvation from all his
present shortcomings. It is true that outwardly the
body still exists, even after the inner act of redemption
has taken place. Even when the man who died with
Christ has arisen and has become a new man, he is
nevertheless still subject to corporeal limitations. The
redeemed man is still in the world and must fight with
its influences. But what man gains in the union with
the body of Christ is the " Spirit " of Christ, which holds
the members of the body together, shows itself to be
active in everything which belongs to the body, and acts
in man as a supernatural power. This spirit, as it dwells
henceforth in the redeemed man, works and directs and
drives him on to every action; lifts man in idea far above
all the limitations of his fleshly nature; strengthens him
in his weakness ; shows him existence in a new light, so
that henceforth he feels himself no longer bound; gives

him the victory over the powers of earth, and enables him to anticipate, even in this life, the blessedness of his real and final redemption in a life to come.* But the spirit of Christ as such is equally the divine spirit. So that the redeemed, as they receive the spirit of Christ, are the " sons " of God himself, and this is expressed by saying that with the spirit they "inherit the glorious freedom of the children of God."† For, as Paul says, " the Lord is the spirit; but where the spirit is, there is freedom."‡

So that when the Christian feels himself transformed into a "new creature," equipped with power of knowledge and of virtue, blest in the consciousness of his victorious strength over carnal desires, and wins his peace in faith, this is only the consequence of a superhuman spirit working in him. Hence the Christian virtues of Brotherly Love, Humility, Obedience, &c., are necessary consequences of the possession of the Spirit : "If we live by the Spirit, by the Spirit let us also walk." § And if the faithful suddenly develop a fulness of new and wonderful powers, which exceed man's ordinary nature— such as facility in " tongues," in prophecy, and in the healing of the sick—this is, in the superstitious view of the age, only to be explained by the indwelling activity of a supernatural spirit-being that has entered man from the outside. Certainly it does not seem clear, in the Pauline conception of the redemption, how this heavenly spirit can at the same time be the spirit of man—how it can be active in man without removing the particular and original spirit of man, and without reducing the individual to a passive tool, to a lifeless puppet without self-determination and responsibility; how the man "possessed " by such a spirit can nevertheless feel

---

* Gal. ii. 20 ; Rom. viii. 4, 26.　　　　† *Id.* viii. 14 *sqq.*
‡ 2 Cor. iii. 17.　　　　§ Gal. v. 26.

himself free and redeemed by the Spirit. For it is in truth an alien spirit, one that does not in essence belong to him, which enters man through the union with Christ. Yet it is supposed to be the spirit, not merely of the individual man, but also Christ's personal spirit. One and the same spirit putting on a celestial body of light must be enthroned on the right hand of the Father in heaven, and must also be on earth the spirit of those who believe in it, setting itself to work in them as the source of Gnosis, of full mystic knowledge; and, as the power of God, as the spirit of salvation, must produce in them supernatural effects.* It must be on the one hand an objective and actual spirit-being which in Christ becomes man, dies, and rises again; and on the other hand an inner subjective power, which produces in each individual man the extinction of the flesh and a new birth which is to be shared by the faithful as the fruit of their individual redemption. That is perhaps comprehensible in the mode of thought of an age for which the idea of personality had as yet no definite meaning, and which consequently saw no contradiction in this, that a personal Christ-spirit should at the same time inhabit a number of individual spirits; and which did not differentiate between the one, or rather the continual, act of redemption by God and its continual temporal repetition in the individual. We can understand this only if the Pauline Christ is a purely metaphysical being. It is, on the contrary, quite incomprehensible if Paul is supposed to have gained his idea of the mediator of salvation from any experience of an historical Jesus and his actual death. Only because in his doctrine of the saving power of the Christ-spirit Paul had thought of no particular human personality could he imagine the immanence of the divine in the world to be mediated by that spirit. Only because he

* 1 Cor. ii. 9, 14; Rom. xii. 2.

connected no other idea with the personality of Jesus
than the Book of Wisdom or Philo did with their particular
immanence principles, does he declare that Christ brings
about salvation. So that Christ, as the principle of
redemption, is for Paul only an allegorical or symbolical
personality and not a real one. He is a personality such
as were the heathen deities, who passed as general cosmic
powers without prejudice to their appearing in human
form. Personality is for Paul only another mode of
expressing the supernatural spirituality and directed
activity of the principle of redemption, in distinction
from the blindly working powers and material realities of
religious naturalism. It serves merely to suggest
spirituality to an age which could only represent spirit
as a material fluid. It corresponds simply to the popular
conception of the principle of redemption, which treated
this as bound up with the idea of a human being. But
it in no way referred to a real historical individual, showing, in fact, just by the uncertainty and fluctuation of the
idea, how far the Christ of the Pauline doctrine of
redemption was from being connected with a definite
historical reality.

Not because he so highly esteemed and revered Jesus
as an historical personality did Paul make Christ the
bearer and mediator of redemption, but because he knew
nothing at all of an historical Jesus, of a human individual of this name, to whom he would have been able
to transfer the work of redemption. " Faithful disciples,"
Wrede considers, " could not so easily believe that the
man who had sat with them at table in Capernaum, or
had journeyed over the Sea of Galilee with them, was
the creator of the world. For Paul this obstacle was
absent."* But Paul is nevertheless supposed to have
met James, the " Brother of the Lord," and to have had

* *Op. cit.*, 86.

dealings with him which would certainly have modified his view of Jesus, if here there were really question of a corporeal brotherhood. What a wonderful idea our theologians must have of a man like Paul if they think that it could ever have occurred to him to connect such tremendous conceptions with a human individual Jesus as he does with his Christ! It is true that there is a type of religious ecstasy in which the difference between man and God is completely lost sight of; and, especially at the beginning of our era, in the period of Cæsar-worship and of the deepest religious superstition, it was not in itself unusual to deify, after his death, a man who was highly esteemed. A great lack of reason, a great mental confusion, an immense flight of imagination, would be necessary to transform a man not long dead, who was still clearly remembered by his relatives and contemporaries, not merely into a divine hero or demi-god, but into the world-forming spiritual principle, into the metaphysical mediator of redemption and the " second God." And if, as even Wrede acknowledges in the above-quoted words, personal knowledge of Jesus was really an " obstacle " to his apotheosis, how is it to be explained that the " First Apostles " at Jerusalem took no exception to that representation of Paul's ? They surely knew who Jesus had been; they knew the Master through many years' continual wandering with him. And however highly they may always have thought of the risen Jesus, however intimately they may have joined in their minds the memory of the man Jesus with the prevailing idea of the Messiah, according to the prevalent theological opinion, even they are supposed to have risen in no way to such a boundless deification of their Lord and Master as Paul undertook a comparatively short while after Jesus' death.

" Paul already believed in such a heavenly Being, in a

divine Christ, before he believed in Jesus." * The truth
is that he never believed at all in the Jesus of liberal
theology. The "man" Jesus already belonged to his
faith in Christ, so far as Christ's act of redemption was
supposed to consist in his humbling himself and becoming man—and no historical Jesus was necessary for
that. For Paul also, just as for the whole heathen world,
the man actually sacrificed in God's place was at best
merely a chance symbol of the God presenting himself
as victim. Hence it cannot be said that the man Jesus
was but " the bearer of all the great attributes, " which
as such had been long since determined; † or, as Gunkel
puts it, that the enthusiastic disciples had transferred to
him all that the former Judaism had been wont to ascribe
to the Messiah; and that consequently the Christology
of the New Testament, in spite of its unhistorical nature,
was nevertheless " a mighty hymn which History sings
to Jesus " (!).‡ I If we once agree as to the existence
of a pre-Christian Jesus—even even Gunkel, apart from
Robertson and Smith, has worked for the recognition of
this fact—then this can in the first place produce
nothing but a strong suspicion against the historical Jesus;
and it seems a despairing subterfuge of the "critical"
theology to seek to find capital, from the existence of
a pre-Christian Jesus, for the "unique" significance of
their " historical " Jesus.

Christ's life and death are for Paul neither the moral
achievement of a man nor in any way historical facts,
but something super-historical, events in the supersensible world.§ Further, the " man " Jesus comes in
question for Paul, just as did the suffering servant of God
for Isaiah, exclusively as an Idea, and his death is, like
his resurrection, but the purely ideal condition whereby

* Wrede, *Id.*   † *Id.*
‡ *Op. cit.*, 94.   § Wrede, *op. cit.*, 85.

redemption is brought about. "If Christ hath not been raised, your faith is vain." * On this declaration has till now been founded the chief proof that an historical Jesus was to Paul the pre-supposition of his doctrine. But really that declaration in Paul's mouth points to nothing but the faith of his contemporaries, who expected natural and religious salvation from the resurrection of their God, whether he were called Adonis, Attis, Dionysus, Osiris, or anything else.

The fact is therefore settled, that Paul knew nothing of an historical Jesus; and that even if he had known anything of him, this Jesus in any case plays no part for him, and exercised no influence over the development of his religious view of the world. Let us consider the importance of this : the very man from whom we derive the first written testimony as to Christianity, who was the first in any way to establish it as a new religion differing from Judaism, on whose teachings alone the whole further development of Christian thought has depended—this Paul knew absolutely nothing of Jesus as an historical personality. In fact, with perfect justice from his point of view he was even compelled to excuse himself, when others wished to enlighten him as to such a personality ! At the present day it will be acknowledged by all sensible people that, as Ed. von Hartmann declared more than thirty years ago, without Paul the Christian movement would have disappeared in the sand, just as the many other Jewish religions have done—at best to afford interest to investigators as an historical curiosity—and Paul had no knowledge of Jesus ! The formation and development of the Christian religion began long before the Jesus of the Gospels appeared, and was completed independently of the historical Jesus

* 1 Cor. xv. 17.

of theology. Theology has no justification for treating Christianity merely as the " Christianity of Christ," as it now is sufficiently evident ; nor should it present a view of the life and doctrines of an ideal man Jesus as the Christian religion.*

The question raised at the beginning, as to what we learn from Paul about the historical Jesus, has found its answer—nothing. There is little value, then, in the objection to the disbelievers in such a Jesus which is raised on the theological side in triumphant tones: that the historical existence of Jesus is "most certainly established" by Paul. This objection comes, in fact, even from such people as regard the New Testament, in other respects, with most evidently sceptical views. The truth is that the Pauline epistles contain nothing which would force us to the belief in an historical Jesus; and probably no one would find such a person in them if that belief was not previously established in him. It must be considered that, if the Pauline epistles stood in the edition of the New Testament where they really belong—that is, before the Gospels—hardly any one would think that Jesus, as he there meets him, was a real man and had wandered on the earth in flesh and blood ; but he would in all probability only find therein a detailed development of the "suffering servant of God," and would conclude that it was an irruption of heathen religious ideas into Jewish thought. Our theologians are, however, so strongly convinced of it *a priori*—that the Pauline representation of Christ actually arose from the figure of Jesus wandering on earth—that even M. Brückner confesses, in the preface to his work, that he had been " himself astonished " (!) at the result of his inquiry—the independence of the Pauline

* Cf. as to the whole question my essay on " Paulus u. Jesus " (" Das Freie Wort " of December, 1909).

representation of Christ from the historical personality, Jesus.*

Christianity is a syncretic religion. It belongs to those multiform religious movements which at the commencement of our era were struggling with one another for the mastery. Setting out from the Apocalyptic idea and the expectation of the Messiah among the Jewish sects, it was borne on the tide of a mighty social agitation, which found its centre and its point of departure in the religious sects and Mystery communities. Its adherents conceived the Messiah not merely as the Saviour of souls, but as deliverer from slavery, from the lot of the poor and the oppressed, and as the bearer of a new justice.†

It borrowed the chief part of its doctrine, the specific point in which it differed from ordinary Judaism, the central idea of the God sacrificing himself for mankind, from the neighbouring peoples, who had brought down this belief into Asia, in connection with fire-worship, from its earlier home in the North. Only in so far as that faith points in the end to an Aryan origin can it be said that Jesus was "an Aryan"; any further statements on this point, such as, for example, Chamberlain makes in his "Grundlagen des neunzehnten Jahrhunderts," are pure fancies, and rest on a complete misunderstanding of the true state of affairs. Christianity, as the religion of Christ, of the "Lord," who secularised the

---

* It is true that other theologians think differently on this point, as, *e.g.*, Feine in his book, "Jesus Christus und Paulus" (1902), declares that Paul had "interested himself very much in gaining a distinct and comprehensive picture of Jesus' activity and personality" (!) (229).

† Kalthoff has in his writings laid especial stress on this social significance of Christianity. Cf. also Steudel, "Das Christentum und die Zukunft des Protestantismus" ("Deutsche Wiedergeburt," iv., 1909, 26 *sq.*), and Kautsky, "Der Ursprung des Christentums," 1908.

Jewish Law by his voluntary death of expiation, did not "arise" in Jerusalem, but, if anywhere, in the Syrian capital Antioch, one of the principal places of the worship of Adonis. For it was at Antioch where, according to the Acts,* the name "Christians" was first used for the adherents of the new religion, who had till then been usually called Nazarenes.†

That certainly is in sharpest contradiction to tradition, according to which Christianity is supposed to have arisen in Jerusalem and to have been thence spread abroad among the heathen. But Luke's testimony as to the arising of the community of the Messiah at Jerusalem and the spreading of the Gospel from that place can lay no claim to historical significance. Even the account of the disciples' experience at Easter and of

---

* xl. 26.

† In the same way Vollers also, in his work on "Die Welt-religionen" (1907), seeks to explain the faith of the original Christian sects in Jesus' death and resurrection as a blend of the Adonis (Attis) and Christ faiths. He regards this as the essence of that faith, that the existing views of the Messiah and the Resurrection were transferred to one and the same person; and shows from this of what great importance it must be that this faith met a well-prepared ground, in North Syria, Anatolia, and Egypt, where it naturally spread. But he treats the Jewish Diaspora of these lands as the natural mediator of the new preaching or "message of Salvation" (Gospel), and finds a proof of his view in this, "that the sphere of the greatest density of the Diaspora almost completely coincides with those lands where the growing and rising youthful God was honoured, and that these same districts are also the places in which we meet, only a generation after Jesus' death, the most numerous, flourishing, and fruitful communities of the new form of belief. It is the Eastern Mediterranean or Levantine horse-shoe shaped line which stretches from Ephesus and Bithynia through Anatolia to Tarsus and Antioch, thence through Syria and Palestine by way of the cult-centres Bubastes and Sais to Alexandria. Almost directly in the middle of these lands lies Aphaka, where was the chief sanctuary of the "Lord" Adonis, and a little south of this spot lies the country where the Saviour of the Gospels was born (*op. cit.*, 152).

the first appearances after the Resurrection, from their contradictory and confused character appear to be legendary inventions.* Unhistorical, and in contradiction to the information on this point given by Matthew and Mark, is the statement that the disciples stayed in Jerusalem after Jesus' death, which is even referred by Luke to an express command of the dead master.† Unhistorical is the assemblage at Pentecost and the wonderful " miracle " of the outpouring of the Holy Ghost, which, as even Clemen agrees, probably originated from the Jewish legends, according to which the giving of the Law on Sinai was made in seventy different languages, in order that it might be understood by all peoples.‡ But also Stephen's execution and the consequent persecution of the community at Jerusalem are legendary inventions.§ The great trouble which Luke takes to

---

* Cf. O. Pfleiderer, " Die Entstehung des Christentums," 1905, 109 *sqq.*

† Luke xxiv. 33, xlix. 52 ; Acts i. 4, 8, 12 *sqq.*

‡ " Religionsgesch. Erklärung d. N.T.," 261. Cf. also Joel iii. 1 and Isa. xxviii. 11, and the Buddhist account of the first sermon of Buddha : " Gods and men streamed up to him, and all listened breathlessly to the words of the teacher. Each of the countless listeners believed that the wise man looked at him and spoke to him in his own language; though it was the dialect of Magadha which he spoke." Seydel, " Evangelium von Jesus," 248 ; " Buddha-Legende," 92 *sq.*

§ Stephen's so-called "martyrdom," whose feast falls on December 26th, the day after the birth of Christ, owes its existence to astrology, and rests on the constellation of Corona (Gr., Stephanos), which becomes visible at this time on the eastern horizon (Dupuis, *op. cit.,* 267). Hence the well-known phrase " to inherit the martyr's crown." Even the theologian Baur has found it strange that the Jewish Sanhedrin, which could not carry into effect any death sentence without the assent of the Roman governor, should completely set aside this formality in the case of Stephen ; and he has clearly shown how the whole account of Stephen's martyrdom is paralleled with Christ's death (Baur, " Paulus," 25 *sqq*).

represent Jerusalem as the point whence the Christian movement set out, clearly betrays the tendency of the author of the Acts to misrepresent the activity of the Christian propaganda, which really emanated from many centres, as a bursting out of the Gospel from one focus. It is meant to produce the impression that the new religion spread from Jerusalem over the whole world like an explosion ; and thus its almost simultaneous appearance in the whole of Nearer Asia is explained. For this reason " devout Jews of all nations " were assembled in Jerusalem at Pentecost, and could understand each other in spite of their different languages. For this reason Stephen was stoned, and the motive given for that persecution which in one moment scattered the faithful in all directions.*

Now it is certainly probable that there was in Jerusalem, just as in many other places, a community of the Messiah which believed in Jesus as the God sacrificing himself for humanity. But the question is whether this belief, in the community at Jerusalem, rested on a real man Jesus ; and whether it is correct to regard this community, some of whose members were personally acquainted with Jesus, and who were the faithful companions of his wanderings, as the " original community " in the sense of the first germ and point of departure of the Christian movement. We may believe, with Fraser, that a Jewish prophet and itinerant preacher, who by chance was named Jesus, was seized by his opponents, the orthodox Jews, on account of his revolutionary agitation, and was beheaded as the Haman of the current year, thereby giving occasion for the foundation of the community at Jerusalem.† Against this it may be said that our informants as to the beginning of the Christian propaganda certainly vary, now making one assertion,

---

* Smith, *op. cit.*, 23–31.   † Frazer, "Golden Bough," iii. 197.

now another, without caring whether these are contradictory ; and they all strive to make up for the lack of any certain knowledge by unmistakable inventions. If the doctrine of Jesus was, as Smith declares, pre-Christian, " a religion which was spread among the Jews and especially the Greeks within the limits of the century [100 B.C. to 100 A.D.], more or less secretly, and wrapped up in ' Mysteries,' " then we can understand both the sudden appearance of Christianity over so wide a sphere as almost the whole of Nearer Asia, and also the fact that even the earliest informants as to the beginning of the Christian movement had nothing certain to tell. This, however, seems quite irreconcilable with the view of a certain, definite, local, and personal point of departure for the new doctrine.* The objection will be raised : what about the Gospels ? They, at least, clearly tell the story of a human individual, and are inexplicable, apart from the belief in an historical Jesus.

The question consequently arises as to the source from which the Gospels derived a knowledge of this Jesus ; for on this alone the belief in an historical Jesus can rest.

* Smith, *op. cit.*, 80 *sq.*

II

THE JESUS OF THE GOSPELS

HOWEVER widely views may differ even now in the sphere of Gospel criticism, all really competent investigators agree on one point with rare unanimity : the Gospels are not historical documents in the ordinary sense of the word, but creeds, religious books, literary documents revealing the mind of the Christian community. Their purpose is consequently not to give information as to the life and teachings of Jesus which would correspond to reality, but to awaken belief in Jesus as the Messiah sent from God for the redemption of his people, to strengthen and defend that belief against attacks. And as creeds they confine themselves naturally to recounting such words and events as have any significance for the faith ; and they have the greatest interest in so arranging and representing the facts as to make them accord with the content of that faith.

(a) The Synoptic Jesus.

Of the numerous Gospels which were still current in the first half of the second century, as is well known, only four have come down to us. The others were not embodied by the Church in the Canon of the New Testament writings, and consequently fell into oblivion. Of these at most a few names and isolated and insignificant fragments remain to us. Thus we know of a Gospel of Matthew, of Thomas, of Bartholomew, Peter, the twelve apostles, &c. Of our four Gospels, two bear the names of apostles and two the names of companions and pupils of apostles, viz., Mark and Luke. In this, of course, it is in no way meant that they were really written by these persons. According to Chrysostom these names were first assigned to them towards the end of the second century. And the titles do not run : Gospel of Matthew, of Mark, and so on, but " according to " Matthew, " according to " Mark, Luke, and John ; so that they indicate at most only the persons or schools whose particular conception of the Gospel they represent.

Of these Gospels, again, that of John ranks as the latest. It presupposes the others, and shows such a dogmatic tendency, that it cannot be considered the source of the story. Of the remaining Gospels, which on account of their similarity as to form and matter have been termed " Synoptic " (*i.e.*, such as must be dealt with in connection with each other and thus only give a real idea of the Saviour's personality), that of Mark is generally regarded as the oldest. Matthew and Luke rely on Mark, and all three, according to the prevailing view, are indebted to a common Aramiac source, wherein Jesus' didactic sermons are supposed to have been contained. Tradition points to John Mark, the nephew of Barnabas, pupil of Peter, and Paul's companion on his first missionary journey and later a sharer in the captivity at Rome, as the author of the Gospel of Mark. It is believed that this was written shortly after the destruction of Jerusalem (70)—*i.e.*, at least forty years after Jesus' death (!). This tradition depends upon a note of the Church historian Eusebius (d. about 340 A.D.), according to which Papias, Bishop of Hierapolis in Asia Minor, learnt from the " elder John " that Mark had set forth what he had heard from Peter, and what this latter

had in turn heard from the "Lord." On account of its
indirect nature and of Eusebius' notorious unreliability
this note is not a very trustworthy one,* and belief in it
should disappear in view of the fact that the author of
the Gospel of Mark had no idea of the spot where Jesus
is supposed to have lived. And yet Mark is supposed to
have been born in Jerusalem and to have been a missionary! As Wernle shows in his work, " Die Quellen des
Lebens Jesu," Mark stands quite far from the life of
Jesus both in time and place (!) ; indeed, he has no clear
idea of Jesus' doings and course of life.† And Wrede
confirms this in his work, " Das Messias-geheimnis "
(1901), probably the clearest and deepest inquiry into the
fundamental problem of the Gospel of Mark which we
possess. Jesus is for Mark at once the Messiah and the
Son of God. " Faith in this dogma must be aroused, it
must be established and defended. The whole Gospel is
a defence. Mark wishes to lead all his readers, among
whom he counts the Heathens and Gentile Christians,
to the recognition of what the heathen centurion said,

---

* As to the small value of Papias' statement, cf. Gfrörer, "Die
heilige Sage," 1838, i. 3–23 ; also Lützelberger, "Die kirchl. Tradition
über den Apostel Johannes," 76–93. The whole story, according to
which Mark received the essential content of the Gospel named
after him from Peter, is based on 1 Peter v. 13, and merely serves
the purpose of increasing the historical value of the Gospel o
Mark. "As the first Gospel was believed to be the work of the
Apostle Matthew, and the second (Luke) the work of an assistant
of Paul, it was very easy to ascribe to the third (Mark) at least a
similar origin as the second, i.e., to trace it back in an analogous
way to Peter ; as it would have seemed natural for the chief of the
apostles, longest dead, to have had his own Gospel, one dedicated to
him, as well as Paul. The passage 1 Peter v. 13, " My son Mark
saluteth you," gave a suitable opportunity for bestowing a name on
the book," (Gfrörer, op. cit., 15 ; cf. also Brandt, " Die evangelische
Geschichte u. d. Ursprung des Christentums," 1893, 535 sq.).

† Op. cit., 58.

'Truly this man was the Son of God !'* The whole account is directed to this end."†

Mark's main proof for this purpose is that of miracles. Jesus' doctrines are with Mark of so much less importance than his miracles, that we never learn exactly what Jesus preached. "Consequently the historical portrait is very obscure : Jesus' person is distorted into the grotesque and the fantastic " (!)‡ Not only does Mark often introduce his own thought into the tradition about Jesus, and so prove perfectly wrong, and indeed absurd, the view held, for instance, by Wernle, that Jesus had intentionally made use of an obscure manner of speech and had spoken in parables and riddles so as not to be understood by the people ;§ but also the connection which he has established between the accounts, which had first gone from mouth to mouth for a long time in isolation, is a perfectly disconnected and external one. At first the stories reported by Mark were totally disconnected with one another. There is no evidence at all of their having followed each other in the present order (!).|| So that only the matter, not what Mark made of it, is of historical value.¶ Single stories, discourses, and phrases are bound into a whole by Mark ; and often enough it may be seen that we have here a tradition which was first built up in the earliest Christianity long after Jesus' death. Experiences were at first gradually fashioned into a story—and the miracle-stories may especially be regarded in this way. In spite of all these trimmings and alterations, and in spite of the fact that neither in the words of Jesus nor in the stories is it for the most part any longer possible to separate the actual from the

---

* xv. 39.   † 60.   ‡ *Id.*

§ The proper explanation for this should lie in the fact that the Jesus-faith was set up as a sect-faith and not for "outsiders."

|| 63 *sqq.*   ¶ 68.

traditional, which for forty years was not put into writing—in spite of all this, the historical value of the traditions given us by Mark is " very highly " estimated. For not only is " the general impression of power, originality, and creation " " valuable," which is given in this account of Mark's, but also there are so many individual phrases " corresponding to reality." Numerous accounts, momentary pictures and remarks, " speak for themselves." The modesty and ingenuousness (!), the freshness and joy (!) with which Mark recounts all this, show distinctly that he is here the reporter of a valid tradition, and that he writes nothing but what eye-witnesses have told him (!). "And so finally, in spite of all, this Gospel remains an extraordinarily valuable work, a collection of old and genuine material, which is loosely arranged and placed under a few leading conceptions ; produced perhaps by that Mark whom the New Testament knows, and of whom Papias heard from the mouth of the elder John." *

One does not trust one's eyes with this style of attempting to set up Mark as an even half-credible " historical source." This attempt will remind us only too forcibly of Wrede's ironical remarks when he is making fun of the " decisions as you like it " that flourish in the study of Jesus' life. " This study," says Wrede, " suffers from psychological suggestion, and this is one style of historical solution." † One believes that he can secure this, another that, as the historical nucleus of the Gospel ; but neither has objective proofs for his assertions.‡ If we wish to

* 70.

† 8.

‡ It strikes the reader, who stands apart from the controversy, as comical to find the matter characterised in the theological works on the subject as " undoubtedly historical," " distinct historical fact," " true account of history," and so forth; and to consider that what

work with an historical nucleus, we must really make certain of a nucleus. The whole point is, that in an anecdote or phrase something is proved, which makes any other explanation of the matter under consideration improbable, or at least doubtful.* It seems very questionable, after his radical criticism of the historical credibility of Mark's Gospel, that Wrede saw in it such a "historical kernel"— though this is supposed by Wernle to "speak for itself." Moreover, Wrede's opinion of the "historian" Mark is not essentially different from Wernle's. In his opinion, for example, Jesus' disciples, as the Gospel portrays them, with their want of intelligence bordering on idiocy, their folly, and their ambiguous conduct as regards their Master, are "not real figures." † He also concedes, as we have stated, that Mark had no real idea of the historical life of Jesus,‡ even if "pallid fragments" (!) of such an idea entered into his superhistorical faith-conception. "The Gospel of Mark," he says, "has in this sense a place among the histories of dogma." § The belief that in it the development of Jesus' public life is still perceptible appears to be decaying.|| "It would indeed be in the highest degree desirable that such a Gospel were not the oldest." ¶

Thus, then, does Mark stand as an historical source. After this we could hardly hope to be much strengthened in our belief in Jesus' historical reality by the other two Synoptics. Of these, Luke's Gospel must have been written, in the early part of the second century, by an

---

holds for one as "historically certain" is set aside by another as "quite certainly unhistorical." Where is the famous "method" of which the "critical" theologians are so proud in opposition to the "laity," who allow themselves to form judgments as to the historical worth or worthlessness of the Gospels ?

* Wrede, *op. cit.*, 91.   † 104.   ‡ 129.
§ 131. || 148.   ¶ 148.

unknown Gentile Christian ; and Matthew's is not the work of a single author, but was produced—and unmistakably in the interests of the Church—by various hands in the first half of the second century.* But now both,

* Cf. Pfleiderer, "Entstehung des Christentums," 207, 213. All estimates as to the time at which the Gospels were produced rest entirely on suppositions, in which points of view quite different from that of purely historical interest generally predominate. Thus it has been the custom on the Catholic side to pronounce, not Mark or Luke, but Matthew, to be the oldest source. " Proofs " for this are also given—naturally, as it is indeed the " Church " Gospel : it contains the famous passage (xvi. 18, 19) about Peter's possession of the keys ; how, then, should this not be the oldest ? And lately Harnack (" Beiträge zur Einl. in das N.T.," iii., " Die Apostelgeschichte," 1908) has tried to prove that the Acts, with the Gospel of Luke, had been already produced in the early part of the year 60 A.D. But he does not dare to come to a real decision ; and his reasons are opposed by just as weighty ones which are against that " possibility " suggested by him (*op. cit.*, 219 *sqq.*). Such is, first, the fact that all the other early Christian writings which belong to the first century, as the Epistle of Barnabas and the Shepherd of Hermas, evidently know nothing of them. In the Epistle of Barnabas, written about 96 A.D., we read that Jesus chose as his own apostles, as men who were to proclaim his Gospel, " of all men the most evil, to show that he had come to call, not the righteous, but sinners, to repentance " (iv.). As to this Lützelberger very justly remarks, " That is more even than our Gospels say. For these are content to prove that Jesus did not come for the righteous by saying that he ate with publicans and was anointed by women of evil life ; while in this Epistle even the Apostles must be most wicked sinners, so that grace may shine forth to them. This passage was quite certainly written neither by an Apostle nor by a pupil of an Apostle ; and also it was not written after our Gospels, but at a time when the learned Masters of the Church had still a free hand to show their spirit and ingenuity in giving form to the evangelical story " ("Die hist. Tradition," 236 *sq.*). But also the so-called Epistle of Clement, which must have been written at about the same time, is completely silent as to the Gospels, while the " Doctrine of the Twelve Apostles," which perhaps also belongs to the end of the first century, cites Christ's words, such as stand in the Gospels, but not as sayings of Jesus. Moreover, according to Harnack, the " Doctrine of the Twelve Apostles " is the Christian elaboration of an

as we have said, are based on Mark. And even if in their representations they have attained a certain "peculiar value" which is wanting in Mark—*e.g.*, a greater number of Jesus' parables and words—even if they have embellished the story of his life by the addition of legendary passages (*e.g.*, of the history of the time preceding the Saviour, of many additions to the account of the Passion and Resurrection, &c.), this cannot quite establish the existence of an historical Jesus. It is true that Wernle takes the view that in this respect "old traditions" have been preserved "with wonderful fidelity" by both the Evangelists; but, on the other hand, he concedes as to certain of Luke's accounts that even if he had used old traditions they need not have been as yet written, and certainly they need not have been "historically reliable." It seems rather peculiar when, leaving completely on one side the historical value of the tradition, he emphatically declares that even such a strong interest, as in his opinion the Evangelists had in the shaping and formation of their account, could not in any way set aside "the worth of its rich treasure of parables and stories, through which Jesus himself [!] speaks to us with freshness and originality" (!). He also strangely sums up at the end, "that the peculiar value of both Gospels, in spite of their very mixed nature, has claim enough on our gratitude" (!).* This surely is simply to make use of the Gospels' literary or other value in the interest of the belief in their historical credibility.

But there is still the collection of sayings, that "great authority on the matter," from which all the Synoptics, and especially Luke and Matthew, are supposed to have

early Jewish document; whence we may conclude that its Words of Christ have a similar origin in Jewish thought to that from which the Gospels obtained them. (Cf. Lützelberger, *op. cit.*, 259–271.)
  * 81.

derived the material for their declarations about Jesus. Unfortunately this is to us a completely unknown quantity, as we know neither what this "great" authority treats of, nor the arrangement of the matter in it, nor its text. We can only say that this collection was written in the Aramaic tongue, and the arrangement of its matter was not apparently chronological, but according to the similarity of its contents. Again, it is doubtful whether the collection was a single work, produced by one individual; or whether it had had a history before it came to Luke and Matthew. All the same, "the collection contains such a valuable number of the Lord's words, that in all probability an eye-witness was its author" (!).* As for the speeches of Jesus constructed from it, they were never really made as speeches by Jesus, but owe the juxtaposition of their contents entirely to the hand of the compiler. Thus the much admired Sermon on the Mount is constructed by placing together individual phrases of Jesus, which belong to all periods of his life, perhaps made in the course of a year. The ideas running through it and connecting the parts are not those of Jesus, but rather those of the original community; "nevertheless, the historical value of these speeches is, on the whole, very great indeed. Together with the 'Lord's words' of Mark they give us the truest insight into the spirit of the Gospel" (!).†

Such are the authorities for the belief in an historical Jesus! If we survey all that remains of the Gospels, this does indeed appear quite "scanty," or, speaking plainly, pitiable. Wernle consoles himself with, "If only it is certain and reliable." Yes, if! "And if only it was able to give us an answer to the chief question: Who was Jesus?"‡ This much is certain: a "Life of

* 71.   † 81 *sq.*   ‡ *Id.*

Jesus" cannot be written on the basis of the testimony before us. Probably all present-day theologians are agreed on this point; which, however, does not prevent them producing new essays on it, at any rate for the "people," thus making up for the lack of historical reliability by edifying effusions and rhetorical phrases. "There is no lack of valuable historical matter, of stones for the construction of Jesus' life; they lie before us plentifully. But the plan for the construction is lost and completely irretrievable, because the oldest disciples had no occasion for such an historical connection, but rather claimed obedience to the isolated words and acts, so far as they aroused faith." But would they have been less faith-arousing if they had been arranged connectedly, would the credibility of the accounts of Jesus have been diminished and not much rather increased, if the Evangelists had taken the trouble to give us some more information as to Jesus' real life? As things stand at present, hardly two events are recounted in the same manner in the Gospels, or even in the same connection. Indeed, the differences and contradictions— and this not only as to unimportant things, such as names, times and places, &c.—are so great that these literary documents of Christianity can hardly be surpassed in confusion.* But even this is, according to Wernle, "not so great a pity, if only we can discover with sufficient clearness, what Jesus' actions and wishes were on important points." † Unfortunately we are not in a position to do even this. For the ultimate source of our information, which we arrive at in our examination of the authorities is completely unknown to

---

* The laity has, as is well known, but a slight suspicion of this. So S. E. Verus' "Vergleichende Übersicht der vier Evangelien " (1897), with the commentary, is to be recommended.

† 83.

us—the Aramaic collection of sayings, and those very old traditions from which Mark is supposed to have derived his production, gleanings of which have been preserved for us by Luke and Matthew. But even if we knew these also, we would almost certainly not have "come to Jesus himself." " They contain the possibility of dispute and misrepresentation. They recount in the first place the faith of the oldest Christians, a faith which arose in the course of four hundred years, and moreover changed much in that time." * So that at most we know only the faith of the earliest community. We see how this community sought to make clear to itself through Jesus its belief in the Resurrection, how it sought to "prove" to itself and to others the divine nature of Jesus by the recital of tales of miracles and the like. What Jesus himself thought, what he did, what he taught, what his life was, and—might we say it?—whether he ever lived at all—that is not to be learnt from the Gospels, and, according to all the preceding discussion, cannot be settled from them with lasting certainty.

Of course the liberal theologian, for whom everything is compatible with an historical Jesus, has many resources. He explains that all the former discussion has not touched the main point, and that this point is—What was Jesus' attitude to God, to the world, and to mankind? What answer did he give to the questions: What matters in the eyes of God? and What is religion? This should indicate that the solution of the problem is contained in what has preceded, and that this solution is unknown to us. But such is not the case. Wernle knows it, and examines it " in the clear light of day." "From his numerous parables and sermons and from countless momentary recollections it comes to us as clearly and

* 83.

distinctly as if Jesus were our contemporary [!]. No man
on earth can say that it is either uncertain or obscure
how Jesus thought on this point, which is to us [viz.,
to the liberal theologians] even at the present day the
chief point." "And if Christianity has forgotten for
a thousand years what its Master desired first and
before all, to-day [*i.e.*, after the clear solutions of
critical theology] it shines on us once more from the
Gospels as clearly and wonderfully, as if the sun were
newly risen, driving before its conquering rays all
the phantoms and shadows of night."* And so Wernle
himself, to whom we owe this consoling assurance, has
written a work, "Die Aufänge unserer Religion"
(1901), which is highly esteemed in theological circles,
and in which he has given a detailed account, in a tone
of overwhelming assurance, of the innermost thoughts,
views, words, and teachings of Jesus and of his followers,
just as if he had been actually present.

We must be careful of our language. These are
indeed the views of a man who must be taken seriously,
with whom we have been dealing above, a "shining
light" of his science! The often cited work on "Die
Quellen des Lebens Jesu" belongs to the series of
"Popular Books on the History of Religion," which
contains the quintessence of present-day theological study,
and which is intended for the widest circles interested
and instructed in religion. We may suppose, probably
with justice, that that work expresses what the liberal
theology of our day wishes the members of the community subject to it to know and to believe. Or is it
only that the popular books on the history of religion
place the intellectual standard of their readers so low
that they think they can strengthen the educated in their
belief in an historical Jesus by productions such as

* 85 *sq.*

Wernle's? We consider the more "scientifically" elaborated works of other important theologians on the same subject. We think of Beyschlag, Harnack, Bernard Weiss, of Pfleiderer, Jülicher, and Holtzmann. We consult Bousset, who defended against Kalthoff, with such great determination and warmth, the existence of an historical Jesus. Everywhere there is the same half-comic, half-pathetic drama : on the one hand the evan-gelical authorities are depreciated and the information is criticised away to such an extent that hardly anything positive remains from it ; on the other hand there is a pathetic enthusiasm for the so-called "historical kernel." Then comes praise for the so-called critical theology and its "courageous truthfulness," which, however, ultimately consists only in declaring evident myths and legends to be such. This was known for a long time previously among the unprejudiced. There usually follows a hymn to Jesus with ecstatic raising of the eyes, as if all the statements concerning him in the Gospels still had validity. What then does Hausrath say ?—" To conceal the miraculous parts of the [evangelical] accounts and then to give out the rest as historical, has not hitherto passed as criticism." * Can we object to Catholic

---

* "Jesus u. d. neutestamentl. Schriftsteller," ii. 43. Let us take the final paragraph in E. Petersen's "Die wunderbare Geburt des Heilandes," which reaches the zenith in proving the mythical nature of the evangelical account of the Saviour's birth : "If, not because we wish it, but because we are forced to do so by the necessity of History, we remove the sentence, 'Conceived of the Holy Ghost, born of the Virgin Mary'—Jesus nevertheless remains the 'Son of God.' He remains such because he experienced God as his father, and because he stands at God's side for us. Also, in spite of our setting aside the miraculous birth as unhistorical, we are quite justi-fied in declaring 'Thou art Christ, the Son of the living God.'" M. Brückner speaks similarly at the close of his otherwise excellent work. "Der sterbende und auferstehende Gottheiland." For the person to whom such phraseology is not—futile, there is no help.

theology because it looks with open pity on the whole of Protestant "criticism," and reproaches it with the inconsistency, incompleteness, and lack of results, which is the mark of all its efforts to discover the beginnings of Christianity.* Is it not right in rejoicing at the blow which Protestantism has sustained and from which it must necessarily suffer through all such attempts at accepting the Gospels as basis for a belief in an historical Jesus? Certainly what Catholic theologians bring forward in favour of the historical Jesus is so completely devoid of any criticism or even of any genuine desire to elucidate the facts, that it would be doing them too much honour to make any more detailed examination of their works on this point. For them the whole problem has a very simple solution in this: the existence of the historical Jesus forms the unavoidable presupposition of the Church, even though every historical fact should register its veto against it; and as one of its writers has put it, that is at bottom the long-established and unanimous view of all our inquiries into the subject under discussion: "The historical testimony for the authenticity of the Gospels is as old, as extensive, and as well established as it is for very few other books of ancient literature [!]. If we do not wish to be inconsistent we cannot question their authenticity. Their credibility is beyond question; for their authors were eye-witnesses of the events [!] related, or they gained their information from such; they were as competent judges [!] as men loving the truth can well be; they could, and in fact were obliged to speak the truth." †

* Cf. "Jesus Christus," a course of lectures delivered at the University of Freiburg i. B., 1908.

† Schäfer, "Die Evangelien und die Evangelienkritik," 1908, 123. The story of the Church's development in the first century is a story of shameless literary falsifications, of rough violence in matters of

How distinguished, as compared with this kind of theologian, Kalthoff seems! It is true that we are obliged to allow for the one-sidedness and insufficiency of his positive working out of the origin of Christianity, of his attempt to explain it, on the basis of Mark's handling of the story, purely on the lines of social motives, and to represent Christ as the mere reflection of the Christian community and of its experiences. Quite certainly he is wrong in identifying the biblical Pilate with Pliny, the governor of Bithynia under Trajan, and in the proof based on this; and this because in all probability Pliny's letter to the Emperor is a later Christian forgery.* But Kalthoff is quite right in what he says about modern critical theology and its historical Jesus. The critical theologians may think themselves justified in treating this embarrassing opponent as "incompetent," or in ignoring him on account of the mistaken basis of argument; but all the efforts made with such great perseverance and penetration by historical theologians to derive from the authorities before us proof of the existence of a man Jesus in the traditional sense have led, as Kalthoff very justly says, to a purely negative conclusion. "The numerous passages in the Gospels which this theology, in maintaining its historical Jesus, is obliged to place on one side and pass over, stand from a literary point of view exactly on the same footing as those passages from which it constructs its historical Jesus; and consequently they claim historical value equal to these latter. The Synoptic Christ, in whom modern

---

faith, of unlimited rial of the credence of the masses. So that for those who know history the iteration of the "credibility" of the Christian writers of the age raises at most but an ironical smile. Cf. Robertson, "History of Christianity," 1910.

* Cf. Hochart, "Études au sujet de la persécution des Chrétiens sous Néron," 1885, cp. 4.

theology thinks it finds the characteristics of the historical Jesus, stands not a hair's breadth nearer to a human interpretation of Christianity than the Christ of the fourth Gospel. What the Epigones of liberal theology think they can distil from this Synoptic Christ as historical essence has historical value only as a monument of masterly sophistry, which has produced its finest examples in the name of theological science."* Historical research should not have so long set apart from all other history that of early Christianity as the special domain of theology and handed it over to churchmen, as if for the decision of the questions on this point quite special talent was necessary—a talent far beyond the ordinary sphere of science and one which was only possessed by the Church theologian. The world would then long since have done with the whole literature of the "Life of Jesus."

The sources which give information of the origin of Christianity are of such a kind that, considering the present standard of historical research, no historian would care to undertake an attempt to produce the biography of an historical Christ.† They are, we can add, of such a nature that a real historian, who meets them without a previous conviction or expectation that he will find an historical Jesus in it, cannot for a moment doubt that he has here to do with religious fiction,‡ with myth

* A. Kalthoff, " Das Christusproblem, Grundzüge zu einer Sozial-theologie," 1902, 14 *sq.*

† Kalthoff, " Die Entstehung des Christentums : Neue Beiträge zum Christusproblem," 1904, 8.

‡ If v. Soden (" Hat Jesus gelebt? " vii. 45) has proved wrong the comparison with the Tell-legend, and thinks I have " probably once more " forgotten that Schiller first transformed a very meagre legend, which was bound up in a single incident, from grey antiquity into a living picture, he can know neither Tschudi nor J. v. Müller. Cf. Hertslet, " Der Treppenwitz der Weltgeschichte," 6 Aufl., 1905, 216 *sqq.*

in an historical form, which does not essentially differ from other myths and legends—such as perhaps the legend of Tell.

SUPPLEMENT : *Jesus in Secular Literature.*

There seems to be but little hope of considerably adding to the weight of the reasons in favour of the historical existence of Jesus by citing documents of secular literature. As is well known, only two passages of the Jewish historian Josephus, and one in each of the Roman historians, Tacitus and Suetonius, must be considered in this connection. As for the testimony of Josephus in his "Antiquities," which was written 93 A.D., the first passage (viz., xviii. 3, 3) is so evidently an after-insertion of a later age, that even Roman Catholic theologians do not venture to declare it authentic, though they always attempt, with pitiful *naïveté,* to support the credibility of pre-Christian documents of this type.* But the other passage, too (xx. 9, 1), which states that James was executed under the authority of the priest Ananos (A.D. 62), and refers to him as "the Brother of Jesus, the so-called Christ," in the opinion of eminent theologians such as Credner,† Schürer,‡ &c., must be regarded as a forgery ; § but

---

* The passage runs : "At this time lived Jesus, a wise man, if he may be called a man, for he accomplished miracles and was a teacher of men who joyously embrace the truth, and he found a great following among Jews and Greeks. This one was the Christ. Although at the accusation of the leading men of our people Pilate sentenced him to the cross, those who had first loved him remained still faithful. For he appeared again to them on the third day, risen again to a new life, as the prophets of God had foretold of him, with a thousand other prophecies. After him are called the Christians, whose sect has not come to an end."

† "Einl. ins N.T.," 1836, 581.

‡ "Gesch. d. jüd. Volkes," i. 548.

§ Origen, though he collected all Josephus' assertions which could

even if its authenticity were established it would still prove nothing in favour of the historical Jesus. For, first, it leaves it undecided whether a bodily relationship is indicated by the word "Brother," or whether, as is much more likely, the reference is merely to a religious brotherhood (see above, 170 *sq*.). Secondly, the passage only asserts that there was a man of the name of Jesus who was called Christ, and this is in no way extraordinary in view of the fact that at the time of Josephus, and far into the second century, many gave themselves out as the expected Messiah.*

The Roman historians' testimony is in no better case than that of Josephus. It is true that Tacitus writes in his "Annals" (xv. 44), in connection with the persecution of the Christians under Nero (64), that "the founder of this sect, Christ, was executed in Tiberius' reign by the procurator Pontius Pilate"; and Suetonius states in his biography of the Emperor Claudius, chap. xxv., that he "drove out of Rome the Jews, who had caused great disturbances at the instigation of Chrestus." What does this prove? Are we so certain that the passage cited from Tacitus as to the persecution of the Christians under Nero is not after all a later insertion and falsification of the original text? This is indeed the case, judging from Hochart's splendid and exhaustive inquiry. In fact, everything points to the idea that the "first persecution of the Christians," which is previously mentioned by no writers, either Jewish or heathen, is nothing but the product of a Christian's imagination in

---

serve as support to the Christian religion, does not know the passage, but probably another, in which the destruction of Jerusalem was represented as a punishment for James' execution, which is certainly a forgery.

* Cf. Kalthoff, "Entstehung d. Chr.," 16 *sq*. As to the whole matter, Schürer, *op. cit.*, 544–549.

the fifth century.* But let us admit the authenticity of Tacitus' assertion; let us suppose also that by Suetonius' Chrestus is really meant Christ and not a popular Jewish rioter of that name; let us suppose that the unrest of the Jews was not connected with the expectation of the Messiah, or that the Roman historian, in his ignorance of the Jewish dreams of the future, did not imagine a leader of the name of Chrestus.† Can writers of the first quarter of the second century after Christ, at which time the tradition was already formed and Christianity had made its appearance in History as a power, be regarded as independent authorities for facts which are supposed to have taken place long before the birth of the Tradition? Tacitus can at most have heard that the Christians were followers of a Christ who was supposed to have been executed under Pontius Pilate. That was probably even at that time in the Gospels—and need not, therefore, be a real fact of history. And if it has been proved, according to Mommsen, that Tacitus took his material from the protocols of the Senate and imperial archives, there has equally been, on the other

---

* V. Soden proves the contrary in his work, " Hat Jesus gelebt ? " (1910), "in order to show the reliability of Drew's assertions," from Clement's letter of 96 A.D., from Dionysius of Corinth (about 170) from Tertullion and Eusebius (early fourth century, not third, as v. Soden writes); and wishes to persuade his readers that the persecution under Nero is testified to. The authenticity of the letter of Clement is, however, quite uncertain, and has been most actively combated, from its first publication in 1633 till the present day, by investigators of repute, such as Semler, Baur, Schwegler, Volkmar, Keim, &c. But as for the above-cited authors, the unimportance of their assertions on the point is so strikingly exhibited by Hochart that we have no right to call them up as witnesses for the authenticity of the passage of Tacitus.

† Cf. Hochart, *op. cit.*, 280 *sqq.*; H. Schiller, "Gesch. d. röm Kaiserzeit," 447, note.

hand, a most definite counter-assertion that he never consulted these authorities.*

Lately, Tacitus proving to be slightly inconsistent, it has been usual to refer to Pliny's letter to the Emperor Trajan, asserting that the historical Jesus is certified to in this. The letter hinges on the question of what Pliny's attitude as Governor of Bithynia must be to the Christians; so that naturally the Christians are much spoken of, and once even there is mention of Christ, whose followers sing alternate hymns to him " as to a God " (quasi deo). But Jesus as an historical person is not once mentioned in the whole letter; and Christ was even for Paul a " Quasi-god," a being fluctuating between man and God. What then is proved by the letter of Pliny as to the historical nature of Jesus? It only proves the liberal theologians' dilemma over the whole question, that they think they can cite these witnesses

* " Consulting the archives has been but little customary among ancient historians; and Tacitus has bestowed but little consideration on the Acta Diurna and the protocols of the Senate " (" Handb. d. klass. Altertumsw.," viii., 2 Abt., Aft. 2, under " Tacitus "). Moreover, the difficulties of the passage from Tacitus have been fully realised by German historians (H. Schiller, *op. cit.*, 449; " De. Gesch. d. röm Kaiserreiches unter der Regierung des Nero," 1872, 434 *sqq.*, 583 *sq.*), even if they do not generally go as far as to say that the passage is completely unauthentic, as Volney did at the end of the eighteenth century (" Ruinen," Reclam, 276). Cf. also Arnold, " Die neronische Christenverfolgung. Eine historiche Untersuchung zur Geschichte d. ältesten Kirche," 1888. The author does indeed adhere to the authenticity of the passage in Tacitus, but as a matter of fact he presupposes it rather than attempts to prove it; while in many isolated reflections he gives an opinion against the correctness of the account given by Tacitus, and busies himself principally in disproving false inferences connected with that passage, such as the connection of the Neronic persecution with the Book of Revelation. The conceivable possibility that the persecution actually took place, but that at all events the sentence of Tacitus may be a Christian interpolation, Arnold seems never to have considered.

again and again for strengthening the belief in an historical Jesus, as, *e.g.* Melhorn does in his work " Wahrheit und Dichtung im Leben Jesu " (in " Aus Natur und Geisteswelt," 1906), trying to make it appear that these witnesses are in any way worthy of consideration. Joh. Weiss also—according to the newspaper account —in his lecture on Christ in the Berlin vacation-course of March, 1910, confessed that " statements from secular literature as to the historical nature of Jesus which are absolutely free of objection are very far from having been authenticated." Even an orthodox theologian like Kropatscheck writes in the " Kreuzzeitung " (April 7, 1910): " It is well known that the non-Christian writers in a very striking way ignore the appearing of Christ. The few small notices in Tacitus, Suetonius, &c., are easily enumerated. Though we date our chronology from him, his advent made no impression at all on the great historians of his age. The Talmud gives a hostile caricature of his advent which has no historical value. The Jewish historian, Flavius Josephus, from whom we might have expected information of the first rank, is absolutely silent. We are referred to our Gospels, as Paul also says little of the life of Jesus; and we can understand how it is that attempts are always being made to remove him, as an historical person, from the past." The objection to this, that the secular writers, even though they give no positive testimony for Jesus' historical existence, have never brought it in question, is of very little strength. For the writings considered in it, viz., Justin's conversation with the Jew Trypho, as well as the polemical work of Celsus against Christianity, both belong to the latter half of the second century, while the passages in the Talmud referred to are probably of a later date, and all these passages are merely based on the tradition. So that this "proof from silence" is in reality no proof. It is, rather, necessary to explain why the whole of the first century, apart from the Gospels, seems to know nothing of Jesus as an historical personality. The Frenchman Hochart ridicules the theological attitude: "It seems that the most distinguished men lose a part of their brilliant character in the study of martyrology. Let us leave it to German theologians to study history in their way. We Frenchmen wish throughout our inquiries to preserve our clearness of mind and healthy common-sense. Let us not invent new legends about Nero: there are really too many already."*

(b) The Objections against a Denial of the Historicity of the Synoptic Jesus.

There the matter ends : we know nothing of Jesus, of an historical personality of that name to whom the events and speeches recorded in the Gospels refer. "In default of any historical certainty the name of Jesus has become for Protestant theology an empty vessel, into which that theology pours the content of its own meditations."† And if there is any excuse for this, it is that that name has never at any time been anything but such an empty vessel : Jesus, the Christ, the Deliverer, Saviour, Physician of oppressed souls, has been from first to last a figure borrowed from myth, to whom the desire for redemption and the naïve faith of the Western Asiatic peoples have transferred all their conceptions of the soul's welfare. The "history" of this Jesus in its general characteristics had been determined even before the evangelical Jesus. Even Weinel, one of the most zealous and enthusiastic adherents of the modern Jesus-worship,

---

* *Op. cit.*, 227.
† Kalthoff, "Christusproblem," 17.

confesses that " Christology was almost completed before Jesus came on earth."*

It was not, however, merely the general frame and out-lines of the "history" of Jesus which had been determined in the Messiah-faith, in the idea of a divine spirit sent from God, of the "Son of Man" of Daniel and the Jewish Apocalyptics, &c., not merely that this vague idea was filled out with new content through the Redeemer-worship of the neighbouring heathen peoples. Besides this, many of the individual traits of the Jesus-figure were present, some in heathen mythology, some in the Old Testament; and they were taken thence and worked into the evangelical representation. There is, for instance, the story of the twelve-year old Jesus in the Temple. " Who would have invented this story? " asks Jeremias. " Nevertheless," he thinks it " probable " that in this Luke was thinking of Philo's description of the life of Moses; he calls to mind that Plutarch gives us a quite similar statement concerning Alexander, whose life was consciously decorated with all the traits of the Oriental King-redeemer.† Perhaps, however, the account comes from a Buddhist origin. The account of the temptation of Jesus also sounds very much like the temptation of Buddha, so far as it is not derived from the temptation of Zarathustra by Ahriman‡ or the temptation of Moses by the devil, of which the Rabbis told,§ while Jesus is said to have entered upon his ministry in his thirtieth year,|| because at that age the Levite was fitted for his sacred office.¶ Till then (*i.e.*, till his baptism) we learn nothing

---

* Weinel, " Jesus im 19 Jahrhundert," 1907, 68.
† " Babylonisches im Neuen Testament," 109 *sq.*
‡ " Zerduscht Nameh," ch. xxvi.
§ Gfrörer, " Jahrhundert des Heils," Part II., 380 *sqq.*
|| Luke iii. 23.
¶ Numb. iv. 3.

of Jesus' life. Similarly Isa. liii. 2, jumps from the early youth of the Servant of God (" He grew up as a tender plant, as a root out of a dry ground: he hath no form nor comeliness, is despised and rejected of men ") straight to his passion and death ; while the Gospels attempt to fill in the interval from Jesus' baptism up to his passion by painting in further so-called Messianic passages from the Old Testament and Words of Jesus. We know how the early Christians liked to rediscover their faith in the Scriptures and see it predicted, and with what zeal they consequently studied the Old Testament and altered the " history " of their Jesus to make it agree with those predictions, thus rendering it valuable as corroboration of their own notions. In this connection it has been shown above how the " ride of the beardless one " influenced the collection of the tribute and his direct attack on the shop-keepers and money-changers in the evangelical account of Jesus' advent to the Temple at Jerusalem.* But the more detailed development of this scene is determined by Zech. ix. 9, Mal. iii. 1–3, and Isa. i. 10 *sqq.*, and the words placed in Jesus' mouth on this occasion are taken from Isa. lvi. 7 and Jer. vii. 1 *sqq.*, so that this " most im-portant " event in Jesus' life can lay no claim to historical actuality.†

And again the account of the betrayal, of the thirty pieces of silver, and of Judas' death, have their source in the Old Testament, viz., in the betrayal and death of Ahitophel.‡ To what extent in particular the figures of Moses, with reference to Deut. xviii. 15 and xxxiv. 10, of

---

* Matt. xxi. 12 *sqq.*

† Zech. xiv. 21 runs in the Targum translation : "Every vessel in Jerusalem will be consecrated to the Lord, &c., and at that time there will no longer be shopkeepers in the House of the Lord." In this there may have been a further inducement for the Evangelists to state that Jesus chases the tradesmen from the Temple.

2 Sam. xvii. 23 ; cf. also Zech. xi. 12 *sq.* ; Psa. xli. 10.

Joshua, of Elijah and Elisha, influenced the portrayal of the evangelical Jesus has also been traced even by the theological party.* Jesus has to begin his activities through baptism in the Jordan, because Moses had begun his leadership of Israel with the passage through the Red Sea and Joshua at the time of the Passover led the people through the Jordan, and this passage (of the sun through the watery regions of the sky) was regarded as baptism.† He has to walk on the water, even as Moses, Joshua, and Elias walked dryshod through the water. He has to awaken the dead, like Elijah;‡ to surround himself with twelve or seventy disciples and apostles, just as Moses had surrounded himself with twelve chiefs of the people and seventy elders, and as Joshua had chosen twelve assistants at the passage of the Jordan;§ he has to be transfigured,‖ and to ascend into heaven like Moses¶ and Elijah.** Elijah (Eli-scha) and Jeho-schua (Joshua, Jesus) agree even in their names, so that on this ground alone it would not have been strange if the Prophet of the Old Testament had served as prototype of his evangelical namesake.†† Now Jesus places himself in many ways above the Mosaic Law, especially above the commands as to food,‡‡ and in this at least one might find a trait answering to reality. But in the Rabbinical writings we find : " It is written, §§ the Lord sets loose

* Gförer, "Jahr. d. Heils," ii. 318 *sqq.*
† Cf. 1 Cor. x. 1 *sq.*
‡ 2 Kings iv. 19 *sqq.*
§ Numb. i. 44 ; Jos. iii. 12 ; iv. 1 *sqq.* Cf. " Petrus-legende," 51 *sq.*
‖ Cf. p. 127, note.
¶ Josephus, " Antiq.," iv. 8, 48 ; Philo, " Vita Mos.," iii.
** 2 Kings ii. 11.
†† *E.g.* also the account of the arrest of Jesus (Matt. xxvi. 51 *sqq.*) cf. 2 Kings vi. 10–22.
‡‡ Matt. ix. 11 *sq.*, xii. 8 *sq.*, xv. 1 *sqq.*, 11 and 20, xxviii. 18.
§§ Psa. cxlvi. 7.

that which is bound; for every creature that passes as unclean in this world, the Lord will pronounce clean in the next." * So that similarly the disposition of the Law belongs to the general characteristics of the Messiah, and cannot be historical of Jesus, because if it were the attitude of the Jewish Christians to Paul on account of his disposition of the Law would be incomprehensible.† The contrary attitude, which is likewise represented by Jesus, ‡ was already foreseen in the Messianic expectation. For while some hoped for a lightening and amendment of the Law by the Messiah, others thought of its aggravation and completion. In Micah iv. 5 the Messiah was to exert his activity, not merely among the Jews, but also among the Gentiles, and the welfare of the kingdom of the Messiah was to extend also to the latter. According to Isaiah lx. and Zechariah xiv., on the contrary, the Gentiles were to be subjected and brought to nothing, and only the Jews were worthy of participation in the kingdom of God. For that reason Jesus had to declare himself with like determination for both conceptions, § without any attempt being made to reconcile the contradiction contained in this.‖ That the parents of Jesus were called Joseph and Mary, and that his father was a " carpenter," were determined by tradition, just as the name of his birthplace, Nazareth, was occasioned by the name of a sect (Nazaraios=Protector), or by the fact that one sect honoured the Messiah as a " branch of the root of Jesse " (nazar Isai).¶ It was a Messianic tradition that he began his activity in Galilee and wandered about

* Bereshith Rabba zu Gen. xli. 1.
† Cf. esp. Acts xi. 2 .
‡ Matt. v. 17 *sqq.*
§ *Id.* viii. 11 *sqq.*, x. 5, xxiii. 34 *sqq.*, xxviii. 19 *sqq.*
‖ Cf. Lützelberger, "Jesus, was er war und wollte," 1842, 16 *sqq.*
¶ Cf. above, 59 *sqq.*

as Physician, Saviour, Redeemer, and Prophet, as mediator of the union of Israel, and as one who brought
light to the Gentiles, not as an impetuous oppressor full
of inconsiderate strength, but as one who assumed a
loving tenderness for the weak and despairing.* He
heals the sick, comforts the afflicted, and proclaims to the
poor the Gospel of the nearness of the kingdom of God.
That is connected with the wandering of the sun through
the twelve Signs of the Zodiac (Galil=circle), and is based
on Isa. xxxv. 5 *sqq.*, xlii. 1–7, xlix. 9 *sqq.*, as well as on
Isa. lxi. 1, a passage which Jesus himself, according
to Luke iv. 16 *sqq.*, began his teaching in Nazareth by
explaining.† He had to meet with opposition in his
work of salvation, and nevertheless endure patiently,
because of Isa. l. 5. Naturally Jesus, behind whose
human nature was concealed a God, and to whom the
pilgrim " Saviour " Jason corresponded, ‡ was obliged to
reveal his true nature by miraculous healing, and could
not take a subordinate place in this regard among the
cognate heathen God-redeemers. At most we may
wonder that even in this the Old Testament had to
stand § as a model, and that Jesus' doings never surpass
those which the heathens praise in their gods and heroes,
e.g., Asclepius. Indeed, according to Tacitus‖ even the
Emperor Vespasian accomplished such miracles at Alexandria, where, on being persistently pressed by the people,
he healed both a lame man and a blind, and this almost

---

* It is given as a reason for his appearing first in Galilee that the
Galileans were first led into exile, and so should first be comforted,
as all divine action conforms to the law of requital (Gfrörer,
"Jahr. d. Heils," 230 *sq.* Cf. also Isa. viii. 23).

† Cf. above, 173 *sq.*

‡ See above, 171.

§ Exod. xvi. 17 *sqq.*; Numb. xxi. 1 *sqq.*; ⸢Exod. vii. 17 *sqq.*
1 Kings xvii. 5 *sqq.*

‖ "Hist.," iv. 81.

in the same way as Jesus did, by moistening their eyes and cheeks with spittle; which information is corroborated also by Suetonius* and Dio Cassius.† But *the* most marvellous thing is that the miracles of Jesus have been found worth mentioning by the critical theology, and that there is an earnest search for an "historical nucleus," which might probably "underlie them."

All the individual characteristics cited above are, however, unimportant in comparison with the account of the Last Supper, of the Passion, death (on the cross), and resurrection of Jesus. And yet what is given us on these points is quite certainly unhistorical; these parts of the Gospels owe their origin, as we have stated, merely to cult-symbolism and to the myth of the dying and rising divine Saviour of the Western Asiatic religions. No "genius" was necessary for their invention, as everything was given: the derision,‡ the flagellation, both the thieves, the crying out on the cross, the sponge with vinegar (Psa. lxix. 22), the piercing with a lance,§ the soldiers casting dice for the dead man's garments, also the women at the place of execution and at the grave, the grave in a rock, are found in just the same form in the worship of Adonis, Attis, Mithras, and Osiris. Even the Saviour carrying his cross is copied from Hercules (Simon of Cyrene),|| bearing the pillars crosswise, as well as from the story of Isaac, who carried his own wood to the altar on which he was to be sacrificed.¶ But where the authors of the Gospels have really found something new, *e.g.,* in the account of Jesus' trial, of the Roman and Jewish procedure, they have worked it out in such an ignorant way, and to one who knows something about it

* "Vespasian," vii.   ‡ lxvi. 8.
‡ Isa. 1. 6 sq.   § Zech. xii. 10.
|| Cf. "Petruslegende," 24.
¶ Gen xxvi. 6; cf. also Tertullian, "Adv. Jud.," 10.

16

betray so significantly the purely fictitious nature of their account, that here really there is nothing to wonder at except perhaps the *naïvéte* of those who still consider that account historical, and pique themselves a little on their "historical exactness" and "scientific method." *

Is not Robertson perhaps right after all in considering the whole statement of the last fate of Jesus to be the re-writing of a dramatic Mystery-play, which among the Gentile Christians of the larger cities followed the sacramental meal on Easter Day? We know what a great rôle was played by dramatic representations in numerous cults of antiquity, and how they came into especial use in connection with the veneration of the suffering and rising God-redeemers. Thus in Egypt the passion, death, and resurrection of Osiris and the birth of Horus; at Eleusis the searching and lamentation of Demeter for her lost Persephone and the birth of Iacchus; at Lernæ in Argolis and many other places the fate of Dionysus (Zagreus); in Sicyon the suffering of Adrastos, who threw himself on to the funeral pyre of his father Hercules; at Amyclæ the passing away of Nature and its new life in the fate of Hyacinth: these were celebrated in festal

---

* Cf. for this Brandt, " Die Evangelische Geschichte," esp. 53 *sqq.* Even such a cautious investigator as Gfrörer confesses that, after his searching examination of the historical content of the Synoptics, he is obliged to close " with the sad admission " that their testimony does not give sufficient assurance to enable us to pronounce anything they contain to be true, so far as they are concerned, with a good historical conscience. " In this it is by no means asserted that many may not think their views correct, but only that we cannot rely on them sufficiently to rest a technically correct proof on them alone. They tell us too many things which are purely legendary, and too many others which are at least suspicious, for a prudent historian to feel justified in a construction based on their word alone. This admission may be disagreeable—it is also unpleasant to me—but it is genuine, and it is demanded by the rules which hold everywhere before a good tribunal, and in the sphere of history " (" Die hl. Sage," 1838, ii. 243).

pageants and scenic representations, to say nothing of the feasts of the death and resurrection of Mithras, Attis, and Adonis. Certainly Matthew's account, xx.–xxviii. (with the exception of verses 11–15 in the last chapter), with its connected sequence of events, which could not possibly have actually followed each other like this—Supper, Gethsemane, betrayal, passion, Peter's denial, the crucifixion, burial, and resurrection—throughout gives one the impression of a chain of isolated dramatic scenes. And the close of the Gospel agrees very well with this conception, for the parting words and exhortations of Jesus to his people are a very suitable ending to a drama.*

If we allow this, an explanation is given of the " clearness " which is so generally praised in the style of the Gospels by the theologians and their following, and which many think sufficient by itself to prove the historical nature of the Synoptic representation of Jesus.

Of course, Wrede has already warned us "not too hastily to consider clearness a sign of historical truth. A writing may have a very secondary, even apocryphal character, and yet show much clearness. The question always is how this was obtained." † Wernle and Wrede quite agree that at least in Mark's production the clear-

---

* This is the case with the corresponding account in Mark, while in Luke the dramatic presentation seems to be more worked away, and the coherence, through the introduction of descriptions and episodes (disciples at Emmaus) bears more the character of a simple narrative. Cf. Robertson, " Pagan Christs," 186 *sqq.* ; " A Short History," 87 *sqq.* The fact that in almost all representations of this kind both the scene at Gethsemane and the words spoken by Jesus usually serve as signs of his personality (*e.g.* also Bousset's " Jesus "— "Rel. Volksb.," 1904, 56), shows what we must think of the historical value of the accounts of the life of Jesus ; especially when we consider that certainly no listeners were there, and Jesus cannot himself have told his experience to his disciples, as the arrest is supposed to have taken place on the spot.

† " Messiasgeheimnis," 143.

ness is of no account at all, while clearness in the other
Gospels is found just in those parts which admittedly
belong to the sphere of legend. And how clearly and
concretely do not our authors of the various "Lives of
Jesus," not to mention Renan, or our ministers in the
pulpits describe the events of the Gospels, with how many
small and attractive traits do they not decorate these
events, in order that they should have a greater effect on
their listeners! This kind of clearness and personal
stamp is really nothing but a matter of the literary skill
and imagination of the authors in question. The writings
of the Old Testament, and not merely the historical
writings, are also full of a most clear ability for narration
and of most individual characteristics, which prove how
much the Rabbinical writers in Palestine knew of this
side of literary activity. Or is anything wanting to the
clearness and individual characterisation, to which Kalthoff also has alluded, of the touching story of Ruth; of
the picture of the prophet Jonah, of Judith, Esther,
Job, &c? And then the stories of the patriarchs—
the pious Abraham, the good-natured, narrow-minded
Esau, the cunning Jacob, and their respective wives—
or, to take one case, how clear is not the meeting of
Abraham's servant with Rebecca at the well!* Or
let us consider Moses, Elijah, Samson—great figures
who in their most essential traits demonstrably belong to
myth and religious fable! If in preaching our ministers
can go so vividly into the details of the story of the
Saviour that fountains of poetry are opened and there
stream forth from their lips clear accounts of Jesus' goodness of heart, of his heroic greatness, and of his readiness
for the sacrifice, how much more would this have been
so at first in the Christian community, when the new
religion was still in its youth, when the faith in the

* Gen. xxiv.

Messiah was as yet unweakened by sceptical doubts, and when the heart of man was still filled with the desire for immediate and final redemption? And even if we are confronted with a host of minor traits, which cannot so easily be accounted for by religious motives and poetic imagination, must these all refer to the same real personality? May they not be based on events which are very far from being necessarily experiences of the liberal theology's historical Jesus? Even Edward v. Hartmann, who is generally content to adhere to the historical Jesus, suggests the possibility "that several historical personages, who lived at quite different times, have contributed concrete individual characteristics to the picture of Jesus."* There is a great deal of talk about the "uninventable" in the evangelical representation. Von. Soden even goes so far as to base his chief proof for the historical existence of Jesus on this individuality that cannot be invented.† As if there was any such thing as what cannot be invented for men with imagination! And as if all the significant details of Jesus' life were not invented on the lines of the so-called Messianic passages in the Old Testament, in heathen mythology, and in the imported conceptions of the Messiah! The part that is professedly "uninventable" shrinks continuously the more assiduously criticism busies itself with the Gospels; and the word can at present apply only to side-issues and matters of no importance. We are indeed faced with the strange fact, that all the essential part of the Gospels, everything which is of importance for religious faith, such as especially the passion, death, and resurrection of Jesus, is demonstrably invented and mythical; but such parts as can at best only be historical because of their supposed "uninventable"

* E. v. Hartmann, "Das Christentum des Neuen Testaments," 1905, 22.
† *Op. cit.*

nature are of no importance for the character of the Gospel representation !

Now, it has been shown that the Gospel picture of Jesus is not without deficiencies. We may see a proof * of the historical nature of the events referred to in small traits, as, for example, in Jesus' temporary inability to perform miracles,† the circumstance that he is not represented as omniscient,‡ the attitude of his relatives to him.§ So the theologian Schmiedel set up first five and then nine passages as " clearly credible," and pronounced these to be the basis of a really scientific knowledge of Jesus. The passages are Mark x. 17 *sqq.* (Why callest thou me good ?), Matt. xii. 31 *sqq.* (The sin against the Holy Ghost shall not be forgiven), Mark iii. 21 (He is beside himself), Mark xiii. 32 (But the day and the hour is known to no man), Mark xv. 24 (My God, why has thou forsaken me ?), Mark vi. 5 (And he could there do no mighty work), Mark viii. 12 (There shall no sign be given unto this generation), Mark viii. 14–21 (Reproaching the disciples on the occasion of the lack of bread), Matt. xi. 5 (The blind see, the lame walk). All these " bases " evidently have a firm support only on the supposition that the Gospels are meant to paint a stainless ideal, a God, that they are at most but a conception, such, perhaps, as has been set up by Bruno Bauer. But they are useless from the point of view intended, as portraying a man. If, however, the Evangelists' intention was to paint the celestial Christ of the Apostle Paul, the God-man, the abstract spirit-being, as a completely real man for the eyes of the faithful, to place him on the ground of historical reality, and so to treat seriously Paul's "idea" of humanity, they were obliged to give him also human characteristics. And these could be either invented afresh

---

* Cf. H. Jordan, " Jesus und die modernen Jesusbilder, Bibl. Zeit- u. Streitfragen," 1909, 88.

† Mark vi. 1 *sq.*   ‡ Mark xiii. 32.   § Mark iii. 20.

or taken from the actual life of honoured teachers, in
which the fact is acknowledged that, even for the noblest
and best of men, there are hours of despair and grief,
that the prophet is worth nothing in his own fatherland,
or is even unknown to his nearest relatives. Even the
prophet Elijah, the Old Testament precursor of the
Messiah, who has in many ways determined the picture
of Jesus, is said to have had moments of despair in which
he wanted to die, till God strengthened him anew to the
fulfilment of his vocation.* Moreover, Mark x. 17 was
a commonplace in all ancient philosophy from the
time of Plato, and gained that form by an alteration
of the original text (A. Pott, "Der Text des Neuen
Testaments nach seiner gesch. Entwicklung" in "Aus
Natur und Geisteswelt," 1906, p. 63, *sq.*); Mark xiv.
24 is taken from the 22nd Psalm, which has also in other
respects determined the details of the account of the
crucifixion. Mark iii. 21 is, as Schleiermacher showed
and Strauss corroborated, a pure invention of the Evangelist, the words of the Pharisees being put into their
mouths, as their opinion, in order to explain Jesus'
answer by the assertion of his kinship (Strauss, "Leben
Jesu," i. 692; cf. also Psa. lix. 1: "I am become a
stranger unto my brethren, and an alien unto my
mother's children"). Matt. xi. 5 is based on Isaiah
xxxv. 5, xlii. 7, xlix. 9, lxi. 1, which runs in the
Septuagint: "The spirit of the Lord is upon me;
because the Lord hath anointed me to preach good
tidings unto the poor; he hath sent me to bind up the
broken-hearted, to proclaim liberty to the captives, and to
the blind the opening of their eyes; to proclaim the
acceptable year of the Lord, and the day of vengeance of
our God; to comfort all that mourn." † Schmiedel's

---

* 1 Kings xix.; cf. also Isa. xlii. 4.

† Cf. Brandt, *op. cit.*, 553 *sq.*

nine "bases" consequently are at most testimony to a "lost glory"; but the construction of a "really scientific" life of Jesus cannot possibly arise from them.*

Clearness of exposition, then, can never afford a proof of the historical nature of the matter concerned. And how easily is not this clearness imported by us into the evangelical information! We are brought up in the atmosphere of these tales, and carry about with us, under the influence of the surrounding Christianity, an imaginary picture of them, which we unwittingly introduce into our reading of the Gospels. And how subjective and dependent on the reader's "taste" the impression of clearness given by the Gospel picture of Jesus is, to what a great extent personal predilections come in, is evidenced by this fact, that a Vollers could not discover in the Gospels any real man of flesh and blood, but only a "shadowy image," which he analysed into a thaumaturgical (the miracle-worker) and a soteriological (the Saviour) part.† In opposition to the efforts of the historical theology to give Jesus a "unique" position above that of all other founders of religions, Vollers justly remarks how difficult it must be for the purely historical treatment to recognise these and similar assertions. "The improbability, not to say impossibility, of the soteriological picture is too obvious. At bottom this picture of critical theology is nothing but the contemporary transformation of Schleiermacher's ideal man; what must have a hundred years ago appeared comprehensible as the product of a refined Moravianism, in the atmosphere of Fichte, Schelling, and Hegel, is nowadays a mere avoidance of an open and honourable analysis from the point of view that prevails outside of theology, and is principally

---

* Hertlein treats of these Bases of Schmiedel in the " Prot. Monats-heften," 1906, 386 *sq.*; cf. also Schmiedel's reply.

† *Op. cit.*, 141.

known in the spheres of Nature and of History. Who would
deny that the tone of the catechism and of the pulpit,
that full-sounding words of many meanings, even the
concealment and glossing over of unpleasant admissions,
play a part in this sphere such as they could never have in
in any other science? "

We are then reduced to the individual maxims and sermons of Jesus. These must be proved to be intelligible only
as the personal experiences and thoughts of one supreme
individual. Unfortunately just this, as has already been
proved, seems peculiarly doubtful. As for Jesus' sermons,
we have already understood from Wernle that they were
in any case not received from Jesus in the form in which
they have been handed down to us, but were subsequently
compiled by the Evangelists from isolated and occasional
maxims of his.* These single phrases and occasional
utterances of Jesus are supposed to have been taken in
the last resort partly from oral tradition, partly from the
Aramaic collection—that "great source" of Wernle's—
which was translated into Greek by the Gospels. The
existence of this source has been established only very
indirectly, and we know absolutely nothing more of it.
But it is self-evident that even in the translation from
one language into another much of the originality of
those "words of the Lord" must have been lost; and,
as may be shown, the different Evangelists have "translated" the same words quite differently. Whether it
will be possible to reconstruct the original work, as
critical theology is striving to do, from the material
before us, seems very questionable. And we are given

---

* Bousset agrees with this in his work "Was wissen wir von
Jesus?" (1901). "Jesus' speeches are for the most part creations of
the communities, placed together by the community from isolated
words of Jesus." "In this, apart from all the rest, there was a powerful and decided alteration of the speeches" (47 *sqq.*).

no guarantee that we have to do with actual "words of
the Lord" as they were contained in the Aramaic collection.

Even if the Evangelist is supposed to have expressed
the original meaning, what is to assure us that this
phrase was spoken by Jesus just in this way, and not in
other connections, if even the phrases were taken down
as soon as uttered ? But this is admittedly supposed not
to have occurred till after Jesus' death, after his Messianic
significance was clearly recognised, and after people were
making efforts to go back in memory to the Master's
figure and preserve of his sayings any that were serviceable. Bousset, indeed, in his work, "Was wissen wir
von Jesus ? "—which was directed against Kalthoff—has
referred to the "good Oriental memory of the disciples."
All who know the East from personal experience are
in tolerable agreement on one point, viz., how little an
Oriental is able to repeat what he has heard or experienced
in a true and objective fashion. Consequently there are
in the East no historical traditions in our sense of the
word, but all important events are decorated like a novel,
and are changed according to the necessities of the
moment. Such maxims, indeed, as "Love your enemies,"
" To give is more blessed than to receive," " No one but
God is good," " Blessed are the poor," " You are the
light of the world," " Give to Cæsar that which is
Cæsar's," &c., once heard may be " not easily forgotten,"
as the theological phrase runs. But also they are not of
such a kind that the Jesus of liberal theology was necessary for their invention.

We need not here take into consideration how many of
Jesus' expressions may have been imported into the Gospels from the Mystery drama, with whose existence we
must nevertheless reckon, and from which phrases may
have been changed into sayings of the " historical " Jesus.

Such obscure and high-flown passages as, *e.g.*, Matt. x. 32 *sq.*; xi. 15–30, xxvi. 64, and xxviii. 18, give one the impression of coming from the mouth of God's representative on the stage ; and this probability is further increased when we meet quite similar expressions, such as of the "light burden" and the "easy yoke," in the Mysteries of Mithras or of Isis.* Bousset admits that all the individual words which have been handed down to us as expressions of Jesus are "mediated by the tradition of a community, and have passed through many hands." † They are, as Strauss has observed, like pebbles which the waves of tradition have rolled and polished, setting them down here and there and uniting them to this and that mass. "We are," Steck remarks, "absolutely certain of no single word of the Gospels—that it was spoken by Jesus just in this way and in no other." ‡ "It would be very difficult," thinks Vollers, "to refer even one expression, one parable, one act of this ideal man to Jesus of Nazareth with historical certainty, let us say with the same certainty with which we attribute the Epistle to the Galatians to the Apostle Paul, or explain the Johannine Logos as the product of Greek philosophy." § Even one of the leaders of Protestant orthodoxy, Professor Kähler, of Halle, admitted, as was stated in the "Kirchliche Monatsblatt für Rheinland und Westfalen," in a theological conference held in Dortmund, that we possess "no single authentic word" of Jesus. Any attempt, such as Chamberlain has made, to gather from the tradition a certain nucleus of "words of Jesus," is consequently mistaken ; and if nothing is to be a criterion but one's personal feelings, it would be better

* Cf. Robertson, "Christianity and Mythology," 424 *sqq.*, 429.
† *Op. cit.*, 43.
‡ "Protest. Monatshefte," 1903, Märzheft.
§ *Op. cit.*, 161 *sq.*

to confess at once that here there can be no talk of any kind of decision.

It is, then, settled that we cannot with certainty trace back to an historical Jesus any single one of the expressions of the "Lord" that have come down to us. Even the oldest authority, the Aramaic collection, may have contained merely the tradition of a community. Can we then think that the supporters of an "historical" Jesus are right in treating it as nothing more than a "crude sin against all historical methods," as something most monstrous and unscientific, if one draws the only possible inference from the result of the criticism of the Gospels, and disputes the existence at any time of an historical Jesus? There may after all have been such a collection of "words of the Lord" in the oldest Christian communities; but must we understand by this words of a definite human individual? May they not rather have been words which had an authoritative and canonical acceptation in the community, being either specially important or congenial to it, and which were for this reason attributed to the "Lord"—that is, to the hero of the association or cult, Jesus? It has been generally agreed that this was the case, for example, with the directions as to action in the case of quarrels among the members of the community * and with regard to divorce.† Let us also recall to our minds the "words of the Lord" in the other cult-associations of antiquity, the αὐτὸς ἔφα of the Pythagoreans. And how many particularly popular, impressive, and favourite sayings were current in antiquity bearing the names of one of the "Seven Wise Men," without any one dreaming of ascribing to them an historical signification! How then can it be anything but hasty and uncritical to give out the "words of the Lord" in the collection, which are the basis of Jesus' sermons in the

* Matt. xviii. 15 sqq. † Id. xxix. 3 sqq.

Gospels, as sayings of one definite Rabbi—that is, of the "historical" Jesus? One may have as high an opinion of Jesus' words as one likes: the question is whether Jesus, even the Jesus of liberal theology, is their spiritual father, or whether they are not after all in the same position as the psalms or sayings of the Old Testament which are current in the names of David and Solomon, and of which we know quite positively that their authors were neither the one nor the other.

But perhaps those sayings and sermons of Jesus are of such a nature that they could only arise from the "historical Jesus"? Of a great number both of isolated sayings and parables of Jesus—and among these indeed the most beautiful and the most admired, for example, the parable of the good Samaritan, whose moral content coincides with Deut. xxix. 1–4, of the Prodigal Son,[*] of the man that sowed—we know that they were borrowed[†] partly from Jewish philosophy, partly from oral tradition of the Talmud, and partly from other sources. In any case they have no claim to originality.[‡] This holds good even of the Sermon on the Mount, which is, as has been shown by Jewish scholars in particular, and as Robertson has once more proved, a mere patchwork taken from ancient Jewish literature, and, together with the Lord's Prayer, contains not a single thought which has not its prototype in the Old Testament and in the ancient philosophical maxims of the Jewish people.[§] Moreover, the remaining portions, whose genesis from any other quarter is at least as yet unproved, is not at all of such a nature that it could only have arisen in the mind

---

[*] Cf. Pfleiderer, "Urchristentum," i. 447 *sq.*; van den Bergh van Eysinga, *op. cit.*, 57 *sqq.*   [†] Smith, *op. cit.*, 107 *sqq.*

[‡] Cf. Nork, "Rabbinische Quellen und Parallelen zu neutestamentlichen Schriftstellen," 1839.

[§] Cf. Robertson, "Christianity and Mythology," 440–457.

of such a personality as the theological Jesus of Nazareth. At bottom, indeed, he neither said nor taught anything beyond the purer morality of contemporary Judaism—to say nothing at all of the Stoics and of the other ethical teachers of antiquity, in particular those of the Indians. The gravest suspicion of their novelty and originality is awakened at the Gospels' emphasising the novelty and significance of Jesus' sayings by " the ancients said "— " but I say unto you "; attempting thereby to make an artificial contradiction with the former spiritual and moral standpoint of Judaism, even in places where only a look at the Old Testament is necessary to convince us that such a contradiction does not exist, as, for example, in the case of the love of God and of one's neighbour.* Moreover, our cultivated reverence for Jesus and the overwhelming glorification of everything connected with him has surrounded a great many of the " words of the Lord " with a glitter of importance which stands in no relation to their real value, and which they would never have obtained had they been handed down to us in another connection or under some other name.

Let us only think how much that is in itself quite trivial and insignificant has been raised to quite an unjustifiable importance merely through the use of the pulpit and the consecration of divine service. Even though our theologians are not already tired of extolling the " uniqueness," incomparability, and majesty of Jesus' words and parables, they might nevertheless just for once

---

* Cf. v. Hartmann, *op. cit.*, 131–143. It will always be a telling argument against the historical nature of the sayings of Jesus that Paul seems to know nothing of them, that he never refers to them exactly; and that even up to the beginning of the second century, with the exception of a few remarks in Clement and Polycarp, the Apostles and Fathers in all their admonitions, consolations, and reprimands, never make use of Jesus' sayings to give greater force to their own words.

consider how much that is of little worth, how much that is mistaken, spiritually insignificant and morally insufficient, even absolutely doubtful, there is in what Jesus preached.* In this connection it has always been the custom to extenuate the tradition by referring to the inexactitude or to fly in the face of any genuine historical method by tortuous elucidations of the passages in question, by unmeaning references to the temporal and educational limitations even of the " superman," and by suppression of the disagreeable parts.

How much trouble have not our theologians taken, and do they not even now take, to show even one single point in Jesus' doctrines which may justify their declaring with a good conscience his "uniqueness" in the sense understood by them, and may justify their raising their purely human Jesus as high as possible above his own age ! Not one of all the passages quoted to this end has been allowed to remain. The Synoptic Jesus taught neither a new and loftier morality, nor a " new meekness," nor a deepened consciousness of God; neither the "indestructible value of the individual souls of men " in the present-day individualistic sense, nor even freedom as against the Jewish Law, nor the immanence of the kingdom of God, nor anything else, that surpassed the capabilities of another intellectually distinguished man of his age. Even the love, the general love, of one's neighbour, the preaching of which is with the greater portion of the laity the chief claim to veneration possessed by the historical Jesus, in the Synoptics plays no very important part in Jesus' moral conception of life; governing no wider sphere than had already been allowed it in the Old Testament.† And if the pulpit eloquence of

* V. Hartmann, *op. cit.*, 44 *sq.*

† Let us hear what Clemen says against this : " In its reduction of the Law to the Commandment of love, though this was already

nineteen hundred years has nevertheless attempted to lay
stress on this point, it is because it counts on the faithful
not having in mind the difference between the Gospels,
and on their peacefully permitting the Gospel of John,
the one and only "gospel of love," which, however, is not
supposed to be "historical," to be substituted for the
Synoptic Gospels. And so we actually see the glorification
of Jesus' doctrines which, a short time ago, flourished
so luxuriantly, appearing recently in more and more
moderate terms.*

Thus it was for a time customary in theology, under
the influence of Holtzmann and Harnack, to consider the
ethical deepening and return of God's "fatherly love" as
the essentially new and significant point in Jesus' "glad
tidings," and to write about it in unctuous phrases.
Recently, even this seems to have been abandoned, as,
for example, Wrede openly confesses, with respect to the
"filiation to God," that this conception existed in
Judaism very long before Christ; also that Jesus did not
especially preach God as the loving "Father" of each
individual, that indeed he did not once place in the foreground the name of God as the Father.† But so much

prominent in the Old Testament [!] and even earlier had here and
there [!] been characterised as the chief Commandment, Christianity
is completely original [!]. And for Jesus the subordination of religious
duties to moral was consequent on this, though in this respect he
would have been equally influenced by the prophets of the Old
Testament" (*op. cit.*, 135 *sq.*).

* "We must (as regards the moral ideals of Jesus) pay just as much
attention to what he does not treat of, to what he set aside, as to
what he clung to, indeed, setting it in opposition to all the rest. At
least this wonderfully sure selection is Jesus' own. We may produce
analogies for each individual thing, but the whole is unique and cannot
be invented" (v. Soden, *op. cit.*, 51 *sq.*). This method, practised by
liberal theology, of extolling their Jesus as against all other mortals,
and of raising him up to a "uniqueness" in the absolute sense, can
make indeed but a small impression on the impartial.

† Wrede, "Paulus," 91.

the more decidedly is reference made to the "enormous effects" which attended Jesus' appearance, and the attempt is made to prove from them his surpassing greatness, "uniqueness," and historical reality. As if Zarathustra, Buddha, and Mohammed had achieved less, as if the effects which proceed from a person must stand in a certain relation to his human significance, and as if those effects were to be ascribed to the "historical" and not rather to the mythical Jesus—that is, to the idea of the God sacrificing himself for humanity! As a matter of fact, his faith in the immediate proximity of the Messianic kingdom of God, and the demand for a change of life based on this, which is really "unique" in the traditional Jesus, is without any religious and ethical significance for us, and is at most only of interest for the history of civilisation. On the other hand, such part of his teaching as is still of importance to us is not "unique," and only has the reputation of being so because we are accustomed by a theological education to treat it in the light of the Christian dogmatic metaphysics of redemption. Plato, Seneca, Epictetus, Laotse, or Buddha in their ethical views are not behind Jesus with his egoistical pseudo-morals, his basing moral action on the expectation of reward and punishment in the future, his narrow-minded nationalism, which theologians in vain attempt to debate away and to conceal; and his obscure mysticism, which strives to attain a special importance for its maxims by mysterious references to his "heavenly Father." * And as for the "great impres-

---

* We admit that besides the eschatological grounding of his moral demands, Jesus also makes use occasionally of expressions that pass beyond the idea of reward. But they are quite isolated—as, e.g., Matt. v. 48, "Be ye perfect, even as your Father in Heaven is perfect," a phrase which is, moreover, in accord with Lev. xi. 44 and xix. 3—and without any fundamental significance. In general, and

sion " which Jesus is supposed to have made on his own people and on the following age, and without which the history of Christianity is supposed to be inexplicable, Kalthoff has shown with justice that the Gospels do not in any way reflect the impression which a person produced, but only such as the accounts of Jesus' personality would have made on the members of the Christian community. " Even the strongest impression proves nothing as to the historical truth of these accounts. Even an account of a fictitious personage may produce the deepest impression on a community if it is given in historical terms. What an impression Goethe's " Werther " produced, though the whole world knew that it was only a

in particular even in the Sermon on the Mount, that " Diamond in the Crown of Jesus' ethics," the idea of reward and punishment is prevalent (Matt. v. 12 and 46; vi. 1, 4, 6, 14, 18; v. 20; vi. 15; vii. 1, &c.). Views may still differ widely as to whether it is historically correct to estimate, as Weinel would like to, Jesus' ethics in this connection really by the few sayings which go beyond that idea. (Cf. v. Hartmann, *op. cit.*, 116–124.) The favourite declaration, however, is quite unhistorical, that Jesus was the first who introduced into the world the principle of active love ; and that the Stoics, as Weinel represents, only taught the doing away with all our passions, even that of love ; or indeed that Jesus, who wished salvation only to benefit the Jews, who forbade his people to walk in the ways of the Gentiles, and who hesitated to comply with the Canaanite woman's prayer, " raised to the highest degree of sincerity" the " altruistic ideal," and that in principle he broke down the boundaries between peoples and creeds with his " Love thy enemy," (Weinel, *op. cit.*, 55, 57). As against this cf. the following passage from Seneca : " Everything which we must do and avoid may be reduced to this short formula of human obligation : We are members of a mighty body. Nature has made us kindred, having produced us from the same stuff and for the same ends. She has implanted in us a mutual love, and has arranged it socially. She has founded right and equity. Because of her commands to do evil is worse than to suffer evil. Hands ready to aid are raised at her call. Let that verse be in our mouths and our hearts : I am a man, nothing human do I despise ! Human life consists in well-doing and striving. It will be cemented into a society

romance! Yet it stirred up countless disciples and imitators." *

In this we have at the same time a refutation of the popular objection that to deny the historical existence of Jesus is to misunderstand "the significance of personality in the historical life of peoples and religions." Certainly, as Mehlhorn says, active devotion above all is enkindled to persons in whom this personality strikes us in an evident, elevating, and animating way.† But in order to enkindle devotion and faith in Jesus Christ the elevating personality of a Paul sufficed, whether or not he was the author of the epistles current in his name; the missionary activity of apostles, working, like him,

of general aid not by fear but by mutual love. What is the rightly constituted, good and high-minded soul, but a God living as a guest in a human body? Such a soul may appear just as well in a knight as in a freedman or in a slave. We can soar upwards to heaven from any corner. Make this your rule, to treat the lower classes even as you would wish the higher to treat you. Even if we are slaves, we may yet be free in spirit. The slaves are men, inferior relatives, friends; indeed, our fellow-slaves in a like submission to the tyranny of fate. A friendship based on virtue exists between the good man and God, yes, more than a friendship, a kinship and likeness; for the good man is really his pupil, imitator, and scion, differing from God only because of the continuance of time. Him the majestic father brings up, a little severely, as is the strict father's wont. God cherishes a fatherly affection towards the good man, and loves him dearly. If you wish to imitate the gods, give also to the ungrateful; for the sun rises even on the ungodly and the seas lie open even to the pirate, the wind blows not only in favour of the good, and the rain falls even on the fields of the unjust. If you wish to have the gods well-disposed towards you, be good: he has enough, who honours and who imitates them." Cf. also Epictetus: "Dare, raising your eyes to God, to say, Henceforth make use of me to what end thou wilt! I accent, I am thine, I draw back from nothing which thy will intends. Lead me whithersoever thou wilt! For I hold God's will to be better than mine." (Cf. also Matt. xxvi. 39.)

* Kautsky, "Ursprung des Christentums," 17.

† *Op. cit.*, 8.

in the service of the Jesus-creed, was enough, since they moved from place to place, and, often undergoing great personal sacrifice and privation, with danger to their own lives demanded adoration of the new God. Those in need of redemption could never find any real religious support outside of the faith in a divine redeemer, they could never find satisfaction and deliverance but in the idea of the God sacrificing himself for mankind—the God whose redeeming power and whose distinct superiority to the other Mystery-deities the apostles could portray in such a lively and striking fashion. That an idea can only be effective and fruitful by means of a great personality is a barren formula.* In thinking they can with this argument support their faith in an historical Jesus liberal theologians avail themselves of an irrelevant bit of modern street-philosophy without noticing that in their case it proves nothing at all. Where, then, is the "great personality" which gave to Mithraism such an efficacy that in the first century of our era it was able to conquer from the East almost the whole of the West and to make it doubtful for a time whether the world was to

---

* "How is it conceivable," even Pfleiderer asks, "that the new community should have fashioned itself from the chaos of material without some definite fact, some foundation-giving event which could form the nucleus for the genesis of the new ideas? Everywhere in the case of a new historical development the powers and impulses which are present in the crowd are first directed to a definite end and fastened into an organism that can survive by the purpose giving action of heroic personalities. And so the impulse for the formation of the Christian community must have come from some definite point, which, from the testimony of the Apostle Paul and of the earliest Gospels, we can only find in the life and death of Jesus" ("Entstehung des Chr.," 11). But that the "testimony" for an his torical Jesus is not testimony, and that the "definite fact," the "foundation-giving event," is to be looked for, if anywhere, in Paul himself and nowhere else—such is the central point of all this analysis.

be Mithraic or Christian ? In such influential religions as those of Dionysus and Osiris, or indeed in Brahmanism, we cannot speak of great personalities as their "founders"; and as for Zarathustra, the pretended founder of the Persian, and Moses, the founder of the Israelite religion, they are not historical persons; while the views of different investigators differ as to the historical existence of the reputed founder of Buddhism. Of course, even in the above-mentioned religions the particular ideas would have been brought forward by brilliant individuals, and the movements depending on them would have been first organised and rendered effective by men of energy and purpose. But the question is whether persons of this type are necessarily "great," even "unique," in the sense of liberal theology, in order to be successful. So that to set aside Paul, whose inspiring personality gifted with a genius for organisation we know from his epistles, —to set him aside in favour of an imaginary Jesus, to base the importance of the Christian religion on the "uniqueness" of its supposed founder, and to base this uniqueness in turn on the importance of the religious movement which resulted from it, is to abandon the critical standpoint and to turn about in circles. "It is an empty assertion," says Lützelberger, "without any real foundation, that the invention of such a person as the Gospels give us in their Jesus would have been quite impossible, as we find in him such a peculiar and sharply defined character that imagination would never have been able to invent and adhere to it. For the personality which meets us in the Gospels is by no means one that is sharply drawn and true to itself; but the story shows us rather a man who from quite different mental tendencies spoke now one way and now another, and is perfectly different in the first and fourth Gospels. Only with the greatest trouble can a homogeneous and coherent whole be formed from the descriptions in the Gospels. So that we are absolutely wrong in concluding from the originality of the person of Christ in the Gospels to their historical credibility." The conclusion is much more justifiable that if such a person with such a life-history and such speech had stood at the beginning of the Christian Church, the history of its development must have been quite a different one, just as the history of Judaism would have been different if a Moses with his Law had stood at its head.*

And now if we compare the praises of Buddha in the Lalita Vistara with the description of Jesus' personality given in the New Testament, we will be convinced how similarly—even if we exclude the hypothesis of a direct influence—and under what like conditions the kindred religion took shape: "In the world of creatures, which was long afflicted by the evils of natural corruption, thou didst appear, O king of physicians, who redeemest us from all evil. At thy approach, O guide, unrest disappears, and gods and men are filled with health. Thou art the protector, the firm foundation, the chief, the leader of the world, with thy gentle and benevolent disposition. Thou art the best of physicians, who bringest the perfect means of salvation and healest suffering. Distinguished by thy compassion and sympathy, thou governest the things of the world. Distinguished by thy strength of mind and good works, completely pure, thou hast attained to perfection, and, thyself redeemed, thou wilt, as the prophet of the four truths, redeem other creatures also. The power of the Evil One has been overcome by wisdom, courage, and humility. Thou hast brought it about,—the highest and immortal glory. We greet thee as the conqueror of the army of the Deceiver. Thou whose word is without

* *Op. cit.,* 61 *sq.*

fault, who freest from error and passion, hast trod the path of eternal life; thou dost deserve in heaven and on earth honour and homage unparalleled. Thou quickenest Gods and men with thy clear words. By the beams which go forth from thee thou art the conqueror of this universe, the Master of Gods and men. Thou didst appear, Light of the Law, destroyer of misery and ignorance, completely filled with humility and majesty. Sun, moon, and fires no longer shine before thee and thy fulness of imperishable glory. Thou who teachest us to know truth from falsehood, ghostly leader with the sweetest voice, whose spirit is calm, whose passions are controlled, whose heart is perfectly at rest, who teachest what should be taught, who bringest about the union of gods and men: I greet thee, Sakhyamuni, as the greatest of men, as the wonder of the three thousand worlds, who deservest honour and homage in heaven and on earth, from Gods and men!" Where, then, is the "uniqueness" of Jesus, into which the future divinity of the World-redeemer has disappeared for modern critical theology, and into which it has striven to import all the sentimental considerations which once belonged to the "God-man" in the sense of the Church dogma? "Nothing is more negative than the result of the inquiry into the life of Jesus. The Jesus of Nazareth, who appeared as the Messiah, who proclaimed the morals of the kingdom of God, who founded the kingdom of heaven upon earth, and died to give consecration to his acts, never existed. He is a figure which was invented by Rationalism, restored by Liberalism, and painted over with historical science by modern theologians." With these words of the theologian Schweitzer* the present inquiry may be said to agree.

* "Von Reimarus bis Wrede," 396.

In fact, in the Gospels we have nothing but the expression of the consciousness of a community. In this respect the view supported by Kalthoff is completely right. The life of Jesus, as portrayed by the Synoptics, merely brings to an expression in historical garb the metaphysical ideas, religious hopes, the outer and inner experiences of the community which had Jesus for its cult-god. His opinions, statements, and parables only reflect the religious-moral conceptions, the temporary sentiments, the casting down and the joy of victory, the hate and the love, the judgments and prejudices of the members of the community, and the differences and contradictions in the Gospels prove to be the developing material of the conception of the Messiah in different communities and at different times. Christ takes just the same position in the religious-social brotherhoods which are named after him as Attis has in the Phrygian, Adonis in the Syrian, Osiris in the Egyptian, Dionysus, Hercules, Hermes, Asclepius, &c., in the Greek cult-associations. He is but another form of these club-gods or patrons of communities, and the cult devoted to him shows in essentials the same forms as those devoted to the divinities above named. The place of the bloody expiatory sacrifice of the believers in Attis, wherein they underwent "baptism of blood" in their yearly March festival, and wherein they obtained the forgiveness of their sins and were "born again" to a new life, was in Rome the Hill of the Vatican. In fact, the very spot on which in Christian times the Church of Peter grew above the so-called grave of the apostle. It was at bottom merely an alteration of the name, not of the matter, when the High Priest of Attis blended his rôle with that of the High Priest of Christ, and the Christ-cult spread itself from this new point far over the other parts of the Roman Empire.

(c) THE TRUE CHARACTER OF THE SYNOPTIC JESUS.

The Synoptic Gospels leave open the question whether they treat of a man made God or of a God made man. The foregoing account has shown that the Jesus of the Gospels is to be understood only as a God made man. The story of his life, as presented in the Gospels, is the rendering into history of a primitive religious myth. Most of the great heroes of the legend, which passes as historical, are similar incarnate Gods—such as Jason, Hercules, Achilles, Theseus, Perseus, Siegfried, &c.; in these we have nothing but the old Aryan sun—champion in the struggle against the powers of darkness and of death. That primitive Gods in the view of a later age should become men, without, however, ceasing to be clothed with the glamour of the deity, is to such an extent the ordinary process, that the reverse, the elevation of men to Gods, is as a rule only found in the earliest stages of human civilisation, or in periods of moral and social decay, when fawning servility and worthless flattery fashion a prominent man, either during his life or after his death, into a divine being. Even the so-called "Bible Story" contains numerous examples of such God made men : the patriarchs, Joseph, Joshua, Samson, Esther, Mordecai, Haman, Simon Magus, the magician Elymas, &c., were originally pure Gods, and in the description of their lives old Semitic star-myths and sun-myths obtained a historical garb. If we cannot doubt that Moses, the founder of the old covenant, was a fictitious figure, and that his "history" was invented by the priests at Jerusalem only for the purpose of sanctioning and basing on his authority the law of the priests named after him; if for this end the whole history of Israel was falsified, and the final event in the religious development of Israel, *i.e.*, the giving of the

Law, was placed at the beginning—why cannot what was possible with Moses have been repeated in the case of Jesus? Why may not also the founder of the new covenant as an historical person belong entirely to pious legend? According to Herodotus,* the Greeks also changed an old Phœnician God, Hercules, for national reasons, into a native hero, the son of Amphitryon, and incorporated him in their own sphere of ideas. Let us consider how strong the impulse was, especially among Orientals, to make history of purely internal experiences and ideas. To carry historical matter into the sphere of myth, and to conceive myth as history, is, as is shown by the investigations of Winckler, Schrader, Jensen, &c., for the Orientals such a matter of course, that, as regards the accounts in the Old Testament, it is hardly possible to distinguish their genuinely "historical nucleus" from its quasi-historical covering. And it is more especially the Semitic thought of antiquity which proves to be completely unable to distinguish mythical phantasy from real event! It is, indeed, too often said that the Semite produced and possessed no mythology of his own, as Renan asserted; and no doubt at all is possible that they could not preserve as such and deal with the mythical figures and events whencesoever they derived them, but always tended to translate them into human form and to associate them with definite places and times. "The God of the Semites is associated with place and object, he is a Genius loci," says Winckler.† But if ever a myth required to be clothed in the garment of place and the metaphysical ideas contained in it to be separated into a series of historical events, it was certainly the myth of the God sacrificing himself for humanity, who sojourned among men in human form, suffered with the rest of men and died, returning, after victoriously over-

* ii. 44.   † " Gesch. Israels," ii. 1 *sqq.*

coming the dark powers of death, to the divine seat whence he set out. We understand how the God Jesus, consequent on his symbolical unification with the man sacrificed in his stead, could come to be made human, and how on this basis the faith in the resurrection of God in the form of an historical person could arise. But how the reverse process could take place, how the man Jesus could be elevated into a God, or could ever fuse with an already existing God of like name into the divine-human redeemer—indeed, the Deity—that is and remains, as we have already said, a psychological puzzle. The only way to solve it is to refer to the "inscrutable secrets of the Divine will." In what other way can we explain how "that simple child of man, as he has been described," could so very soon after his death be elevated into that "mystical being of imagination," into that "celestial Christ," as he meets us in the epistles of Paul? There can only have been at most seven, probably three, years, according to a recent estimate hardly one year, between the death of Jesus and the commencement of Paul's activity.* And this short time is supposed to have sufficed to transform the man Jesus into the Pauline Christ! And not only Paul is supposed to have been able to do this; even Jesus' immediate disciples, who sat with him at the same table, ate and drank with him, knowing then who Jesus was, are supposed to have declared themselves in agreement with this, and to have prayed to him whom they had always seen praying to the "Father"! Certainly in antiquity the deification of a man was nothing extraordinary : Plato and Aristotle were, after their death, honoured by their pupils as god-like beings ; Demetrius Poliorcetes, Alexander, the

* Holtzmann, "Zum Thema Jesus and Paulus'" ("Prot. Monats-heft," iv., 1900, 465).

Ptolemies, &c., had divine honours rendered to them even during their lives. But this style of deification is completely different from that which is supposed to have been allotted to Jesus. It is merely an expression of personal gratitude and attachment, of overflowing sentiment and characterless flattery, and never obtained any detailed theological formulation. It was the basis for no new religion. Schopenhauer has very justly pointed out the contradiction between Paul's apotheosis of Jesus and usual historical experience, and remarked that from this consideration could be drawn an argument against the authenticity of the Pauline epistles.* In fact, Holtzmann considers, with reference to this assertion of the philosopher's, the question "whether the figure of Jesus attaining such colossal dimensions in Paul's sight may not be taken to establish the distance between the two as that of only a few years, if there was not immediate temporal contact," as the question "most worthy of discussion, which the critics of the Dutch school have propounded for consideration."† According to the prevalent view of critical theologians, as presented even by Pfleiderer, the apparitions of the " Lord," which after Jesus' death were seen by the disciples who had fled from Jerusalem, the "ecstatic visionary experiences, in which they thought they saw their crucified Master living and raised up to heavenly glory," were the occasion of their faith in the resurrection, and consequently of their faith in Jesus' divine rôle as Redeemer.‡ Pathological states of over-excited men and hysterical women are then supposed to form the "historical foundation" for the genesis of the Christian religion! And

* Parerga, ii. 180.

† Neutest. Theol. ii. 4. Cf. R. H. Grützmacher: " Ist das liberale Christusbild modern ? Bibl. Zeit-und Streitfragen," 39 *sq.*

‡ Pfleiderer, " Entstehung d. Chr.," 108 *sqq.*

with such opinions they think themselves justified in looking down on the rationalist of the eighteenth-century Enlightenment with supreme contempt, and in boasting of the depth to which their religious-historical insight reaches ! But if we really admit, with historical theology, this more than doubtful explanation, which degrades Christianity into the merely chance product of mental excitement, at once the further question arises as to how the new religion of the small community of the Messiah at Jerusalem was able to spread itself abroad with such astounding rapidity that, even so soon as at most two decades after Jesus' death, we meet with Christian communities not only over the whole of Western Asia, but also in the islands of the Mediterranean, in the coast-towns of Greece, even in Italy, at Puteoli, and in Rome ; and this at a time when as yet not a line had been written about the Jewish Rabbi * Even the theologian Schweitzer is obliged to confess of historical theology that "until it has in some way explained how it was that, under the influence of the Jewish sect of the Messiah, Greek and Roman popular Christianity appeared at all points simultaneously, it must admit a formal right of existence to all hypotheses, even the most extravagant, which seek to attack and solve this problem." †

If in all this it is shown to be possible, or even probable, that in the Jesus of the Gospels we have not a deified man, but rather a humanised God, there remains but to find an answer to the question as to what external reasons led to the transplanting of the God Jesus into the soil of historical actuality and the reduction of the eternal or super-historical fact of his redeeming death and of his resurrection into a series of temporal events.

* Cf. Stendel, *op. cit.*, 22.   † "Von Reimarus bis Wrede," 313.

This question is answered at once if we turn our attention to the motives present in the earliest Christian communities known to us, which motives appear in the Acts and in the Pauline epistles. From these sources we know at what an early stage an opposition arose between Paul's Gentile Christianity and the Jewish Christianity, the chief seat of which was at Jerusalem, and which for this reason, as we can understand, claimed for itself a special authority. As long as the former persecutor of the Christian community, over whose conversion they could not at first rejoice too much,* did not obstruct others and seemed to justify his apostolic activity by his success among the Gentiles, they left him to go his way. But when Paul showed his independence by his reserve before the "Brothers" at Jerusalem, and began to attract the feelings of those at Jerusalem by his abrogation of the Mosaic Law, then they commenced to treat him with suspicion, to place every obstacle in the way of his missionary activity, and to attempt, led by the zealous James, to bring the Pauline communities under their own government. Then, seeking a title for the practice of the apostolic vocation, they found it in this—that every one who wished to testify to Christ must himself have seen him after his resurrection.

But Paul could very justly object that to him also the transfigured Jesus had appeared.† Then they made the justification for the apostolic vocation consist in this, that an apostle must not only have seen Christ risen up, but must also have eaten and drunk with him.‡ This indeed was not applicable in the case of Judas, who in the Acts i. 16 is nevertheless counted among the apostles; and it was also never asserted of Matthias, who was chosen in the former's stead, that he had been

* Gal. i. 24.　　† 1 Cor. ii. 1; 2 Cor. xix. 9.　　‡ Acts i. 3, x. 41.

a witness of Jesus' resurrection. Much less even does he
seem to have fulfilled the condition to which advance was
made in the development of the original idea, *i.e.*, that an
apostle of Jesus should have been personally acquainted
with the living Jesus, that he should have belonged to the
" First Apostles " and have been present as eye-witness
and hearer of Jesus' words from the time of John's
baptism up to the Resurrection and Ascension.* Now
Seufert has shown that the passage of the Acts referred
to is merely a construction, a transference of later conditions to an earlier epoch; and that the whole point of it
is to paralyse Paul's mission to the Gentiles and to
establish the title of the Jew-Christians at Jerusalem as
higher than that of his followers.

If with this purpose, as Seufert showed, the organisation of the Apostleship of Twelve arose—an organisation
which has no satisfactory basis or foundation in the
Gospels or in the Pauline epistles—then it is from this
purpose also that we can find cause for the God Jesus to
become a human founder of the apostleship. " An
apostle was to be only such an one as had seen and
heard Jesus himself, or had learnt from those who had
been his immediate disciples. A literature of Judaism
arose which had at quite an early stage the closest
interest in the historical determination of Jesus' life; and
this formed the lowest stratum on which our canonical
Gospels are based." † Judaism in general, and the form of
it at Jerusalem in particular, needed a legal title on which
to base its commanding position as contrasted with the
Gentile Christianity of Paul; and so its founders were

---

* Acts i. 21 *sq.*

† Seufert, " Der Ursprung und die Bedeutung des Apostolates in
der christlichen Kirche der ersten Jahrhunderte," 1887, 143. Cf.
also my " Petruslegende," in which the unhistorical nature of the
disciples and apostles is shown, 50 *sqq.*

obliged to have been companions of Jesus in person, and to have been selected for their vocation by him. For this reason Jesus could not remain a mere God, but had to be drawn down into historical actuality. Seufert thinks that the tracing of the Apostleship of Twelve back to an "historical" Jesus, and the setting up of the demand for an apostle of Jesus to have been a companion of his journeying, took place in Paul's lifetime in the sixth, or perhaps even in the fifth decade.* In this he presupposes the existence of an historical Jesus, while the Pauline epistles themselves contain nothing to lead one to believe that the transformation of the Jesus-faith into history took place in Paul's lifetime. In early Christianity exactly the same incident took place here, on the soil of Palestine and at Jerusalem, as took place later in "eternal" Rome, when the bishop of this city, in order to establish his right of supremacy in the Church, proclaimed himself to be the direct successor of the Apostle Peter, and caused the "possession of the keys" to have been given to this latter by Jesus himself.†

So that there were very mundane and very practical reasons which after all gave the impulse for the God Jesus to be transformed into an historical individual, and for the central point of his action, the crisis in his life, his death and his resurrection, which alone affected religious considerations, to be placed in the capital of the Jewish state, the "City of God," the Holy City of David, of the "ancestors" of the Messiah, with which now the Jews connected religious salvation. But how could this fiction succeed and maintain its ground, so that it was able to become an absolutely vital question for the new religion, an indestructible dogma, a self-evident "fact,"

* Op. cit., 42.
† Cf. my work "Die Petruslegende."

so that its very calling in question seems to the critical theologians of our time a perfect absurdity?

Before we can answer this question we must turn our attention to the Gnostic movement and its relations to the growing Church.

(d) GNOSTICISM AND THE JOHANNINE JESUS.

Christianity was originally developed from Gnosticism (Mandaism). The Pauline religion was only one form of the many syncretising efforts to satisfy contemporary humanity's need of redemption by a fusion of religious conceptions derived from different sources. So much the greater was the danger which threatened to spring up on this side of the youthful Church.

Gnosticism agreed with Christianity in its pessimistic valuation of the world, in its belief in the inability of man to obtain religious salvation by himself, in the necessity for a divine mediation of " Life." Like Christianity, it expected the deliverance of the oppressed souls of men by a supernatural Redeemer. He came down from Heaven upon earth and assumed a human form, establishing, through a mystic union with himself, the connection between the spheres of heaven and earth. He thereby guarantees to mankind an eternal life in a bliss to come. Gnosticism also involves a completely dualistic philosophy in its opposition of God and world, of spirit and matter, of soul and body, &c. ; but all its efforts are directed to overcoming these contradictions by supernatural mediation and magical contrivances. It treats the " Gnosis," the knowledge, the proper insight into the coherence of things, as the necessary condition of redemption. The individual must know that his soul comes from God, that it is only temporarily confined in this prison of the body, and that it is intended for something higher than to be lost here in the obscurity of ignorance, of evil and of sin; so that he is already freed from the trammels of the flesh, and finds a new life for himself. The God-Redeemer descended upon earth to impart this knowledge to mankind; and Gnosticism pledges itself, on the basis of the "revelation" received directly from God, to open to those who strive for the highest knowledge all the heights and depths of Heaven and of earth.

This Gnosticism of the first century after Christ was a wonderfully opalescent and intricate structure—half religious speculation, half religion, a mixture of Theosophy, uncritical mythological superstition, and deep religious mysticism. In it Babylonian beliefs as to Gods and stars, Parsee mythology, and Indian doctrines of metempsychosis and Karma were combined with Jewish theology and Mystery-rites of Western Asia; and through the whole blew a breath of Hellenic philosophy, which chiefly strove to fix the fantastic creatures of speculation in a comprehensible form, and to work up the confusion of Oriental licence and extravagance of thought into the form of a philosophical view of the world. The Gnostics also called their mediating deity, as we have already seen of the Maudaic sect of the Nassenes, "Jesus," and indulged in a picture rendering of his pre-worldly existence and supernatural divine majesty. They agreed with the Christians that Jesus had been "human."

The extravagant metaphysical conception which they had of Jesus at the same time prevented them from dealing seriously with the idea of his manhood. So that they either maintained that the celestial Christ had attached himself to the man Jesus in a purely external way, and indeed, first on the occasion of the baptism in the Jordan, and only temporarily, *i.e.*, up to the Passion —it being only the "man" Jesus who suffered death

(Basilides, Cerinthus) ; or they thought of Jesus as having assumed merely a ghostly body—and consequently thought that all his human actions took place merely as pure appearance (Saturninus, Valentinus, Marcion). But how little they managed to penetrate into the centre of the Christian doctrine of redemption and to value the funda- mental significance of the Christ-figure, is shown by the fact that they thought of Christ merely as one mediator among countless others. It is shown also by the romantic and florid description of the spirits or " æons," who are supposed to travel backwards and forwards between heaven and earth, leading their lives apart. These played a great part in the Gnostic systems.

It was a matter of course that the Christian faith had to take exception to such a fantastic and external treat- ment of the idea of the God-man. The Pauline Chris- tianity was distinct from Gnosticism, with which it was most closely connected, just in this, that it was in earnest with the "manhood" of Jesus. It was still more serious that the Gnostics combined with their extreme dualism an outspokenly anti-Jewish character. For this in the close relationship between Gnosticism and Christianity would necessarily frighten the Jews from the Gospel, and incite only too many against the young religion. But the Jews formed the factor with which early Christianity had first of all to reckon. In addition to this the Gnostics, from the standpoint of their spiritualistic conception of God, turned to contempt of the world and asceticism. They commended sexual continence, rejected marriage, and wished to know nothing either of Christ's or of man's bodily resurrection. But in the West no propaganda of an ascetic religion could succeed. And yet even with the Gnostics, as is so often the case, asceticism only too frequently degenerated into unbridled voluptuousness and libertinage, and the spiritual pride of those chosen by

God to knowledge, who were raised above the **Mosaic Law**, threatened completely to tear apart the connection with Judaism by its radical criticism of the Old Testament. In this Gnosticism not only undermined **the** moral life of the communities, but also brought **the** Gospel into discredit in other parts of the world. As an independent religion, which expressly opposed all **other** worships, and the adherents of which withdrew from **the** religious practices of the State, even from any political activity whatsoever, Christianity brought on itself **the** suspicion of the authorities and the hate of the people, and incurred the prohibition of new religions and **secret** sects (lex Julia majestatis).* So that Gnosticism, **by** taking it from its Jewish native soil, drove Christianity into a conflict with the Roman civil laws.

All these dangers, which threatened Christianity **from** the Gnostic movement, were set aside in one stroke **by** the recognition of the true "manhood" of Jesus, **the** assertion of the "historical" Jesus. This preserved **the** connection, so important for the unhindered spread **of** Christianity in the Roman Empire, with Judaism and **its** "revealed" legality—the heteronomous and ritualistic character of which had indeed been shown by Paul, **and** the moral content of which was nevertheless adhered **to** by the Christians even later. It was made possible, **in** default of any previous written documents of revelation, even yet to regard the Old Testament in essentials as **the** authoritative book of the new faith, and as a preparatory testimony to the final revelation which appeared in Jesus. And most of all, it put a check on Gnostic phantasy, **in** drawing together the perplexing plurality of the Gnostic æons into the one figure of the World-redeemer **and** Saviour Christ, in making the chief dogma the redeeming

* Cf. Hausrath, "Jesus und die neutestamentl. Schriftsteller," ii. 203 *sqq.*

sacrificial death of the Messiah, and in concentrating the religious man's attention on this chief turning-point of all the historical events. This was the reason why the Apologists and "Fathers" of Christianity, Ignatius, Polycarp, Justin, Irenæus, &c., spoke with such decision in favour of the actuality and true manhood of Jesus. It was not perhaps a better historical knowledge which caused them to do this, but the life-instinct of the Church, which knew only too well that its own position and the prosecution of its religious task, in contrast with the excitements of Gnosticism and its seductive attempts to explain the world, was dependent on the belief in an historical Redeemer. So the historical Jesus was from the beginning a dogma, a fiction, caused by the religious and practical social needs, of the growing and struggling Christian Church. This Jesus has, indeed, led it to victory; not, however, as an historical reality, but as an idea; or, in other words, not an historical Jesus, in the proper sense of the word, a really human individual, but the pure idea of such a person, is the patron-saint, the Genius of ecclesiastical Christianity, the man who enabled it to overcome Gnosticism, Mithraism, and the other religions of the Redeemer-Gods of Western Asia.

The importance of the fourth Gospel rests in having brought to a final close these efforts of the Church to make history of the Redeemer-figure Christ. Begun under the visible influence of the Gnostic conception of the process of redemption, it meets Gnosticism later as another Gospel; indeed, it seems saturated through and through with the Gnostic attitude and outlook. To a certain degree it shares with Gnosticism its anti-Jewish character. But at the same time it adheres, with the Synoptics, to Jesus' historical activity, and seeks to establish a kind of mediation between the essentially metaphysical conception of the Gnostics and the essentially human conception of the Synoptic Gospels.

The author who wrote the Gospel in the name of John, the "favourite disciple of Jesus," probably about 140 A.D., agrees with Gnosticism in its dualistic conception of the universe. On one side is the world, the kingdom of darkness, deceit, and evil, in deadly enmity to the divine kingdom of light, the kingdom of truth and life. At the head of the divine kingdom is God, who is himself Light, Truth, Life, and Spirit—following Parsee thought. At the head of the kingdom of earth is Satan (Angromainyu). In the middle, between them, is placed man. But mankind is also divided, as all the rest of existence, into two essentially different kinds. The souls of the one part of mankind are derived from God, those of the other from Satan. The "children of God" are by nature destined for the good and are fit for redemption. The "children of Satan"—among whom John, in agreement with the Gnostics, counts the Jews before all—are not susceptible of anything divine and are assigned to eternal damnation. In order to accomplish redemption, God, from pure "Love" for the world, selected Monogenes, his only-begotten Son, that is, the only being which, as the child of God, was produced not by other beings, but by God himself. The author of the Gospel fuses Monogenes with the Philonic Logos, who in the Gnostic conception was only one of countless other æons, and was a son of Monogenes, the divine reason, and so only a grandson of God. At the same time, he transfers the whole "pleroma" —the plurality of the æons into which, in the Gnostic conception, the divine reality was divided—to the single principle of the Logos, defines the Logos as the unique bearer of the whole fulness of divine glory, as the pre-existent creator of the world; and calls him also, since he is in essence identical with God his "Father," the source of life, the light, the truth, and the spirit of the universe.

And how then does the Logos bring about redemption? He becomes flesh, that is, he assumes the form of the "man" Jesus, without, however, ceasing to be the supernatural Logos, and as such brings to men the "Life" which he himself is, by revealing wisdom and love. As revealer of wisdom he is the "light of the world"; he opens to men the secret of their filial relation to God; he teaches them, by knowing God, to understand themselves and the world; he collects about himself the children of God, who are scattered through the world, in a united and brotherly society; and gives them, in imitating his own personality, the "light of life"—that is, he inwardly enlightens and elevates them. As revealer of love he not only assumes the human form and the renunciation of his divine bliss connected with it, but as a "good shepherd" he lays down his life for his flock; he saves them from the power of Satan, from the terrors of darkness, and sacrifices himself for his people, in order through this highest testimony of his love for men, through the complete surrender of his life, to regain the life which he really is, and to return to his celestial glory. This is the meaning of Christ's work of redemption, that men by faith and love become inwardly united with him and so with God; whereby they gain the "life" in the higher spirit. For though Christ himself may return to God, his spirit still lives on earth. As the "second Paraclete" or agent, the Spirit proceeds with the Saviour's work of redemption, arouses and strengthens the faith in Christ and the love for him and for the Brotherhood, thereby mediating for them the "Life," and leading them after their death into the eternal bliss.

In all this the influence of Gnosticism and of the Philonic doctrine of the Logos is unmistakable, and it is very probable that the author of the fourth Gospel was influenced by the recollection, still living at Ephesus, of the Ephesian Heraclitus' Logos, in his attachment to Philo and to the latter's more detailed exposition of the Hellenic Logos-philosophy. But he fundamentally differs from Philo and Gnosticism in his assertion that the Logos "was made flesh," sojourned on earth in the figure of Jesus of Nazareth, and suffered death. It is true, however, that the Evangelist is more persistent in this assertion than successful in delineating a real man, notwithstanding his use of the Synoptic accounts of the personal fate of Jesus. The idea of the divine nature of the Saviour is the one that prevails in his writings. The "historical picture" which came down to him was forcibly rectified, and the personality of Jesus was worked up into something so wonderful, extraordinary, and supernatural that, if we were in possession of the fourth Gospel alone, in all probability the idea would hardly have occurred to any one that it was a treatment of the life-story of an historical individual. And yet in this the difference between the Johannine and the Synoptic Gospels is only a slight one. For the Synoptic Jesus also is not really a man, but a "superman," the original Christian community's God-man, cult-hero, and mediator of salvation. And if it is settled that the quarrel between the Church teachers and the Gnostic heretics hinged, not on the divinity of Christ, in which they agreed, but rather on the kind and degree of his humanity, then this "paradoxical fact" is by itself sufficient to corroborate the assertion that the divinity of the mediator of redemption was the only originally determined and self-evident presupposition of the whole Christian faith; and that, on the contrary, his humanity was doubtful even in the earliest times, and for this reason alone could become a subject of the bitterest strife.

Indeed, even the author of the fourth Gospel did not bring about a real fusion between the human person Jesus and the mythological person, the Gnostic Son of God, who with Philo wavered, also in the form of the Logos, between impersonal being and allegorical personality. All the efforts to render comprehensible "the interfusion of the divine and the human in the unity of the personal, its basis (essence) being divine, its appearance a human life of Jesus," are frustrated even with the so-called John by one fact. This fact is that a Logos considered as a person can never be at once a human personality and yet have as its basis and essence a divine personality, but can only be demoniacally possessed by this latter, and can never *be* this latter itself. And so, as Pfleiderer says, the Johannine Christ wavers throughout "between a sublime truth and a ghostly monstrosity; the former, in so far as he represents the ideal of the Son of God, and so the religion of mankind, separated from all the accidents and limits of individuality and nationality, of space and time—and the latter so far as he is the mythical covering of a God sojourning on earth in human form." *

It is true that this fusion of the Gnostic Son of God and the Philonic Logos with the Synoptic Jesus first fixed the hazy uncertainty of mythological speculation and abstract thought in the clear form and living individuality of the personal mediator of redemption. It brought this personality nearer to the hearts of the faithful than any other figure of religious belief, and thereby procured for the Christian cult-god Jesus, in his pure humanity, his overflowing goodness and benevolence, such a predominance over his divine competitors, Mithras, Attis, and others, that by the side of Jesus these faded away into empty shadows. The Gnostic ideal man, that

* " Entstehung d. Chr.," 239.

is, the Platonic idea, and the moral ideal of man merged
in him directly into a unity. The miracle of the union
of God and man, over which the ancient world had so
hotly and so fruitlessly disputed, seemed to have found
its realisation in Christ. Christ was the "Wise man" of
the Stoic philosophy, in whom was united for them all
that is most honourable in man ; more than this, he was
the God-man, as he had been preached and demanded by
Seneca for the moral elevation of mankind.* The world
was consequently so ready to receive and so well prepared
for his fundamental ideas that we easily see why the
Church Christianity took its stand on the human personality of its redeeming principle with almost more
decision than on the divine character of Jesus. Nevertheless, in spite of the majesty and sublimity, in spite of the
immeasurable significance which the accentuation of the
true humanity of Jesus has had for the development of
Christianity, it remains true that on the other hand it is
just this which is the source of all the insoluble contradictions, of all the insurmountable difficulties from
which the Christian view of the world suffers. This is
the reason why that great idea, which Christianity
brought to the consciousness of the men of the West,
and through which it conquered Judaism—the idea of the
God-man—was utterly destroyed, and the true content
of this religion was obscured, hidden, and misrepresented
in such disastrous fashion, that to-day it is no longer
possible to assent to its doctrine of redemption without
the sacrifice of the intellect.

* Cf. above, p. 31. *sqq.*

THE RELIGIOUS PROBLEM OF THE PRESENT

THE RELIGIOUS PROBLEM OF THE PRESENT

IN the opinion of liberal theologians, not the God but rather the man Jesus forms the valuable religious essence of Christianity.* In saying this it says nothing less than that the whole of Christendom up to the present day—that is, till the appearance of a Harnack, Bousset, Wernle, and others of like mind—was in error about itself, and did not recognise its own essence. For Christianity, as the present account shows, from the very first conceived the God Jesus, or rather the God-man, the Incarnate, the God-redeemer, suffering with man and sacrificing himself for humanity, as the central point of its doctrine. The declaration of the real manhood of Jesus appears, on the other hand, but as an after-concession of this religion to outer circumstances, wrung from it only later by its opponents, and so expressly championed by it only because of its forming the unavoidable condition of its permanence in history and of its practical success. Only the God, therefore, not the man Jesus, can be termed the "founder" of the Christian religion.

It is in fact the fundamental error of the liberal theology to think that the development of the Christian

* Cf. Arnold Meyer, " Was uns Jesus heute ist. Rel. Volksb.," 1907 —a very impressive presentation of the liberal Protestant point of view; also Weinel, " Jesus im 19ten Jahrhundert."

Church took its rise from an historical individual, from the man Jesus. The view is becoming more common that the original Christian movement under the name of Jesus would have remained an insignificant and transient movement within Judaism but for Paul, who first gave it a religious view of the world by his metaphysics of redemption, and who by his break ·with the Jewish Law really founded the new religion. It will not be long before the further concession is found necessary, that an historical Jesus, as the Gospels portray him, and as he lives in the minds of the liberal theologians of to-day, never existed at all; so that he never founded the insignificant and diminutive community of the Messiah at Jerusalem. It will be necessary to concede that the Christ-faith arose quite independently of any historical personality known to us; that indeed Jesus was in this sense a product of the religious " social soul " and was made by Paul, with the required amount of reinterpretation and reconstruction, the chief interest of those communities founded by him. The "historical" Jesus is not earlier but later than Paul; and as such he has always existed merely as an idea, as a pious fiction in the minds of members of the community. The New Testament with its four Gospels is not previous to the Church, but the latter is antecedent to them; and the Gospels are the derivatives, consequently forming a support for the propaganda of the Church, and being without any claim to historical significance.

Nothing at all, as Kalthoff shows, is to be gained for the understanding of Christianity from the completely modern view that religion is an entirely personal life and experience. Religion is such personal life only in an age which is differentiated into personalities; it is such only in so far as this differentiation has been accomplished. From the very beginning religion makes its appearance as a phenomenon of social life ; it is a group-religion, a folk-religion, a State religion ; and this social character is naturally transferred to the free associations which are formed within the limits of tribe and the State. The talk about personality as the centre of all religious life is with regard to the origin of Christianity absurd and unhistorical, for the reason that Christianity grew up in religious associations, in communities. From this social religion our personal religion has only been developed in a history lasting centuries. Only after great struggles has personal religion been able to succeed against an essentially older form. What devout people of to-day call Christianity, a religion of the individual, a principle of personal salvation, would have been an offence and an absurdity to the whole of ancient Christendom. It would have been to it the sin against the Holy Ghost which was never to be forgiven ; for the Holy Ghost was the spirit of the Church's unity, the connection of the religious community, the spirit of the subordination of the flock to the shepherd. For this reason individual religion existed in old Christendom only through the medium of the association of the community of the Church. A private setting up of one's own religion was heresy, separation from the body of Christ.*

We cannot refuse to concede to the "Catholic" Church, both Roman and Greek, that in this respect it has most faithfully preserved the spirit of the earliest Christendom. This alone is to-day what Christianity in essence once was—the religion of an association in the sense to which we have referred. Thus Catholicism justly refers to "tradition" for the truth of its religious view of the world and for the correctness of its hierarchical claims. But Catholicism itself beyond

* "Entstehung d. Chr.," 98 *sq.*

doubt first established this "tradition" in its own interests. It teaches also an "historical" Jesus, but clearly one that is historical merely by tradition, and of whose actual historical existence not the least indication has yet been established. Protestantism, on the other hand, is completely unhistoric in passing off the Gospels as the sources, as the "revealed" basis of the faith in Christ, as if they had arisen independently of the Church and represented the true beginnings of Christianity. Consequently one cannot base one's religious faith on the Gospel and wish nevertheless to stand outside of that community, since the writings of the New Testament can only pass as the expression of the community's life. One cannot therefore be Christian in the sense of the original community without obliterating one's own personality and uniting oneself as a member with the " Body of Christ "—that is, with the Church. The spirit of obedience and humility, which Christ demanded of his followers, is nothing but the spirit of subordination to the system of rules of conduct observed by the society of worship passing under his name. Christianity in the original sense is nothing but —" Catholic " Christianity ; and this is the faith of the Church in the work of redemption accomplished by the God-man Christ in his Church and by means of the organisation infused with his " spirit."

On purely religious grounds the wrongly so-called " Catholicism " could very probably dispense with the fiction of an historical Jesus, and go back to Paul's standpoint before the origin of the Gospels, if it could have faith to-day in its mythological conception, of the God sacrificing himself for mankind, without that fiction. In its present form, however, it stands or falls as a Church with the belief in the historical truth of the God-redeemer; because all the Church's hierarchical claims and authority are based on this authority having been entrusted to her by an historical Jesus through the apostles. Catholicism relies for this, as it has been said, on "tradition." But Catholicism itself called this tradition into life, just as the priests at Jerusalem worked up the tradition of an historical Moses in order to trace back to him their claim to authority. It is the " Irony of World-History" that that very tradition soon afterwards forced the Church, with regard to the historical Christ, to conceal its real nature from the crowd, and to forbid the laity to read the Gospels, on account of the contradiction between the power of the Church and the traditional Christ it had produced. But the position of Protestantism is even more contradictory and more desperate than that of the Catholic Church, in view of our insight into the fictitious character of the Gospels. For Protestantism has no means but history for the foundation of its religious metaphysics; and history, viewed impartially, leads away from those roots of Christianity to which Protestantism strives, instead of towards them.

If this is true of Protestant orthodoxy it is even more true of that form of Protestantism which thinks it can maintain Christianity apart from its metaphysical doctrine of redemption because this doctrine is " no longer suitable to the age." Liberal Protestantism is and wishes to be nothing but a mere faith in the historical personality of a man who is supposed to have been born 1,900 years ago in Palestine, and through his exemplary life to have become the founder of a new religion; being crucified and dying in conflict with the authorities at Jerusalem, being raised up then as a God in the minds of his enthusiastic disciples. It is a faith in the "loving God the Father," because Jesus is supposed to have believed in him; in the personal immortality of man, because this is supposed to have been the presupposition of Jesus' appearance and doctrines; in the "incomparable" value of moral instructions, because they stand in a book which is supposed to have been produced under the immediate influence of the prophet of Nazareth. Liberal Protestantism supports morality on this, that Jesus was such a good man, and that for this reason it is necessary for each individual man to follow the call of Jesus. But it bases the faith in Jesus once and for all on the historical significance of the Gospels; though it cannot conceal from itself, after careful consideration, that the belief in their historical value rests on extremely weak grounds, and that we know nothing of that Jesus, not even that he ever lived. In any case we know nothing which could be of influential religious significance, and which could not be put together just as well or better from other less doubtful sources.* It is

---

* Weinel, indeed, resolutely denies that this is a real characteristic of liberal Protestantism, and asserts that he has looked for it in vain in any liberal theologian's book. But he need only look in A. Meyer's work, which is cited by me, to find my idea confirmed. There it is said of Jesus *inter alia*: "Not only should we move and live in his love, but we are as he was, of the faith that this love will overcome the world, that it is the meaning, end, and true content of the world; that the power which uniformly and omnipotently fills and guides the world, is nothing but the God in whom he believed [was Jesus then a Pantheist?], and whom he calls his heavenly father. As he believed, so let us also, that whoever trusts in this God and lives in his love has found the meaning of life and the power which preserves him in time and in eternity. Jesus was the founder of our religion, of our faith, and of our inner life" (31). According to Meyer, Jesus attracts us by his manner, his Being, his love and his faith, we feel ourselves bound to him, become kin with him and so live by his strength; he is called "the voice of God to us," "our redeemer," and so forth. Those are simply expressions which applied to God have at least a valid meaning, but applied to the historical man Jesus are nothing but phrases, and are to be explained purely psychologically from the fact that liberalism in honouring the "unique" man Jesus does nevertheless unwittingly allow the belief in his divinity to come

pierced to the heart by the denial of the historical personality of Jesus, not, like Catholicism, merely as a Church, but in its very essence, as a Religion. And as to its real religious kernel it consists in a few fine-sounding phrases and some scattered references to a metaphysics which was once living, but which is now degraded into a mere ornament for modest minds. And after disposing of its would-be historical value there is left only a dimly smouldering spark of "homeless sentiments," which would suit any style of religious faith. Liberal Protestantism proclaims itself as the really "modern" Christianity. Confronted by the philosophic spirit of our day, it lays stress upon having no philosophy. It sets aside all religious speculation as "Myth," if possible with reference to Kant, as this is "modern," without noticing that it is itself most deeply

into play. In this atmosphere, obscured with phrases, the so-called "theology" of liberal Protestantism moves. Moreover, Weinel himself quotes a sentence of Herrmann with approval, which also gives expression to the idea that Jesus is for Protestant liberalism a kind of "demonstration of God" (80), and he adds himself: "It may indeed be that our conception of the significance of Jesus has often been expressed unskilfully enough. It may be that in discourses, lectures, or other popular ways of speaking something is at times said which may be so clumsily put as to give occasion for such things to be said." Indeed, he himself maintains regarding Jesus: "Whoever places the ideal of his life in him, he experiences God in him" (84). He also finds that the desire for God of the Jews, Greeks, Semites, and Germans "could be stilled in him." Taking into account these expressions and the whole tone which it pleases Herr Weinel to adopt towards the opponents of his standpoint, it appears time to remind him once again of E. v. Hartmann's "Die Selbstzersetzung des Christentums" (it is obvious he has only a third-hand acquaintance with the author whose point of view he calls Neo-Buddhism, counting him among the supporters of the morality of pity!) and especially of the chapter on "Die Irreligiosität des liberalen Protestantismus." Here, in connection with the lack of metaphysics displayed by liberal Protestantism (and

imbedded in mythology with its "historical" Jesus. It
believes that, in its exclusive reverence for the man
Jesus, it has brought Christianity to the "height of
present culture." As to this Stendel justly says: "Of
the whole apologetic art with which the modern Jesus-
theology undertakes to save Christianity for our time,
it can be said that there is no historical religion which
could not just as well be brought into accord with
the modern mind as that of the New Testament." *
We have no occasion to weep for the complete collapse of such a "religion." This form of Christianity
has already been proved by Hartmann to be worthless
from the religious point of view;† and it is only a
proof of the fascinating power of phrases, of the laxity
in our creeds, and the thoughtlessness of the mob in
religious matters, that it is even yet alive. For such

admitted even by Weinel) and the latter's principle of love, he says :
" If we transform the whole of religion into Ethics and soften down
the whole of Ethics into love, we thereby renounce everything that
is in religion besides love, and everything which makes love
religious. We thereby confess that the impulse of love is raised into
religion since religion properly so called has been lost. It is true
religion is not a shark, as the inquisitors thought, but at the same
time it is not a sea-nettle. A shark can at least be terrifying, a
sea-nettle is always feeble." Liberal Protestantism, as Hartmann
sums it up, consists "of a shapeless, poor, shallow metaphysic,
which is concealed as far as possible from critical eyes ; of a worship
successfully freed from all mystery, but one that has become thereby
by no means incapable of being objected to ; of an Ethics forcibly
separated from Metaphysics and on that account irreligious. It rests
upon a view of the world which by its worldliness and optimistic
contentment with the world is by no means in a position to give
birth to a religion, and which sooner or later will allow the remnants
of religious feeling which it brought with it to be smothered in
worldly ease."

* *Op. cit.*, 39.

† Cf. E. v. Hartmann, " Die Selbstzersetzung des|Christentums und
die Religion der Zukunft," 2nd ed., 1874, especially chaps. vi. and vii.

reasons it is even allowed, under the lead of the so-called critical theology, to proclaim itself as the pure Christianity, now known for the first time. Thus it finds sympathy. This unsystematic collection of thoughts, arbitrarily selected from the view of the world and of life given by the Gospels, which even so requires to be rhetorically puffed out and artistically modified before it is made acceptable to the present age,—this unspeculative doctrine of redemption, which at bottom is uncertain of itself,—this sentimental, æsthetic, Jesus-worship of a Harnack, Bousset, and the rest on whom W. v. Schnehen so pitilessly broke his lance ;* this whole so-called Christianity of cultured pastors and a laity in need of redemption, would have long since come to grief through its poverty of ideas, its sickening sweetness, if it were not considered necessary to maintain Christianity at all costs, were it even that of the complete deprivation of its spiritual content. The recognition of the fact that the " historical " Jesus has no religious interest at all, but at most concerns historians and philologists, is indeed at present commencing to make its way into wider circles.† If one only knew a way out of the difficulty ! If one were only not afraid of following a clear lead just because one might then possibly be forced beyond the existing religion in the course of his ideas—as the example of Kalthoff showed ! If only one had not such a fearful respect for the past and such a tender " historic unconsciousness " and such immense respect for the " historical basis " of existing religion ! The reference to history and the so-called " historical continuity of the religious development " is indeed on the face of it merely a way

* Cf. W. v. Schnehen, "Der moderne Jesuskultus," 2nd ed., 1906 ; also " Naumann vor dem Bankerott des Christentums," 1007.

† Cf. my work, "Die Religion als Selbstbewusstsein Gottes," 1906, 199 *sq.*

out of a difficulty, and another way of putting the fact
that one is not desired to draw the consequences of his
presuppositions. As if there can still be talk of a "historical basis " where there is no history, but pure myth !
As if the " preservation of historical continuity " could
consist in maintaining as history what are mythical
fictions, just because they have hitherto passed for
historic truth, though we have seen through their purely
fictitious and unreal character ! As if the difficulty of
the redemption of present-day civilisation from the chaos
of superstition, social deceit, cowardice, and intellectual
servitude which are connected with the name of Christianity, lay in a purely spiritual sphere and not rather in
the sentiment, in the slovenly piety, in the heavy weight
of ancient tradition, above all in the economic, social,
and practical relations which unite our churches with
the past ! Faith in the future of Christianity is still
built not so much on the persuasive inner truth of its
doctrine, but much more on the inborn religious feeling
of the members of the community, on the religious education in school and home, and the consequent increasing
store of metaphysical and ethical ideas, on protection by
the State and—on the law of inertia in the spiritual life
of the mob. For the rest, in pulpit, in parish papers, and
in public life, a method of expression is used which is
not essentially different from that of orthodoxy, but is so
adapted as to allow every man to think what he deems
best for himself. We are enthusiastically told that thus
we are able to keep the rudderless ship of Protestantism
still a while above water, and that we have " reconciled "
faith with modern culture in " the further development of
Christianity."

Thus nineteen hundred years of religious development
were completely in error. Is no other course open to
us but a complete break with the Christian doctrine of

redemption ? This doctrine, however—such was the
result of our previous examination—is independent of
the belief in an historical Jesus. Its centre of gravity
lies in the conception of the "incarnation" of God, who
suffers in the world but is finally victorious over this
suffering ; and through union with whom Mankind also
"prevails over the world" and gains a new life in a
higher sphere of existence. That the form of this divine
Redeemer of the world coalesced, in the minds of the
Christian community, with that of a man Jesus ; that,
consequent on this, the act of redemption was fixed as to
time and place, is only the consequence of the conditions
under which the new religion appeared.

For this reason it can only claim, in and for itself, a
transient practical significance, and not a special religious
value ; while on the other hand it has become the doom
of Christianity that just this making into history of the
principle of redemption makes it impossible for us still to
acknowledge this religion. But then the preservation of
historical continuity or the "further development" of
Christianity in its proper sense probably does not consist
in separating this chance historical side of the Christian
doctrine of redemption from its connection with the whole
Christian view of the world and setting it up by itself, but
only in going back to the essential and fundamental idea
of the Christian religion, and stating its metaphysical
doctrine of redemption in a manner more nearly answering
to the ideas of the day.

From the conception of a personal God-redeemer arose
the possibility of sacrificing a man in God's place, and of
seeing the divine and ideal man, that is, the Idea of Man,
in an actual man. From the growing Church's desire
for authority, from its opposition to Gnostic phantasy
with its intellectual volatilising of the religious-moral
kernel of the Pauline doctrine of redemption, and from

the wish not to give up the historical connection with Judaism on opportunist grounds, arose the necessity of portraying the divine-human expiatory sacrifice as the sacrifice of an historical person who had arisen in Judaism. All these different reasons, which led to the formation of the belief in an " historical " Jesus, have no force with us, particularly after it has been shown that the personality of the principle of redemption, this fundamental presupposition of the evangelical " history," is in the end to blame for all the contradictions and shortcomings of that religion. To lead back to its real essence the Christian doctrine of redemption can consequently mean nothing but placing the idea of the God-man, as it lies at the basis of that doctrine, in the central point of the religious view of the world, through the stripping off of the mythical personality of the Logos.

God must become man, so that Man can become God and be redeemed from the bounds of the finite. The idea of Man which is realised in the world must itself be a divine idea, an idea of the Deity, and so God must be the common root and essence of all individual men and things; only then may Man attain his existence in God and freedom from the world, through this consciousness of his supernatural divine essence. Man's consciousness of himself and of his true essence must itself be a divine consciousness. Man, and indeed every man, must be a purely finite phenomenon, an individual limitation, the clothing of the Deity with a human form. In possibility he is a God-man, to be born again an actual God-man through his moral activity, and consequently to become really one with God. In this conception all the contradictions of Christian dogmatism are solved, and the kernel of its doctrine of redemption is preserved without being divested of its true significance by the introduction of mythical phantasy or of historical coincidences, as is the case in Christianity.

If we are still to use the language of the past, and to call the divine essence of mankind the immanent God-head, " Christ," then any advance of religion can only consist in the development and working out of this "inner Christ," that is, of the spiritual-moral tendencies dwelling in mankind, in the carrying of it back to its absolute and divine basis, but not in the historical personification of this inner human nature. Any reality of the God-man consequently consists in " Christ's " activity in Man, in the proving of his "true self," of his personal, spiritual essence, in the raising of one's self to personality on the ground of Man's divine nature, but not in the magical efficacy of an external divine personality. This, indeed, is nothing but the religious ideal of mankind, which men have projected on to an historical figure, in order to assure themselves of the "reality" of the ideal. It is not true that it is " essential " to the religious consciousness to consider its ideal in human form, and that for this reason the historical Jesus is indispensable for the religious life. Were this true, religion would not be, in principle, in a position to raise itself above the mythical and primitive stage of God's externality and appearance to the senses, and to conquer these Gods, working them more and more into the forms of an inner nature. This, however, is the essence of religious development. Religion would otherwise be confined to a lower province in the human life of the spirit ; and it would be over-thrown whenever the fiction of that projection and separation of God from one's own self was seen through. It is only to orthodox Christianity that it is necessary to represent the God in Man as a God outside of Man, as the " unique " personality of a historical God-man ; and that because it still remains with one foot in religious naturalism and mythology, and the historical circumstances of another age occasioned the choice of that representation and falsification of the idea of the God-man.

To think of the world's activity as God's activity; of mankind's development, filled with struggles and sufferings, as the story of a divine struggle and Passion; of the world-process as the process of a God, who in each individual creature fights, suffers, conquers and dies, so that he may overcome the limitations of the finite in the religious consciousness of man and anticipate his future triumph over all the suffering of the world—that is the real Christian doctrine of redemption. To revive in this sense the fundamental conception from which Christianity sprang—and which is independent of any historical reference—is, indeed, to return to this religious starting-point. Protestantism, on the contrary, which repudiates Paul's religion and sets up the Gospels as the foundation of its belief, nevertheless does not go behind Christianity's development into the Church, back to the origin of Christianity, but remains always within this development, and deceives itself if it thinks that it can prevail over the Church from the point of view of the Gospel.*

In such an interpretation and development of the Christian conception of redemption "historical continuity" is preserved just as decidedly as it is in the one-sided making into history of that thought on the side of liberal Protestantism. What is in opposition to it is, on the one hand, completely unhistorical belief in an historical Jesus; on the other hand, the prejudice against the "immanent God," or against Pantheism. But this prejudice is based entirely on that fiction of an

* Cf. my work, "Die Religion als Selbstbewusstsein Gottes," in which the attempt has been made to form a general religious view of the world in the sense mentioned.

historical "mediator" and the hypothesis contained therein of a dualistic separation of world and God. The representatives of the monistic conception — who began to organise themselves a short time ago—should be clearer as to the significance of that conception than they are for the most part even at the present day. They must perceive that the true doctrine of unity can only be the doctrine of the all in one. There must be an idealistic monism in opposition to the naturalistic monism of Haeckel, which is prevalent even to-day. This monism must not exclude but include God's existence; and its present unfruitful negation of all religion must deepen into a positive and religiously valuable view of the world. Then, and not till then, will it be able to effect a genuine separation from the Church, and the monistic movement, still in its childhood, may lead to an inner improvement and renovation of our spiritual life in general. It requires much short-sightedness on the part of the exponents of a purely historical Christianity to suppose that the soulless and poor faith in the personal, or as it is considered better expressed to-day, in the "living" God, in freedom and immortality, supported by the authority of the "unique" personality of a man Jesus who died two thousand years ago, will be in a position permanently to satisfy religious needs, even when the metaphysic of redemption, still connected with it at all points, and the pious attitude based upon this are completely stripped off from it. The earlier the orthodox Christians, by giving up their superstition in an historical Jesus, and the Monists, by sacrificing their equally fatal superstition in the sole reality of matter and in the redeeming truths of physical science which alone can give happiness, come to a mutual reconciliation, the better it will be for both. The more surely we shall avoid the total obliteration of the religious consciousness; and the civilised nations of Europe will be saved from the loss of their spiritual ballast—towards which loss there seems at the present day to be a continuous movement on all sides. At present there are only two possibilities—either to look on quietly while the tidal wave of naturalism, getting ever more powerful from day to day, sweeps away the last vestige of religious thought, or to transfer the sinking fire of religion to the ground of Pantheism, in a religion independent of any ecclesiastical guardianship. The time of dualistic Theism has gone by. At present all the advancing spirits, in spheres most widely different, concur in striving towards Monism. This striving is so deeply grounded and so well warranted, that the Church will not be able to suppress it for ever.* The chief obstacle to a monistic religion and attitude is the belief, irreconcilable with reason or history, in the historical reality of a " unique," ideal, and unsurpassable Redeemer.

* Cf. " Der Monismus, dargestellt in Beiträgen seiner Vertreter," 2 vols., 1908.

INDEX

UNWIN BROTHERS, LIMITED, THE GRESHAM PRESS, WOKING AND LONDON.